IMAGES
of America

SACRAMENTO'S ALKALI FLAT

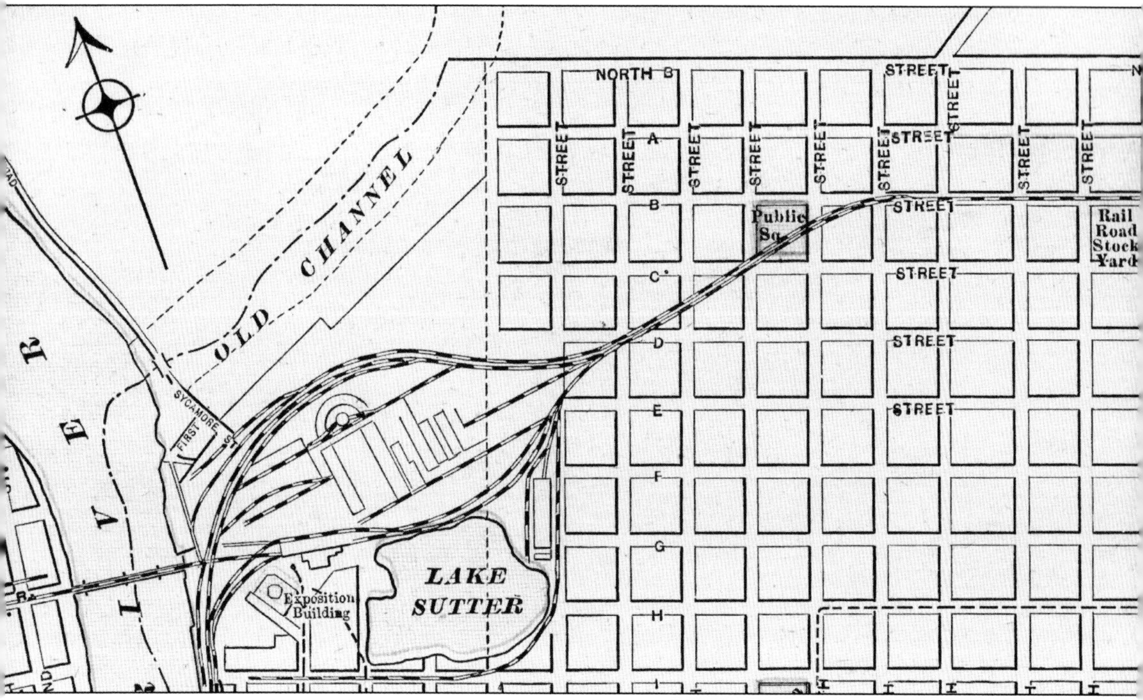

The historical Alkali Flat is shown in this 1893 map. The area within H Street to the south to North B Street to the north and Seventh Street in the west to 13th Street in the east forms the purview of this work. In the upper left-hand portion is the "old channel" of the American River, which was pushed north through Bannon Slough between 1862 and 1869. Four floods between December 1861 and February 1862 prompted rechanneling. (SPL.)

ON THE COVER: Pictured around 1905 is 1110 E Street. Built in 1888, the home was purchased in 1900 from J. R. Hodson by a family of skilled laborers, a more-than-common occurrence in turn-of-the-century Alkali Flat. Standing in the yard are Peter and Mary Sullivan, while on the stairs is their eldest son, George, and his wife, Millie. Both men worked for Southern Pacific, Peter as a foreman and George as a machinist. (Bill Masters.)

IMAGES
of America

SACRAMENTO'S ALKALI FLAT

Special Collections of the
Sacramento Public Library

ARCADIA
PUBLISHING

ISBN 978-0-7385-7151-5

Published by Arcadia Publishing
Charleston SC, Chicago IL, Portsmouth NH, San Francisco CA

Printed in the United States of America

Library of Congress Control Number: 2009930182

For all general information contact Arcadia Publishing at:
Telephone 843-853-2070
Fax 843-853-0044
E-mail sales@arcadiapublishing.com
For customer service and orders:
Toll-Free 1-888-313-2665

Visit us on the Internet at www.arcadiapublishing.com

To James's son, Liam,
and Tom's grandsons, Joel, Eli, and Paul

Contents

ACKNOWLEDGMENTS

We gratefully acknowledge the contributions of the following individuals and organizations: Raul Carillo of the Sacramento Housing and Redevelopment Agency, Sean Wright of the Alkali Flat/Mansion Flats Historic Neighborhood Association, and the members of the Alkali Flat Redevelopment Advisory Committee eagerly accepted our early inquiries, availing us to the community. Neighborhood residents and business owners Laura Lough, Dan Frankenfield, Charlotte Delgado, Dan and Sue Hood, Bill Masters, Phillip Cunningham, Mahlen Picht, Liza Lathe, Lawry Yerby, Ed Quint, Jim Havey, Adrienne Oehler of Porter-Sprague, John Nicolaus of the HLA Group, Harry Sweet and Jay Rudin of KCRA-TV, Sacramento, Saber Shehadeh, Jose Gomez, and the staff of 524 Restaurant all graciously and readily provided photographs, facts, and anecdotes. We'd also like to thank Royal Chicano Air Force members Louie Gonzalez, Dave Contreras, Juanishi Orozco, Rudy Cuellar, Juan Cervantes, and the late Ricardo Favela and his wife, Clara Cid, for their generous aid.

Significant contributions were also made by the following Sacramento Public Library staff and volunteers: technology specialist Antonio Gutierrez; special collections head librarian Clare Ellis; special collections staff members Shaun Tagger, Melissa Walls, and Betty Miner; special collections volunteers Debra Fleming, Amelia Parks, Meredith March, Michael Dolgushkin, and Spencer Yau; Central Library manager Nina Biddle; Central librarians Gerald Ward, Beth Daugherty, and Michael Gillman; central administration staff Paula McDonald and Brenda Haggard; and Diane Balter, authority counsel of the Sacramento Public Library.

We also appreciate the passionate and dedicated assistance of our library and archive colleagues in providing a majority of the images for this volume, in addition to those from the Sacramento Public Library's (SPL) own collection. They include Carson Hendricks, Pat Johnson, Rebecca Crowther, and Dylan McDonald of the Center for Sacramento History (CSH), Julie Thomas and Sheila O'Neill of Sacramento State University's Special Collections and University Archives (CSUS), Katherine Blackmer-Reyes of San Jose State University, and the staff of the California History Room of the California State Library (CSL).

We finally wish to thank photographers Jay Mather, Craig Lee, and Tom Myers and the late Ralph Shaw and Eugene Hepting, whose hobby has provided us with an invaluable window into our history.

INTRODUCTION

Alkali Flat is bordered to the north by North B Street, to the south by H Street, to the west by Seventh Street, and to the east by 13th Street and is effectively blocked on two sides by the old Southern Pacific rail yards and tracks and bounded by the busy downtown district that starts where the Alkali ends. Characterized at different periods by genteel splendor, the empire building of the Central Pacific, a heavy industrial presence, and eventual decline, the district within hailing distance of Sacramento's city hall is first and foremost a neighborhood—Sacramento's oldest.

The chalky mineral residue left behind by waves of flooding from the rivers and delta sloughs prior to the 20th century provided the name popularly associated with the area. Prior to the Gold Rush of 1849 and John Sutter's fort, the Nisenan fished, hunted, and established villages there. Native Americans have long viewed a confluence of rivers to carry a spiritual significance as a point of energy and a gathering spot for life, and the lush forest, tule thickets, and vernal pools fed by the American and Sacramento Rivers embodied that vision. Countless fish, abundant game, fruit, and nuts fed the body, while the majestic, soaring, southern bald eagles and the beauty of a virtual paradise fed the soul.

An account written in 1848 describes an area north of what would become the city of Sacramento as "primeval oak and sycamore surrounding lakes and ponds," but after the great fire in November of 1852 that landscape was drastically altered. Flooding and cholera hadn't completely discouraged survivors and new arrivals, but the destruction of 70 percent of Sacramento's structures left a scorched city searching for a solution. The answer to flooding would come another decade later, following the devastating inundation of 1861–1862, when engineers and laborers actually changed the course of the American River. Brick, however, was Sacramento's solution to fire and soon filled the city's core.

After the great fire of November 1852, the new neighborhood rose just beyond G Street as an enclave of the learned, industrious, and the wealthy. Governors, Supreme Court justices, and the local gentry joined newly rich merchants and business leaders like Maria Hastings, proud owner of a mansion at 1119 D Street and the ornate Orleans Hotel blocks away. Elaborate, eclectic, and sometimes magnificent homes rose from Sixth Street to Twelfth Street and beyond, while the natural break past C Street and the edge of Sutter's Slough marked the beginning of the business district on I Street. Prosperity for merchants and budding local industry was in direct proportion to the growth of the area, and an increased working class needed to consume the goods and pay the rents demanded to the services and institutions to facilitate their needs. Class knew little distinction when it came to schooling, health care, and religious beliefs. Well-off or struggling, Alkali residents had a choice of public schools or private academies, hospitals, and churches. St. Joseph's Academy's square block provided aid to the community in numerous ways, from orphanages to outreach, for over a century.

From its earliest days, the Alkali invited industry, and the businesses that flourished in the land surrounding Sacramento's first grand neighborhood provided basic services and needs. In a city boasting dozens of saloons within staggering distance of each other, breweries were included in the first wave of enterprise, along with dairies to provide butter and milk and blacksmiths to keep horse and wagon on the road. Lumber companies were included to provide building materials, and the huge presence of the Central Pacific Railroad within a dozen years of the Alkali's flowering brought more laborers and residents. These people had new skills, and smaller, local businesses like funeral homes, ice-making plants, taxidermists, and even carriage-makers-turned-automobile-manufacturers set up shop within the neighborhood's boundaries.

Increased industry and populations necessitated improvements in roads and adjustment to the new mobility automobiles and trucks offered. As one of the original roads in and out of Sacramento, Twelfth Street underwent drastic change to serve as both a bridge for the Central Pacific (later Southern Pacific) and conduit to the growing communities beyond the city. Gas stations, automotive repair garages, and stores selling parts and supplies provided a new economic base. They were joined by restaurants, grocery stores, and other staples of a thriving community.

With new workers arriving weekly to toil in the rail yards, breweries, mills, and lumberyards of the Alkali, the magnificent showplaces of the first generation of owners downsized to multifamily dwellings and rental properties to accommodate the influx. No new single-family homes were built in Alkali Flat after 1910, and properties that were once home to the elite might shelter several families forced to live in deteriorating buildings in a depreciated neighborhood. After World War I, no major industry entered the area for over 20 years, and then in 1955 it came in the unlikely form of television station KCRA-TV Channel 3, a partner in land and business with Carl Hansen's Crystal Butter and Dairy just down the street.

History-making moments in Alkali Flat are largely forgotten today, but libraries, archives, and newspaper files supply stories of a past punctuated by startling events and striking occurrences. The first transmission of electricity to the Sacramento region came via Alkali Flat just a year after part of the neighborhood was occupied by the National Guard of California and federal troops. The noisome smell and eventual filling of China Slough, the Garten Gold Cure Institute, "Tom Thumb" weddings, the discovery of a young girl's treasures after a century of rest, and many other stories await discovery in the Alkali's past.

One

Alkali Architecture

by James Scott

Just as Sacramento was finding its urban legs, a November 1852 wildfire devastated nearly 70 percent of the city's core. Mostly untouched and unsettled was an area of lush underbrush and sycamore trees, just north of the central city. It would be here, away from the clutter of juxtaposed wood and canvas, that the city's first residential district would be born out of a combination of building styles. They included prefabricated wood and brick, the former reassuringly marketed as "fire proof wood." By 1855, Sacramento had laid a dizzying 12 million bricks. The neighborhood's earliest homes proved the most visible manifestation of the city's burgeoning aristocracy. In addition to generously sized lots, diverse gardens, and wrought-iron fences, the mid- to late-19th century's architectural styles brought an American concept of European class to a rough-hewn city. Politicians, merchants, and captains of local industry were quick to lay claim to a neighborhood only a stone's throw from business, government, and local society. The advent of the latter 19th century necessitated architectural change, as newborn rail yards placed up to 5,000 laborers amidst what had been a sleepy realm of the rich. Construction of smaller residential units and apartment buildings was ushered in, and the conversion of larger, single-family homes into multiunit structures became popular. The vacuous gaps between the often-gaudy East Lakes and Italianates were filled with smaller, vernacular-style homes, and nearly overnight the class structure of the Alkali was turned on its head. In 1957, city planners determined the average lifespan of a wooden structure in Sacramento was between 40 and 50 years and that the median age of dwellings in 11 blocks of the Alkali was calculated to be 59 years. In spite of this hyper decay of some of the American West's most ornate homes, the dawn of the 1970s and 1980s introduced a band of activist residents and so-called "urban pioneers." Their efforts to rehabilitate most of the neighborhood's antebellum and Victorian homes to their rightful splendor lent an element of energy and stability to a hallowed neighborhood long seeking as much.

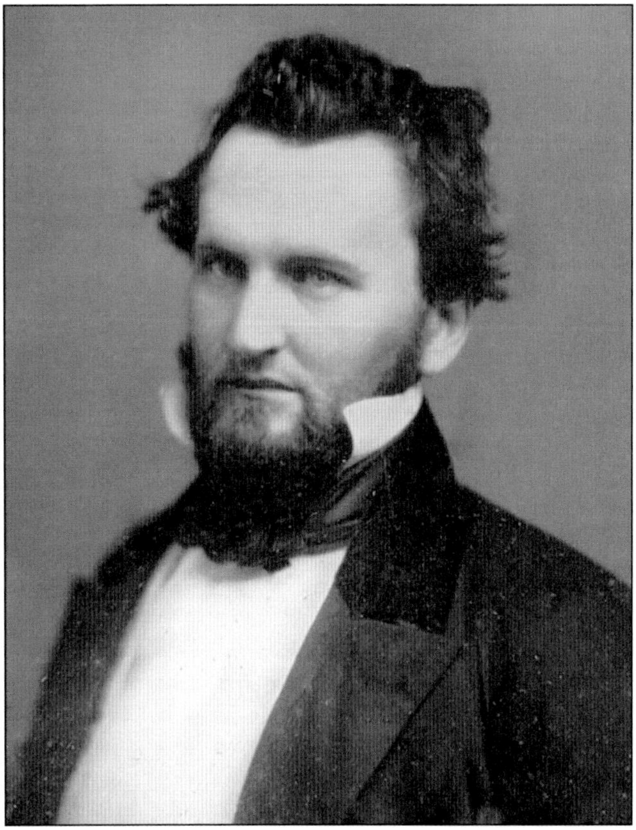

Not only was Indiana-born J. (John) Neely Johnson California's fourth governor, he was also Sacramento's first census taker, having done so in 1850. At the age of 30, Johnson won the gubernatorial ticket as a "Know Nothing"—the country's mid-19th-century anti-immigrant party. In 1856, he took up residence at 1029 F Street, arguably one of the Alkali's best-known and oldest-standing structures, built in 1854 in the Greek Revival style. Just prior to a rainy January 9 inauguration at the capitol, several volunteer military companies, including the city's own Sutter Rifles, paraded before the governor-elect as he stood on the front step of his Alkali Flat home. As seen below, this photograph, pre–J. Neely Johnson Park, was taken in the spring of 1936. (At left, CSL; below, CSH.)

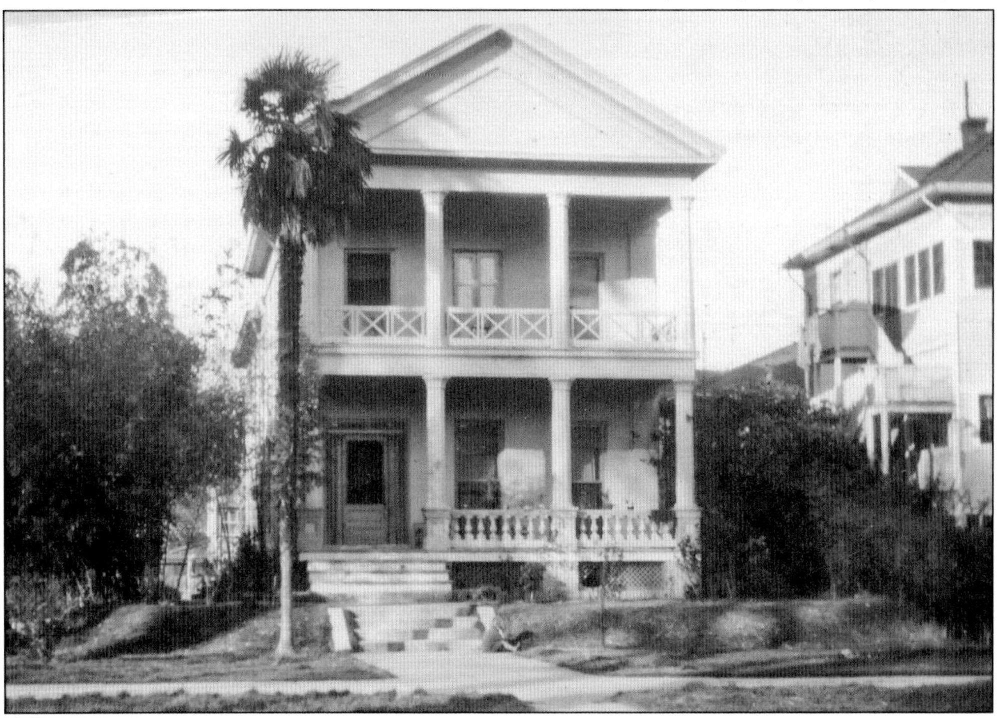

As seen at right and reflecting the conscientious stewardship of owners past and present, the J. Neely Johnson House stands sentinel over F Street today. The structure was converted into an unbelievable nine separate living quarters in the 1960s. Neither two fires in the mid-1970s nor various code violations (plus condemnation by both city health and fire departments) were enough to keep the home from nearing full restoration. In 1976, the home was ultimately converted into two units. The Johnson House's survival, and that of many of the Alkali's 19th-century homes, was due chiefly to the diligence of the Sacramento Old City Association, Sacramento Heritage, Inc., and area preservationists. Below is the house as it sat in the mid-1970s. (Both Tom Myers.)

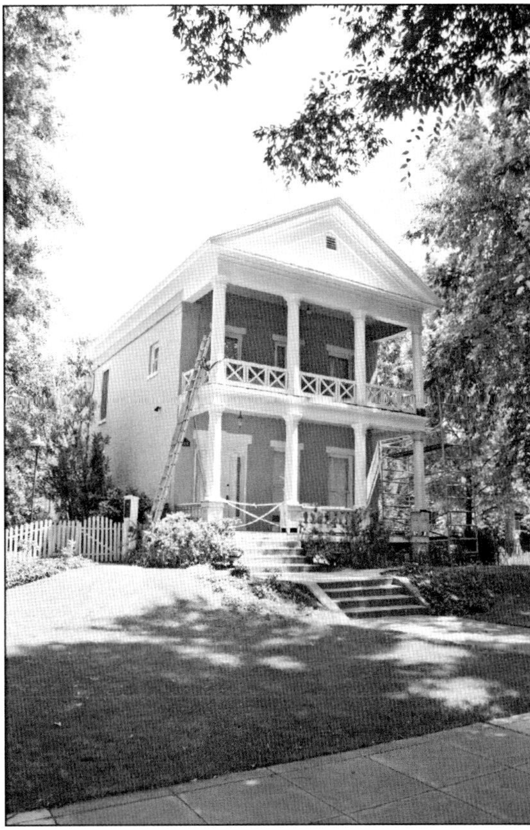

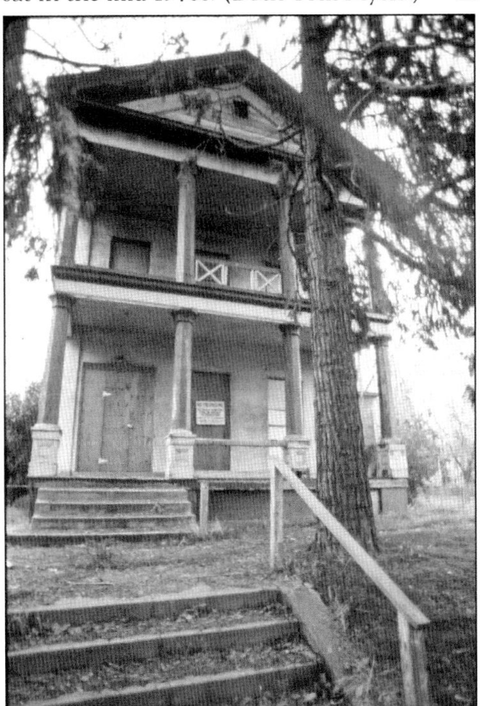

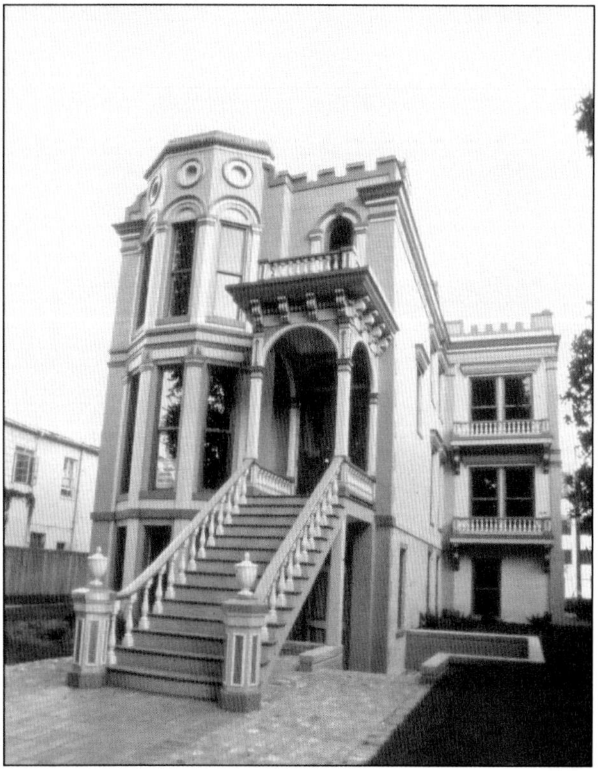

Arguably the most uniquely crafted home in the Alkali is the Isaac Martin Hubbard House, resting at 1010 F Street. Bucking the prevailing styles of the day, it was in 1856 that the energetic and dashing Hubbard built the home commonly referred to as "the castle." He was instrumental in establishing the nation's first transcontinental telegraph and is also credited—along with his father—for building the first railroad bridge across the American River. In an acutely ironic turn of events, the firefighter, engineer, and former sea captain died at the youngish age of 57 after tripping down a line of steps while exiting a building on K Street. Like the Johnson home, Hubbard's residence, as seen below, fell into disrepair in the 1970s and 1980s, but it received resuscitation through the efforts of local preservationists. (Both Tom Myers.)

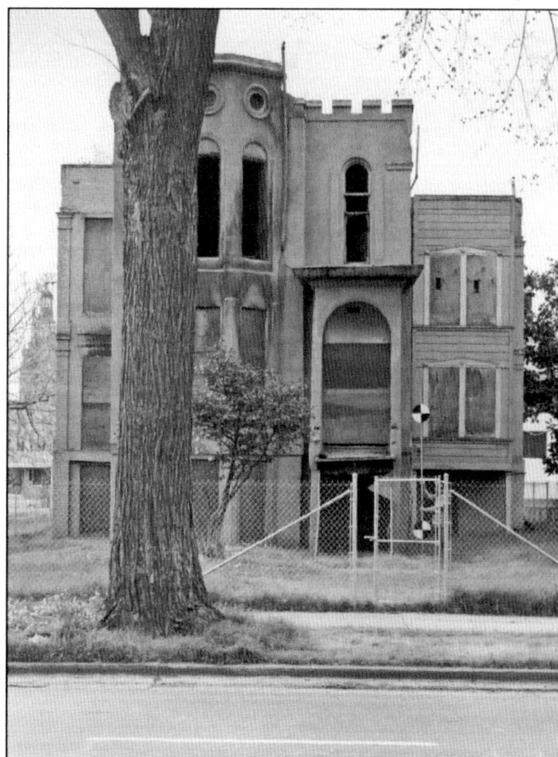

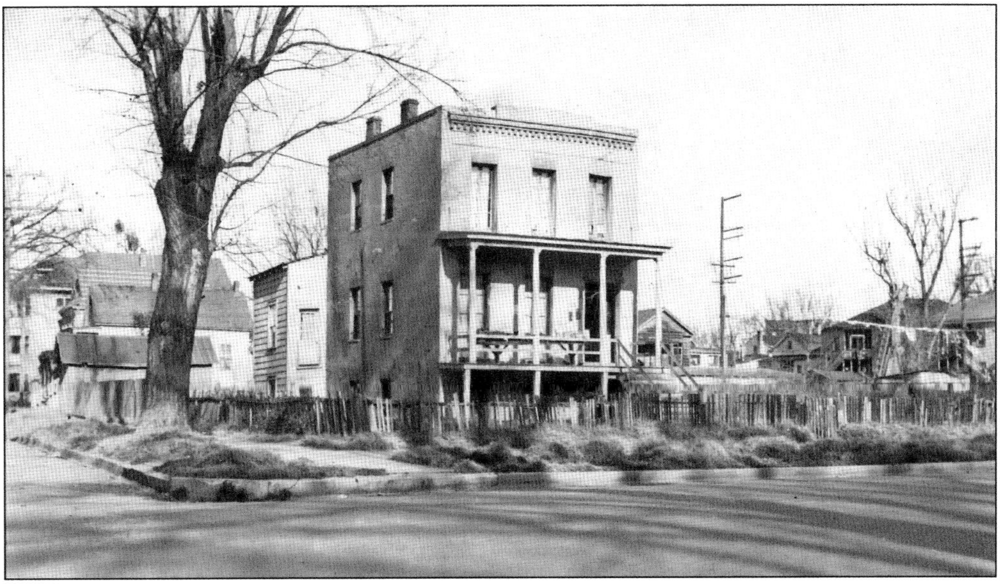

Pictured above in 1935 is a northeasterly view of 903 E Street, one of the very first homes to be built in the Alkali. It was erected out of brick in 1852 for the family of John Kohner, "Old Honest John," a gardener from Baden-Württemberg, Germany. As was customary, the Kohner's lived on the upper two floors during the rainy season, while the steamy summer months pushed them to sleep amidst the coolness of the basement. During the near-biblical flooding of 1861, waters crested and were marked at 8 feet above the home's foundation. The house was razed in 1946 after being condemned by city health and fire departments. During demolition, the 1861 watermark was still visible. The photograph below was taken in 1944, looking northwesterly. (Both CSH.)

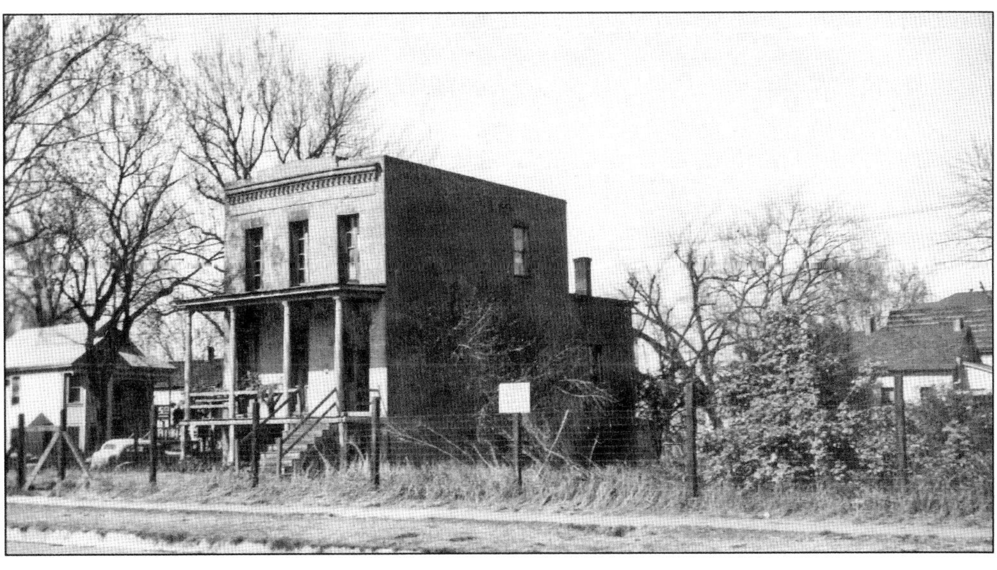

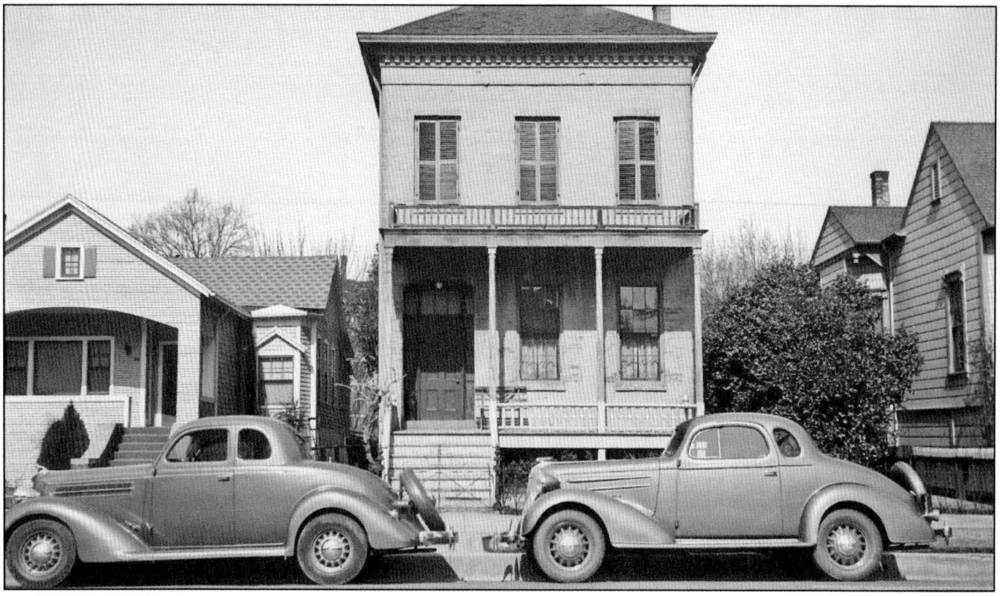

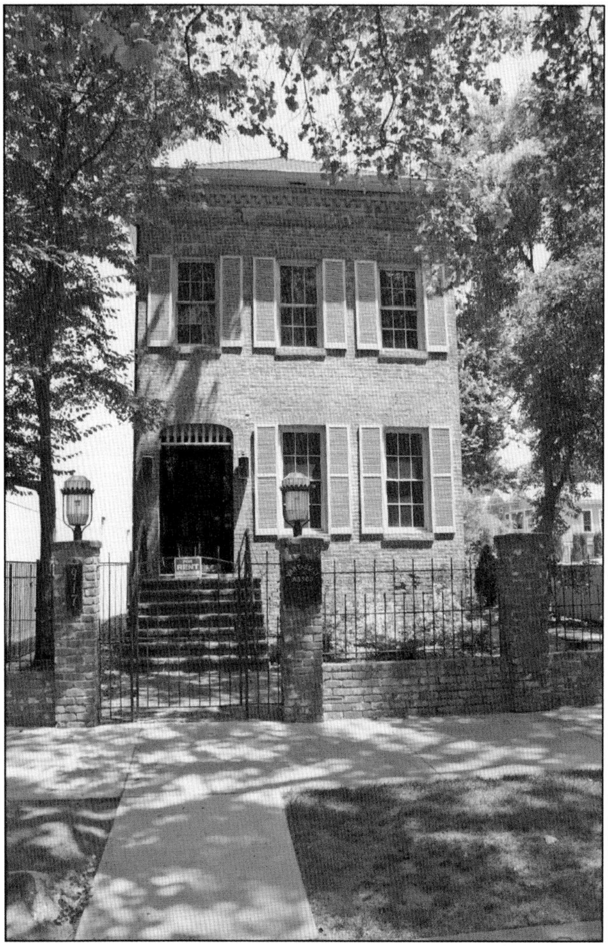

The European revolutions of 1848 sent thousands of political progressives from the Occident to the United States and California. One of them was Antoine "Anthony" Egl, an ethnic German from Hungary and a fruit, nut, and candy merchant. By 1860, Egl's efforts materialized into a palatial Italianate on 917 G Street, pictured above in 1933. A story floats about that the original windows for the home had to be imported from the East Coast because of a dearth of glaziers in young California. What's more, the interior paints of the home were very likely mixed on-site with ingredients making their way to Sacramento from faraway spots like China, Brazil, and India. Pictured at left is the Egl home as it stands today, host to law offices. (Both CSH.)

Albert Van Voorhies arrived in the Sacramento region in 1860 as a trained harness-maker, with little to his name. By 1869, he had parlayed his skill into a healthy business, giving him the means to move his family into 925 G Street, a structure clad with a mélange of Italianate and Georgian styles. In a steamy twist, just after Van Voorhies' death, his widowed wife, at age 55, married the family's chauffeur, Arnold Patterson, age 30. (CSH.)

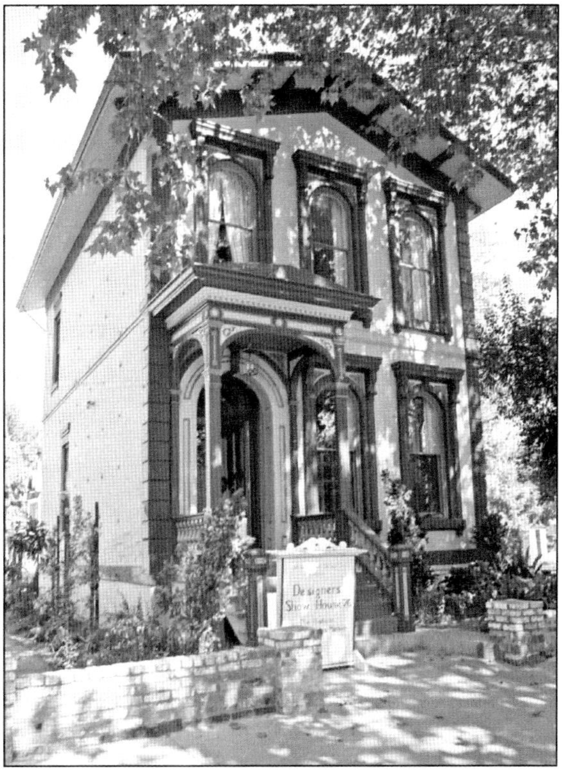

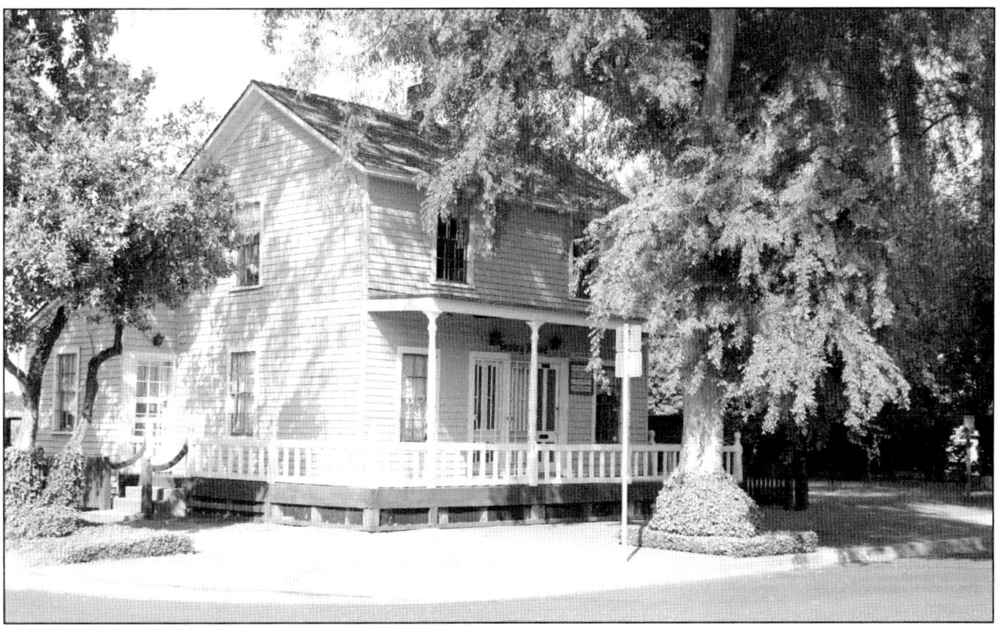

The Wagner House is located at the northeast corner of Seventh and E Streets. The utilitarian-style home was assembled in 1862–1863 by German immigrant Anton Wagner, a local cabinet and saddle maker. It was also a prefabricated structure and had been transported from the East Coast. Also referred to as the "Sentry House," it may have served as a sentry post for Union soldiers during the Civil War. (SPL.)

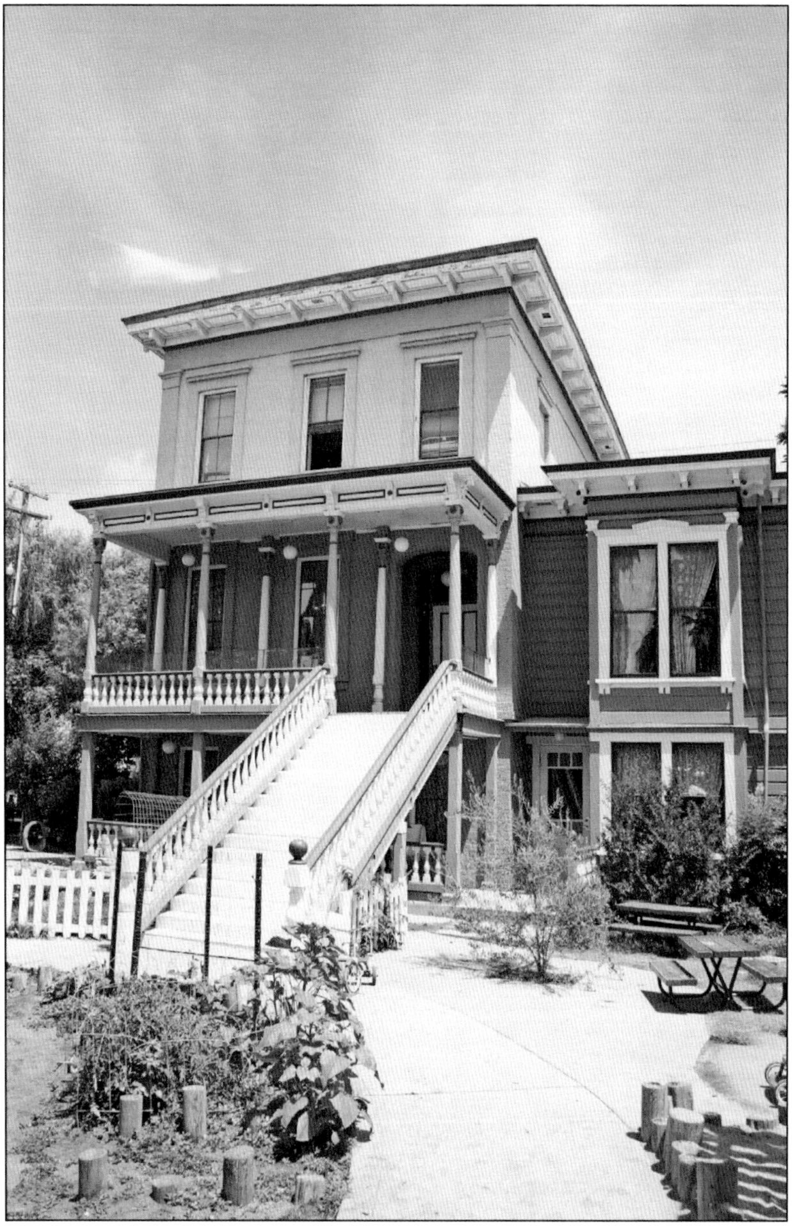

Maria Hastings's 1860 Greek Revival home still stands at 1119 D Street. The native New Yorker is notable for bringing a touch of style to Sacramento during the Gold Rush. Her prefabricated Orleans House on Second Street, between J and K Streets, was not simply a saloon and hotel, but a place where entertainment luminaries like Lola Montez and violin virtuoso Miska Hauser performed to packed rooms. Vigilance committees used the Orleans House in 1851 to circumvent the rule of law, while years later the hotel would serve as the first place of formal assembly for California state officials in Sacramento. Moreover, a story from the *Sacramento Union* in January 1856 referred to the Orleans House as a "political hive" and a "great depot for present and prospective office holders." After falling to the November 1852 fire, the Orleans House was resurrected in brick in time for the horrendous flooding of January 1853. Pictured here in 2009, the Hasting House is now home to a Montessori school. (SPL.)

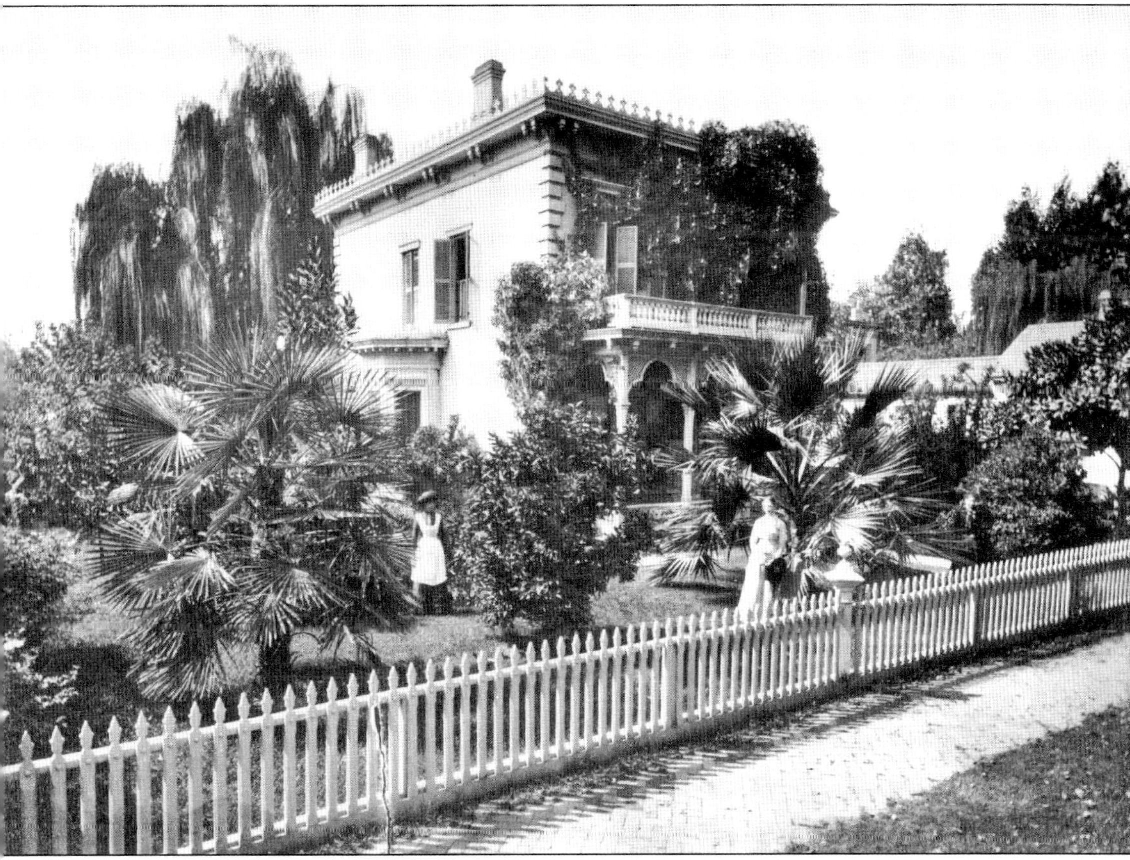

Shrouded in the semitropical greenery so typical of many late-19th-century lots in the Alkali was the home of William F. Knox, at 916 G Street. The Virginia-born Knox came to California as a 49er, but settled into the construction industry where he amassed a modest fortune. In addition to serving on the city's school board and common council, Knox and his business contributed mightily to the building of the Central Pacific Railroad (CPR) and Sacramento County's first courthouse, and he was a primary player in the epic undertaking of raising Sacramento's business district by 18 feet in 1863. The Knox legacy is sullied by his efforts to resist the integration of the city's schools. Despite as much, and at the strong behest of several school principals, on May 25th, 1874, non-white pupils were admitted into Sacramento's grammar and high schools. Knox died suddenly of a heart attack in 1894 and is buried in the Old City Cemetery. (CSL.)

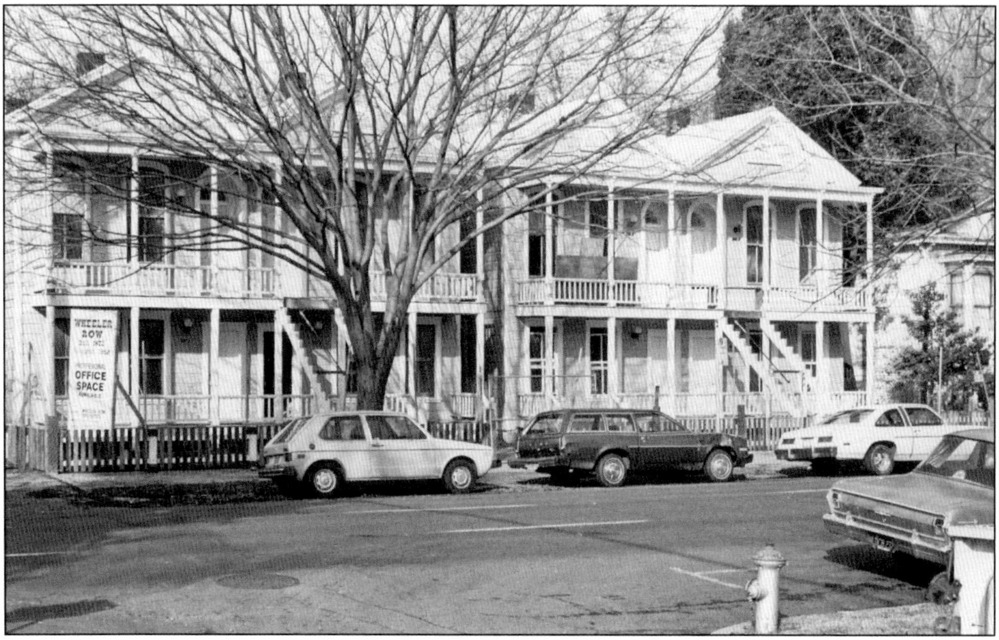

Built in 1872–1873 and pictured here in 1984, Wheeler Row, at 608-614 Tenth Street, holds distinction for being the first documented apartment house in Sacramento. New York native Rev. Osgood C. Wheeler, who came to Sacramento in 1852 to edit the West Coast's first Baptist newspaper, the *Pacific Banner*, was the owner and likely builder of the Delta Style units whose elevated living areas were designed to anticipate flooding. (Dan Hood.)

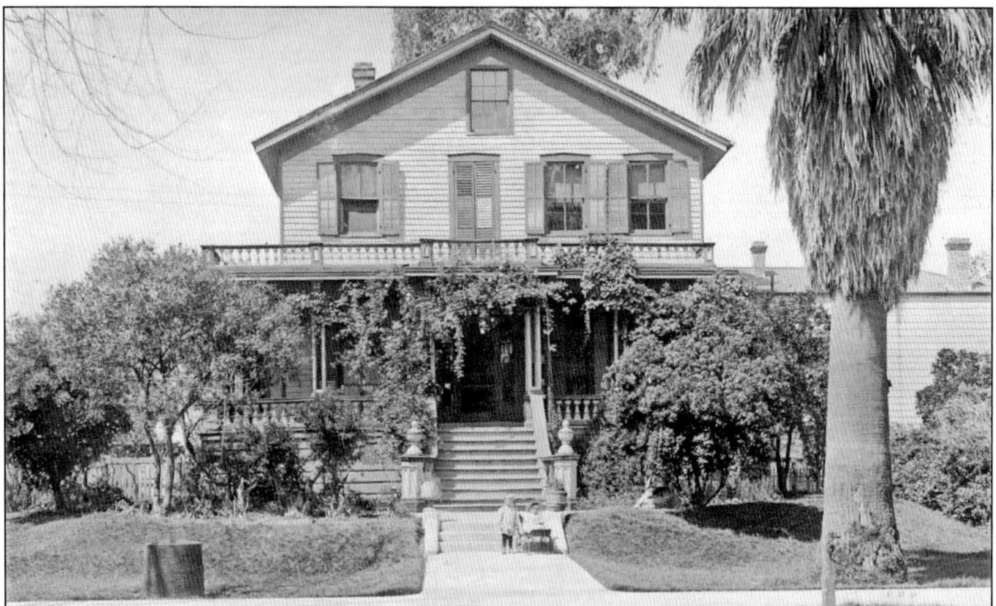

Pictured in 1912 is the 406 Eleventh Street home of German immigrant and widow Dorothea Schubert and her four daughters. The house was moved from Thirteenth and C Streets in 1869. Prior to that, and between 1864 and 1869, it was the hospital of the Central Pacific Railroad. By 1957, the house had been razed. (SPL.)

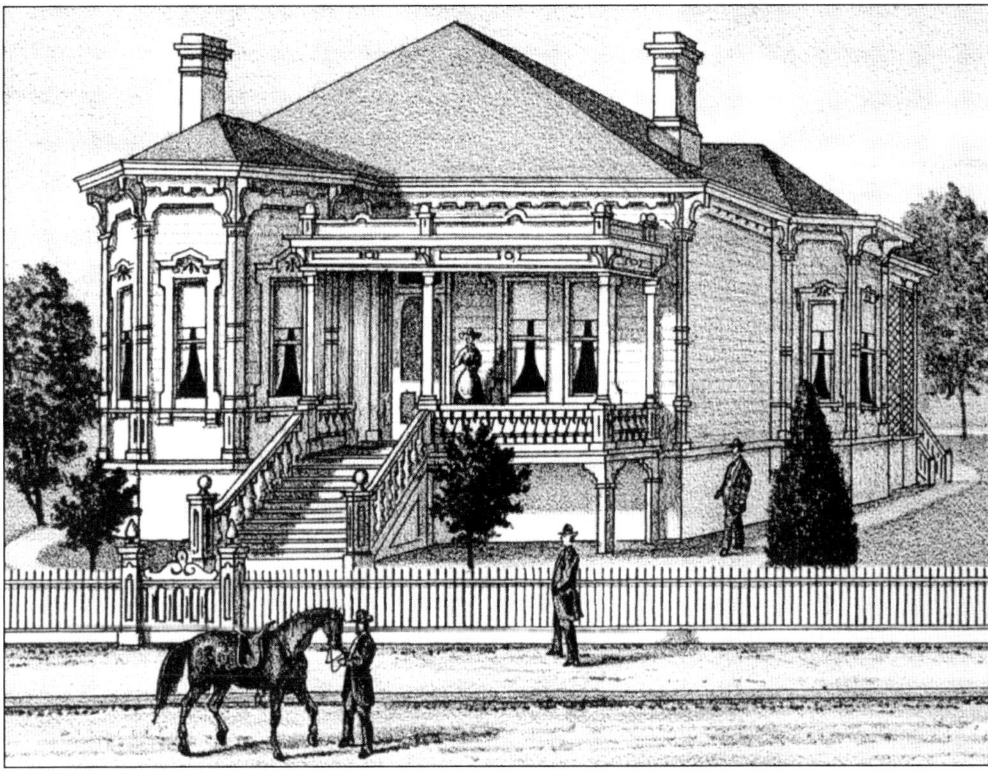

As portrayed here around 1880, W. R. Strong shared his 1018 G Street residence with wife, Jane, son Charles, and daughter Ella. In addition to his business commitments, Strong developed a reputation as a painter and one who would have his work displayed at the 1874 California State Fair. (SPL.)

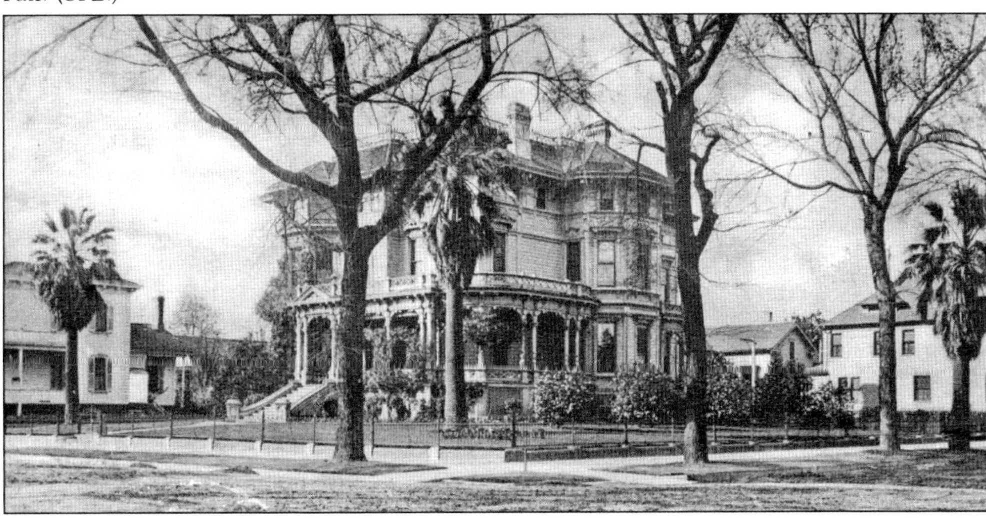

Seen here in 1890, this residence at 917 H Street was built in 1882 by architects Seth Babson and James Seadler in the Victorian Stick style. Its first resident was city pioneer Llewellyn Williams. In 1891, it was sold to Halsey G. Smith for $30,000 in gold. Well after Smith's departure, it was converted into a funeral home in 1907 and then acquired by the University Club in 1971. Today it serves ably as a youth hostel. (SPL.)

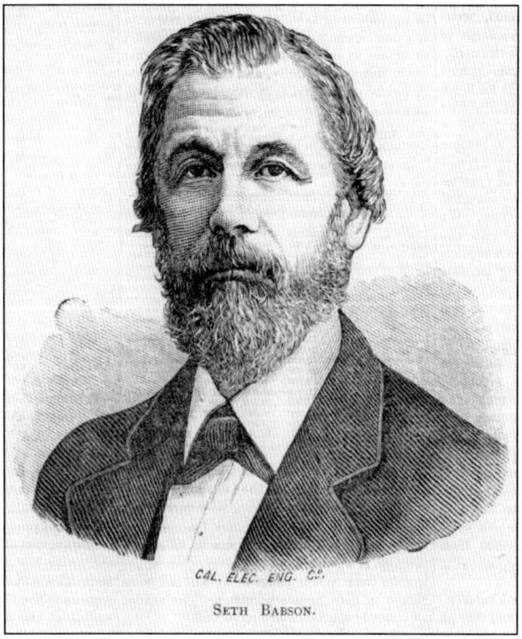

Portrayed here in 1884, Seth Babson was one of the most active of California's early architects, having practiced throughout the state for over 50 years. His work in Alkali Flat included two schools and several homes, most notably those of Halsey G. Smith and Charles Crocker. Outside of the Alkali, Babson was credited with building the Crocker home at Third and O Streets and the Stanford Mansion at Eighth and N Streets. (CSL.)

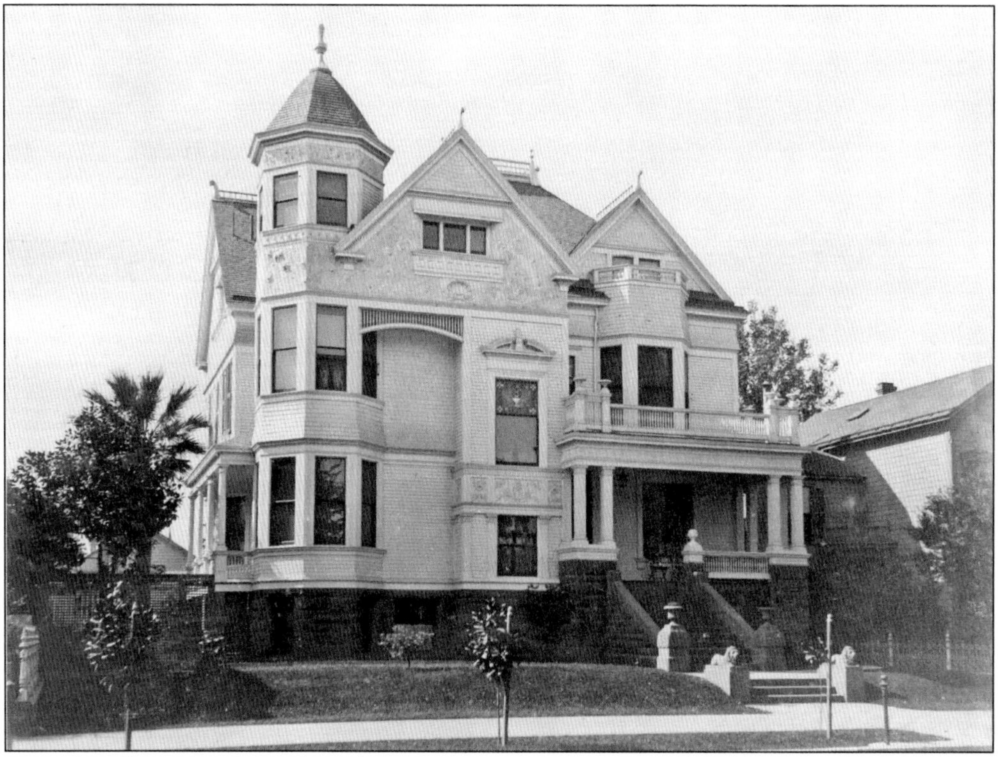

It was from his palatial shingle-style Queen Anne at 1220 H Street that Capt. Frank Ruhstaller kept close watch over his City Brewery. Set on a lot of some 12,800 square feet, the 21-room home was sold a few years after Ruhstaller's death in 1907 for $20,000. In the coming decades, it would be home to the Hermitage Club, then broken into residential units before its razing in the 1960s. (SPL.)

This early 1970s street scene, just outside of Angela's Bargain Center and the five-unit La Rosa Apartments at 500 Tenth Street, illustrates an adapted use of some of the Alkali's vintage architecture. The building itself, constructed between 1905 and 1915 by successful saloon operator Albert C. Huelsman, smites the contemporary design paradigm with a mix of Moorish-style windows and mission-style accents. (SPL.)

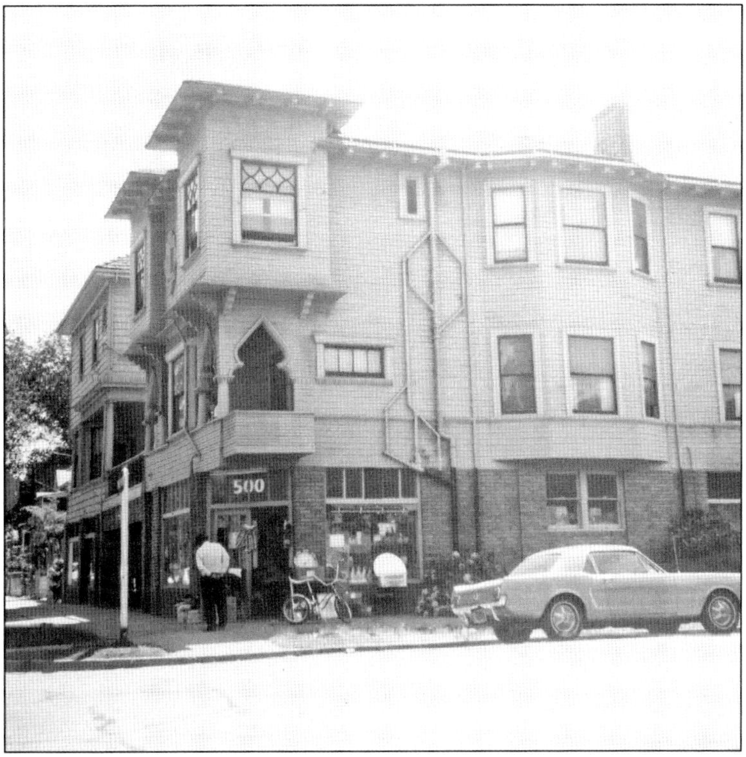

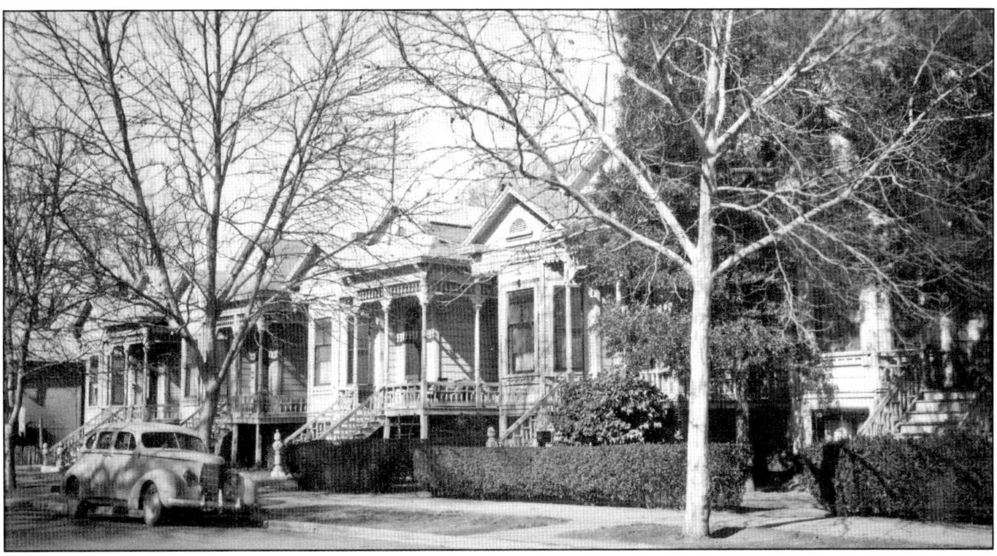

This 1949 photograph shows a row of homes occupied by blue-collar families on the north side of E Street, between Eleventh and Twelfth Streets. Their inhabitants, moving left to right, were Albert Ferguson (laborer at Crystal Cream), Clara Hocking (launderer), John Davis (mechanic at McClellan AFB), Pearl Stoner (launderer), and Walter Murray (mechanic at Sears Roebuck and Company). By 1952, half of them had been removed due to being uninhabitable. (CSH.)

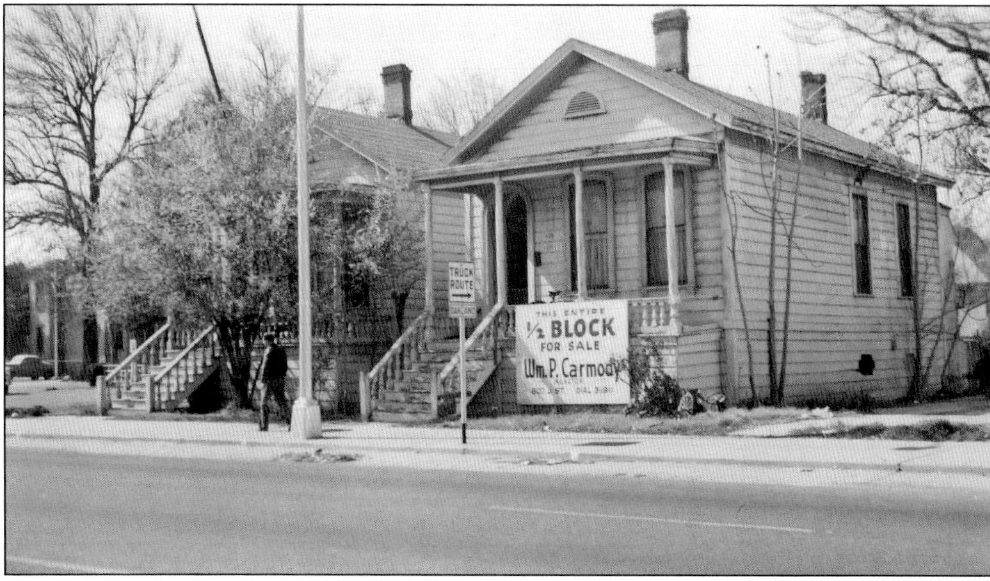

This March 1950 photograph shows deteriorated or dilapidated homes on Twelfth Street, between D and E Streets. By this time, Alkali blocks touching Twelfth Street, between D and G Streets, were finding that between 26 to 50 percent of their residential units were blighted. Moreover, as of 1957, nearly all the dwellings in the Alkali—all built of wood framing—had been constructed in 1919 or earlier. (CSH.)

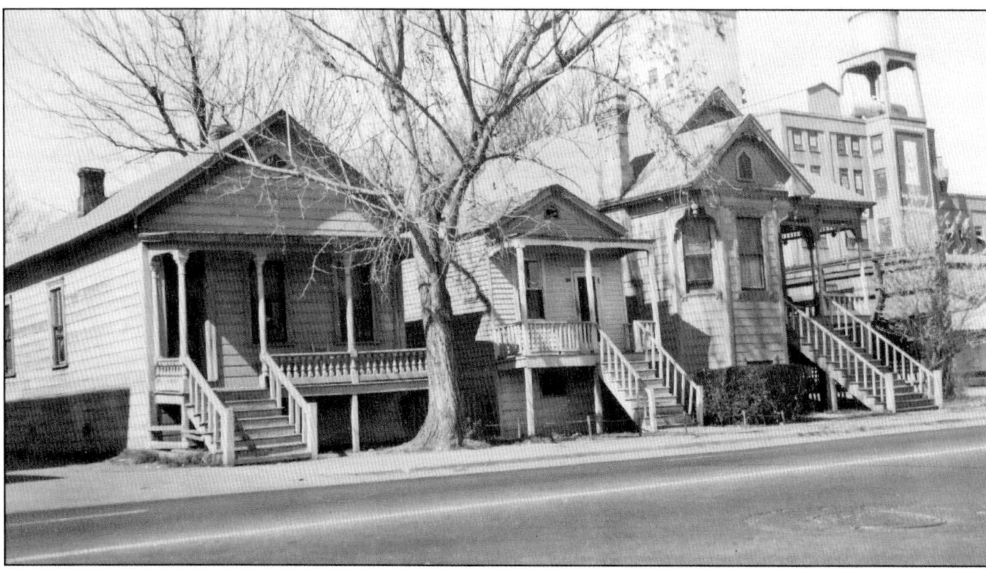

Looking exceptionally like a working-class neighborhood in spring 1950, and under the looming presence of the Globe Mill, is this section of Twelfth Street, between C and D Streets. From left to right, 314, 312, and 310 were occupied by Paul Sanchez (machinist's helper at the Southern Pacific shops), Alejandro Candela (warehouseman at Globe Mill), and Pasquale Salerno (painter) respectively. All three of these homes were built before 1915. (CSH.)

In August 1903, Edward and Augusta Sullivan gave birth to a child at 1100 E Street and decided to name her Helen. She is pictured here in her 1922 graduation photograph from Sacramento High School. Following school, she spent the next 10 years working as a telephone operator and stenographer for the State of California. Helen lived at both 1100 and 1110 at different times from birth through her late 20s. (SPL.)

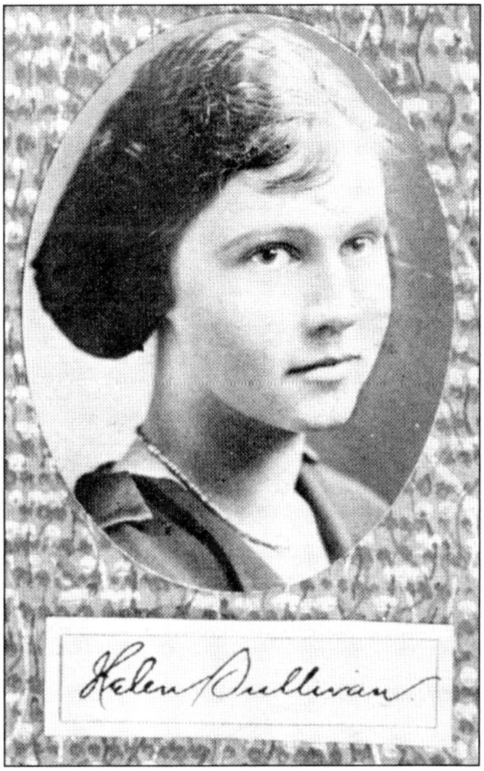

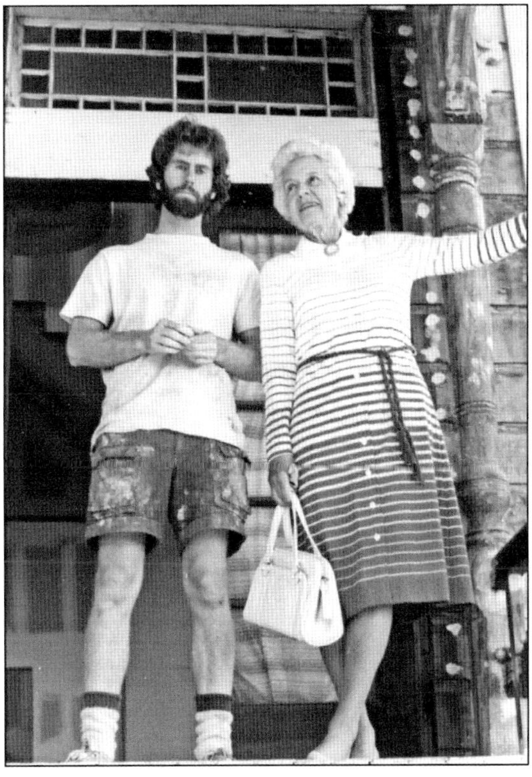

Pictured here in the late 1970s are Helen Sullivan Randolph and Bill Masters standing in front of 1100 E Street. Masters, then employed with AT&T, had just purchased the home and was renovating it when Helen visited. At the time, Helen was living in East Sacramento after residing for nearly two decades just outside the Alkali at Seventeenth and G Streets. She died in May 1990. (Bill Masters.)

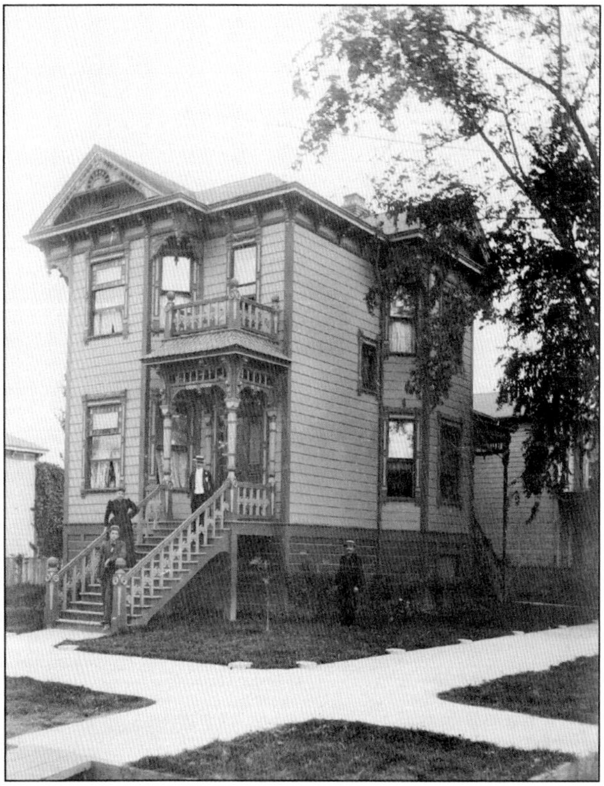

Helen's father, Edward, was a blacksmith for Southern Pacific. At left, he is pictured in the mid-1890s in his late teens at the base of the steps of the 1100 E Street Eastlake-style home. His mother and father, Peter and Mary, who moved to Sacramento from New York, are on the steps, while his brother Frank, a machinist for Southern Pacific, is standing in the yard. Edward and Peter died within five months of one another in 1915, Edward of typhoid fever in August and Peter of a stroke in April. Both are buried at the Old City Cemetery. Etched on Edward's grave is the word "Papa." Below is a picture of the home as it appears today. (Both Bill Masters.)

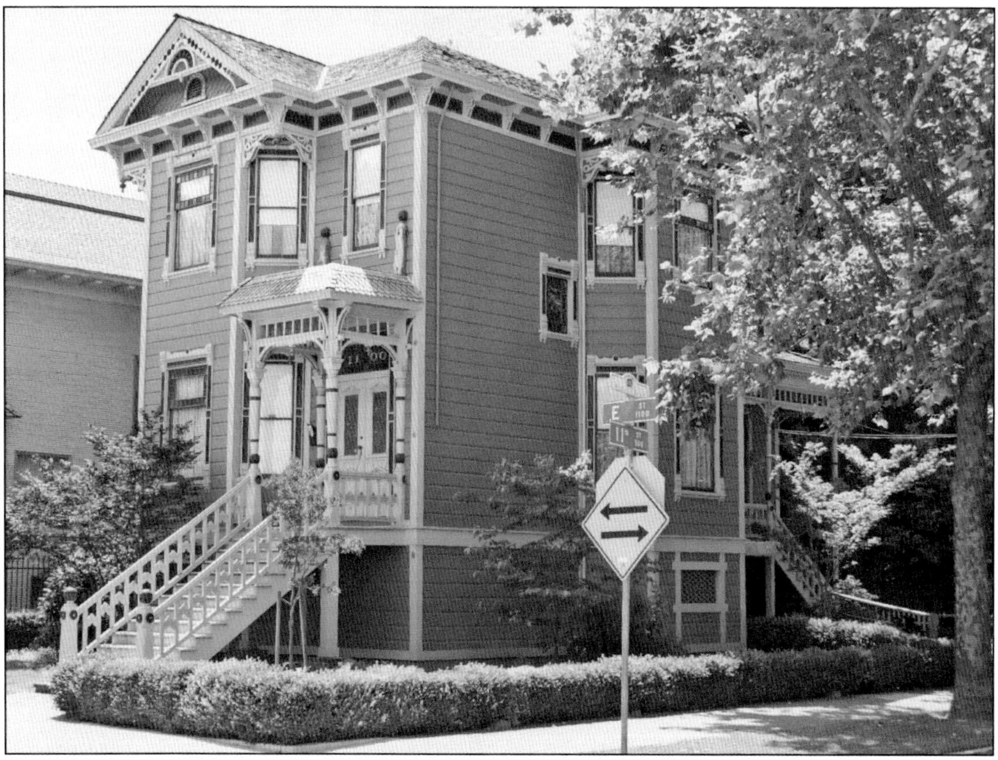

Taken in the winter of 1893 is this photograph of the Sullivans. The eldest boy at 20, George, stands near the door. Frank, 18 years old, leans on the left post. Ed, the youngest son at 13 years old, and Helen's father, is at the top of the steps. Peter and Mary stand farther down the steps. (Bill Masters.)

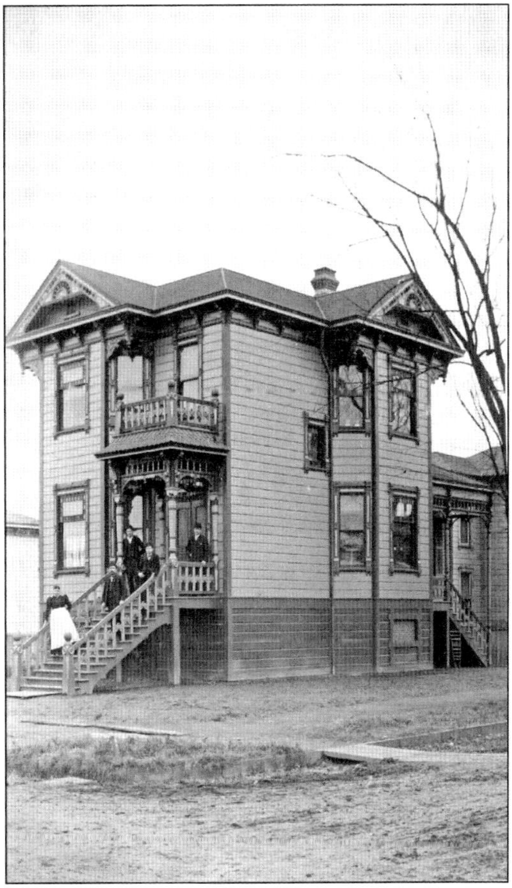

This springtime scene in the Alkali, around 1910, reveals the Sullivan's stately 1100 E Street home and a rare view of a passable Eleventh Street between E and F Streets, where J. Neely Johnson Park sits today. Just to the left of the Sullivan house is 1104, which was built in 1906 with, although not visible, a set of Moorish-style arches reminiscent of the Huelsman Building. (Bill Masters.)

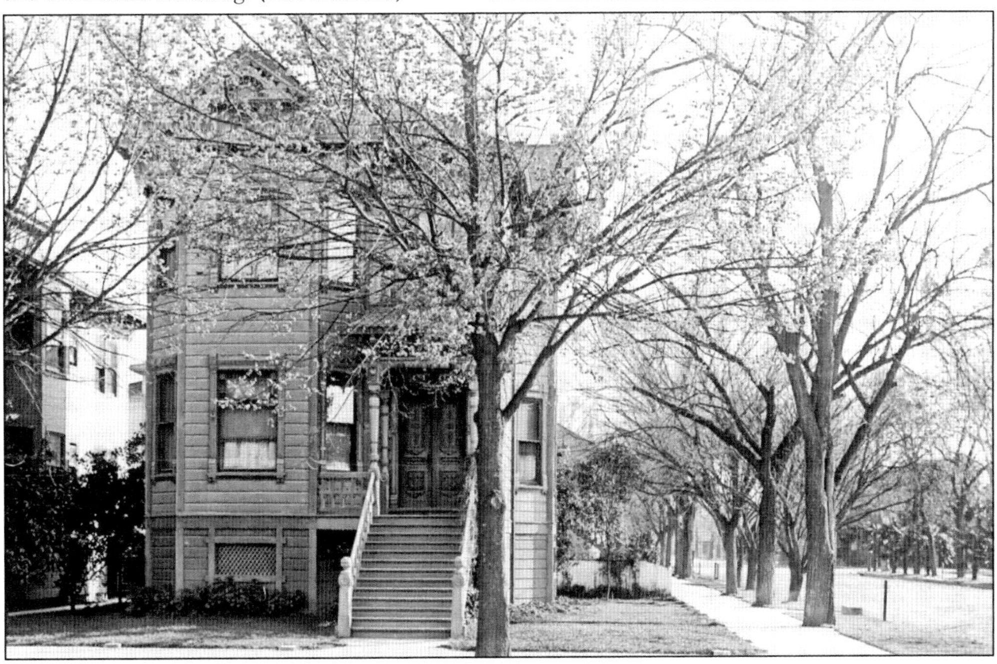

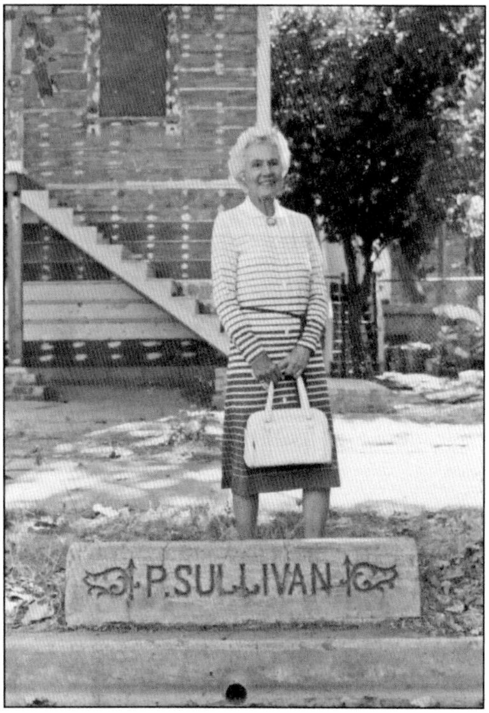

In this late-1970s photograph, Helen Sullivan Randolph proudly stands behind the carriage step designed for her grandfather, Peter Sullivan. Few of the distinctive artifacts remain citywide, let alone the Alkali, where those in existence include that of the Sullivans and the Calvin Crocker house at 530 Tenth Street. (Bill Masters.)

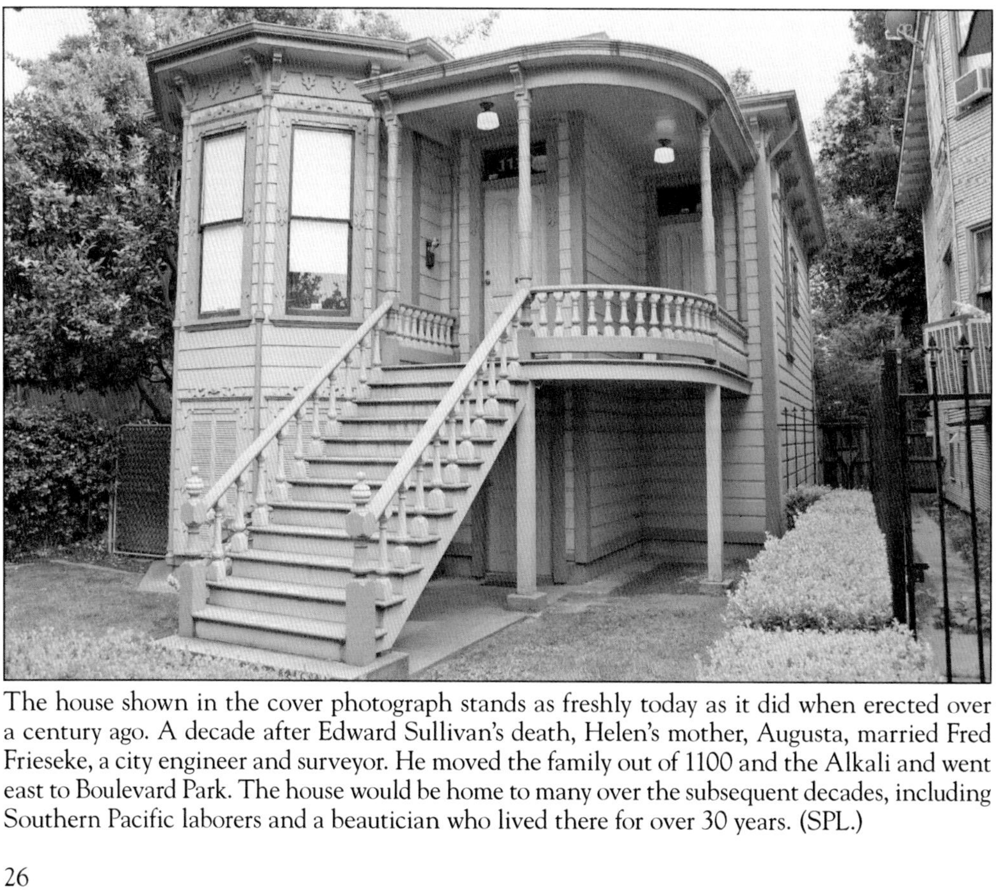

The house shown in the cover photograph stands as freshly today as it did when erected over a century ago. A decade after Edward Sullivan's death, Helen's mother, Augusta, married Fred Frieseke, a city engineer and surveyor. He moved the family out of 1100 and the Alkali and went east to Boulevard Park. The house would be home to many over the subsequent decades, including Southern Pacific laborers and a beautician who lived there for over 30 years. (SPL.)

The Mesick House at 517 Eighth Street is one of only two remaining High Victorians in Sacramento that possess a distinctive mansard roof (the other is the Stanford Mansion on Eight and N Streets). The home was built in the mid-1890s for Mary Mesick. Irish immigrant Owen Pendergast was the home's next resident. He made his living as a rail truck builder and rope splicer for Southern Pacific. Its current owners purchased the dilapidated home (at right) in the early 1980s while also practicing a community activism that has come to typify so many Alkali dwellers. Their stand against area gangs resulted in an attempted firebombing of their home in the early 1990s. They remain, and the house (below) is nearing full rehabilitation. (Both Dan Hood.)

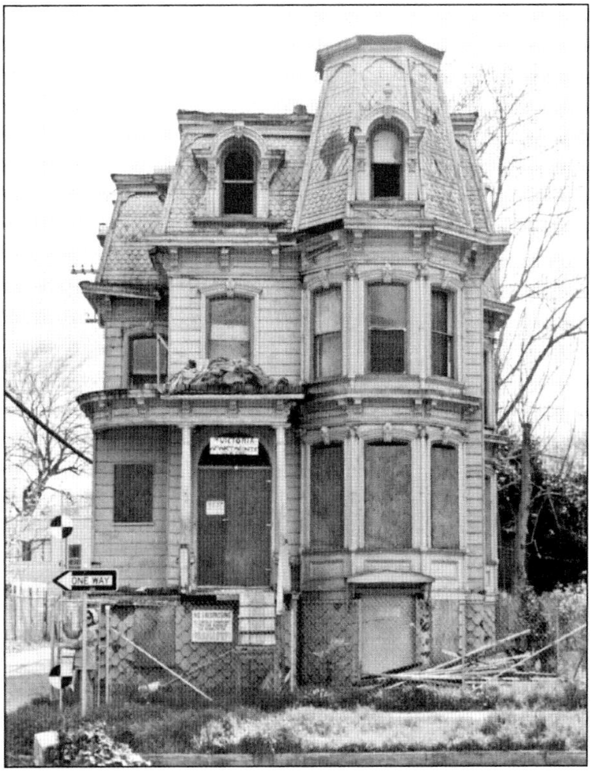

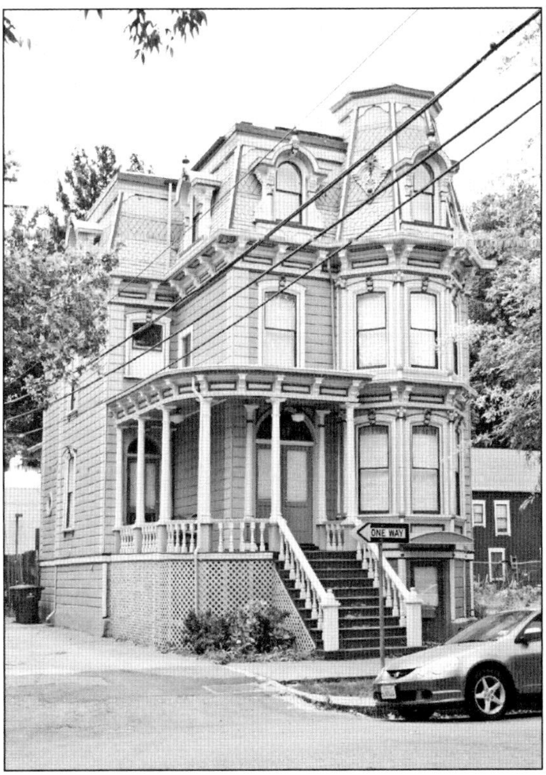

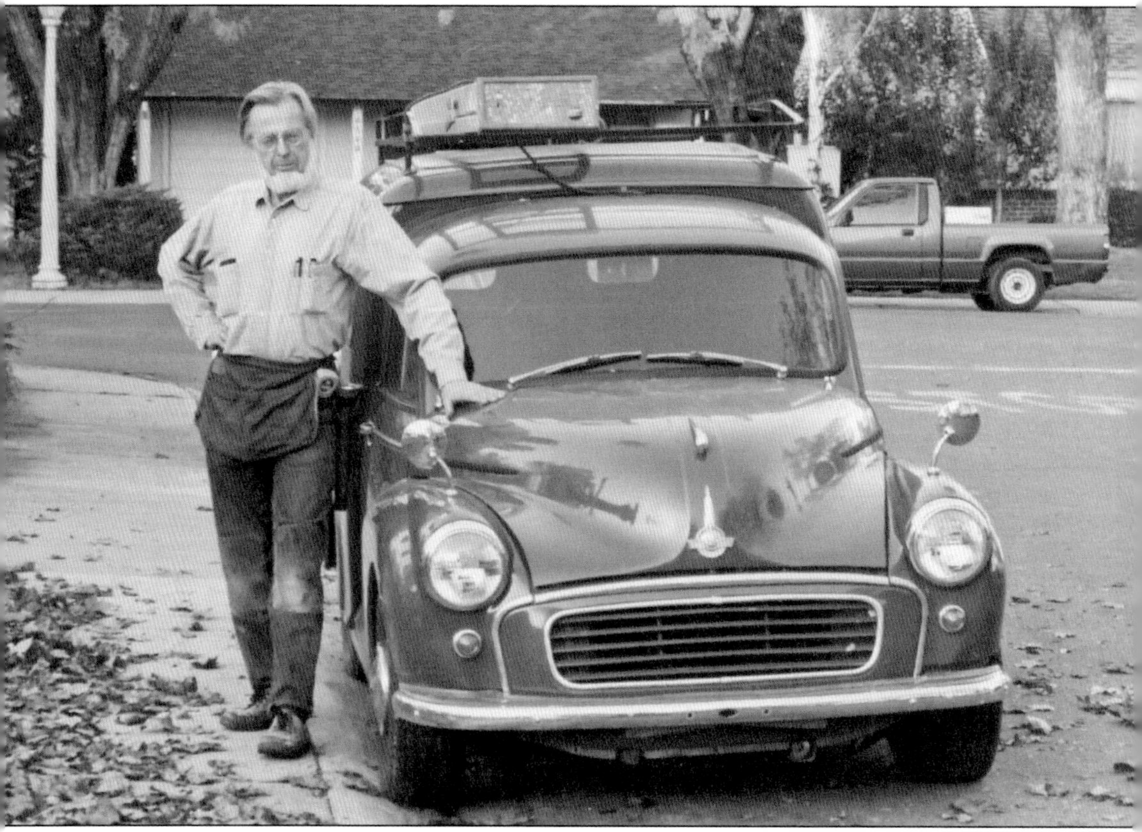

Posing here with his Morris Minor van is Roger Lathe, a longtime resident of Alkali Flat and one of the city's foremost architectural historians. In addition to involving himself in community activism and freelance writing, the self-styled "housewright" was a professional contractor and licensed home inspector. In 1976, he and his wife, Liza, moved from Philadelphia to the Alkali, where for three decades they worked to restore the 1894 home they also lived in. He passed away in February 2009 at the age of 75. In one of his classic "Site Seeing" columns from the September 17, 1990, *Sacramento Bee*, Lathe spoke of his beloved Alkali Flat by imploring Sacramentans to "take time to stroll around to look at the houses other than those open for tour. Appreciate the variety and the contrasts; we live in a display case of urban sociology and social economics as well as historic architecture. . . . Which is why, after a century and a half, it's still premature to be critical of Alkali Flat. It's not finished yet." (Liza Lathe.)

Two

Alkali Institutions

by James Scott and Tom Tolley

As Alkali Flat's residential profile slowly yet surely diversified, and the neighborhood's population surged, a multitude of community institutions soon followed. The boilermaker, blacksmith, launderer, restaurateur, and brewmaster required places for child education, medical care, worship, comfort, and leisure.

Reliable public and/or parochial education was a working-class imperative for much of the 19th and 20th Centuries. Whether through some sincere "passion for schooling" or an adherence to a perceived correlation between academic achievement and economic welfare, parents, at any given time, between 1864 and 1974 relied on the choice of St. Joseph's Academy and at least one public school, at Union, McKinley, or Washington. In addition to Alkali Park and the Emiliano Zapata or J. Neely Johnson "mini-parks," neighborhood schools also offered open space for activity, leisure, and congregation.

Hospitals of the Central Pacific then Southern Pacific Railroad, albeit private and company-operated, provided state-of-the-art health care to thousands of the Alkali's rail-employed residents. Over a one-year period (1870–1871), the CPR Hospital cared for nearly 1,193 employees. While serving at both of the hospital's Alkali locations, medical generalists, like expatriate Scotsman Thomas Ross and Thomas Huntington, became national leaders in industrial orthopedics and the treatment of open-wound injuries.

Although not one stands today, St. Joseph's Academy, Kingsley Chapel (also known as the Central Methodist Episcopal Church), the African Methodist Episcopal Church (AME), and the short-lived Chinese Chapel offered Alkali Flat venues to faith. While the AME was groundbreaking, the Chinese Chapel gave an alternative to native belief systems. The multidimensional St. Joseph's provided Catholics a steady foundation until its ignominious transformation into a county parking lot in the 1970s. And, for nearly 80 years, Alkali Protestants were served by Kingsley Chapel, first on Sixth Street, and then on Eleventh and H Streets.

The art collective of the Royal Chicano Air Force brought multiculturalism and internationally recognized creativity to the Alkali while also inspiring generations of local Chicanos to fight social injustice. During the 1950s and onward, places like Club Reno provided refuge to a burgeoning Latino community. In their own right, the legendary La Raza Bookstore and Galeria Posada further served as incubators of class and ethnic consciousness.

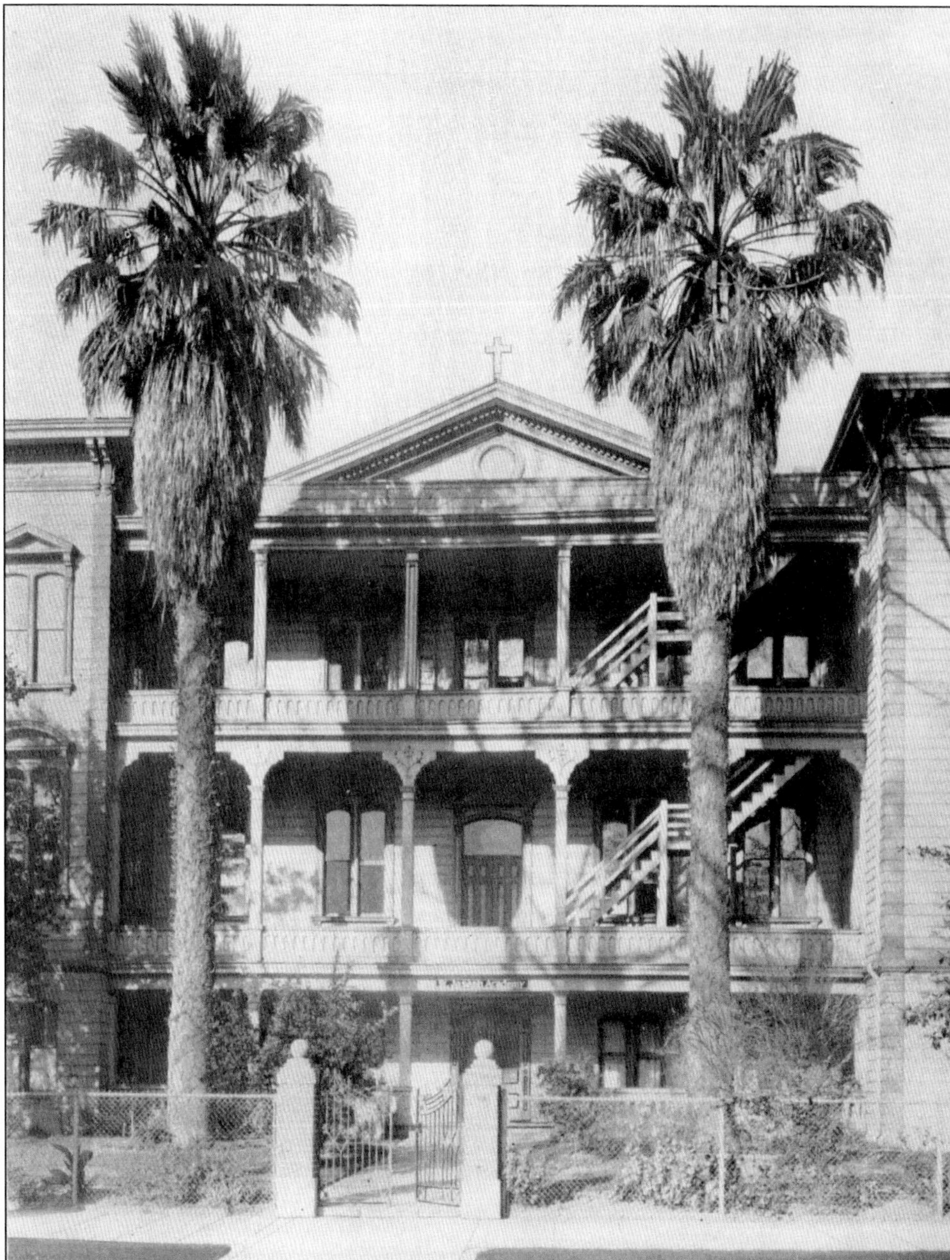

PALM TREES IN FRONT OF THE ACADEMY

The Sisters of Mercy performed works of charity for their Alkali Flat neighbors, feeding the hungry, visiting the sick and imprisoned, and providing aid where needed, but their primary purpose at St. Joseph Academy was seen as the care and education of Sacramento's school-age children. The old academy flanked by the towering palm trees planted in 1879 served as the convent after a new school went up in 1926. By the late 1940s, the structure was considered unfit for use and razed. (SPL.)

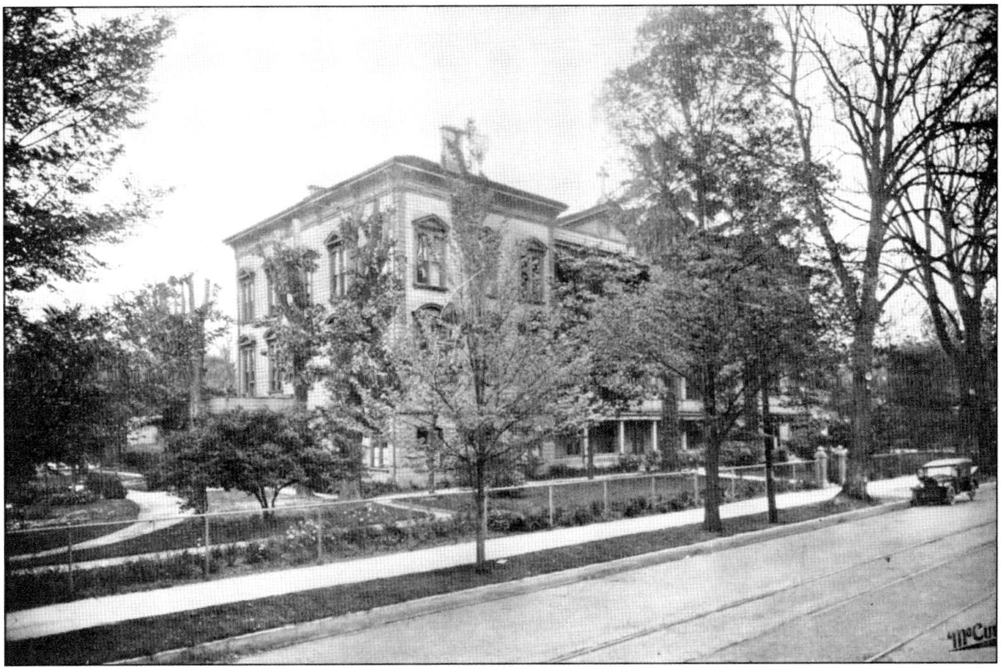

Established as a day and boarding school conducted by the Sisters of Mercy before the end of the Civil War, St. Joseph's Academy occupied the entire block between F and G Streets and Eighth and Ninth Streets in Alkali Flat for over a century. (SPL.)

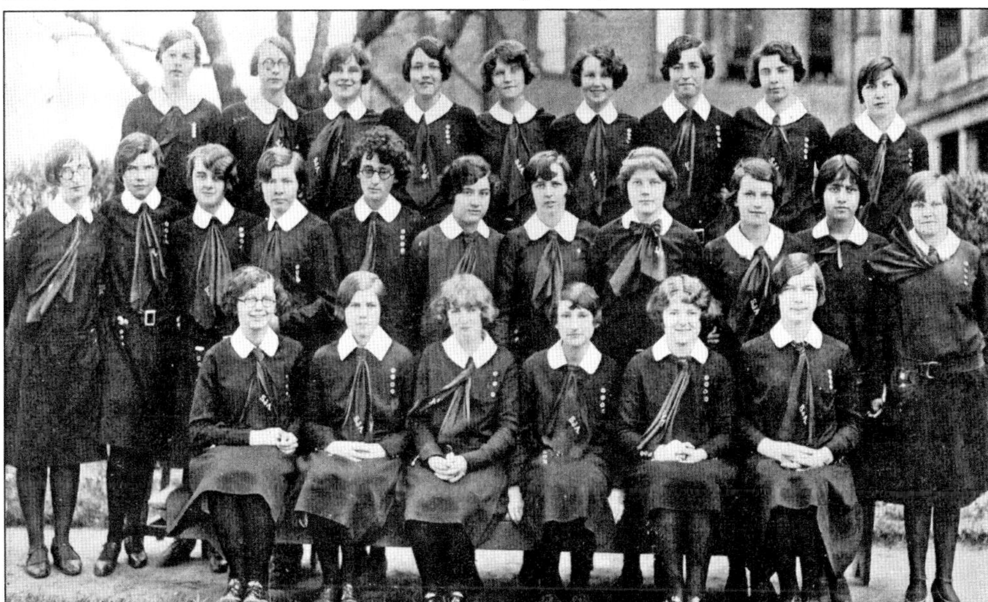

Twenty-six young ladies from the class of 1928 pose proudly for this portrait from the 1927 St. Joseph Academy yearbook. All of them wore dark stockings and uniform dresses with buttons in a row down the left and a tie lettered "SJA." Generations of young women attended the academy, many of them from families prominent or noteworthy, including Beata Hobrecht, the associate editor of *Echoes from SJA*, whose father and uncle founded Hobrecht Lighting in 1909. (SPL.)

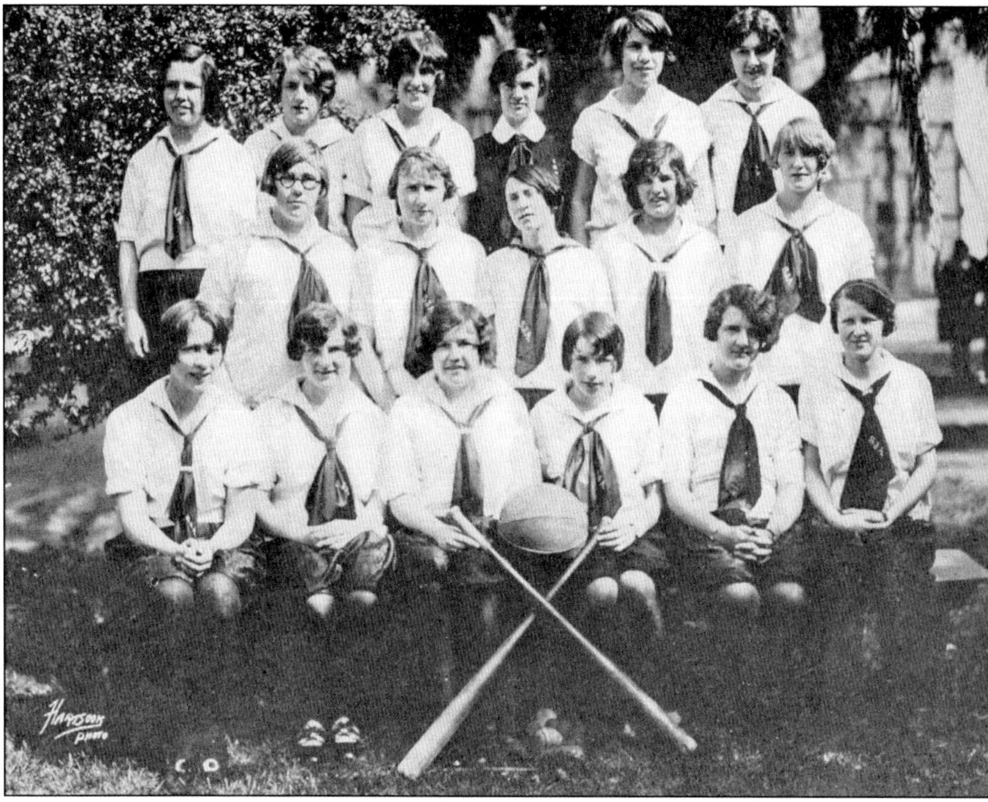

St. Joseph's Academy students took their sports seriously, and the sophomore class of 1926–1927 was the best at baseball and the new game on campus, basketball. Team leader Ila Anderson poses perfectly above the crossed bats and ball symbolizing her charge. Ila's father, Andrew, went from farming in 1920 to employment with the Southern Pacific railroad by 1930, when she was 20. (SPL.)

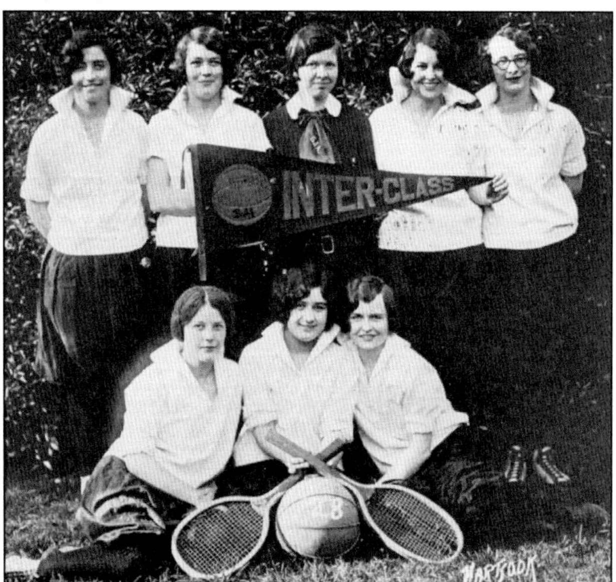

The class of the 1928 "Senior Athletic Group" poses confidently for the yearbook of St. Joseph's Academy, where academics, art, business, and commerce prominently figured into an education. Sports, including baseball, basketball, golf, tennis, and track, were stressed and interclass rivalries as well as league games with other parochial schools kept spirits high and bodies fit. Pictured here from left to right are (first row) Catherine Steele, Beatrice Fugazi, and Alice McBride; (second row) Clare Drysdale, Julia Cavanaugh, team leader Marie Palmiter, Catherine Shannon, and Marie Holzworth. (SPL.)

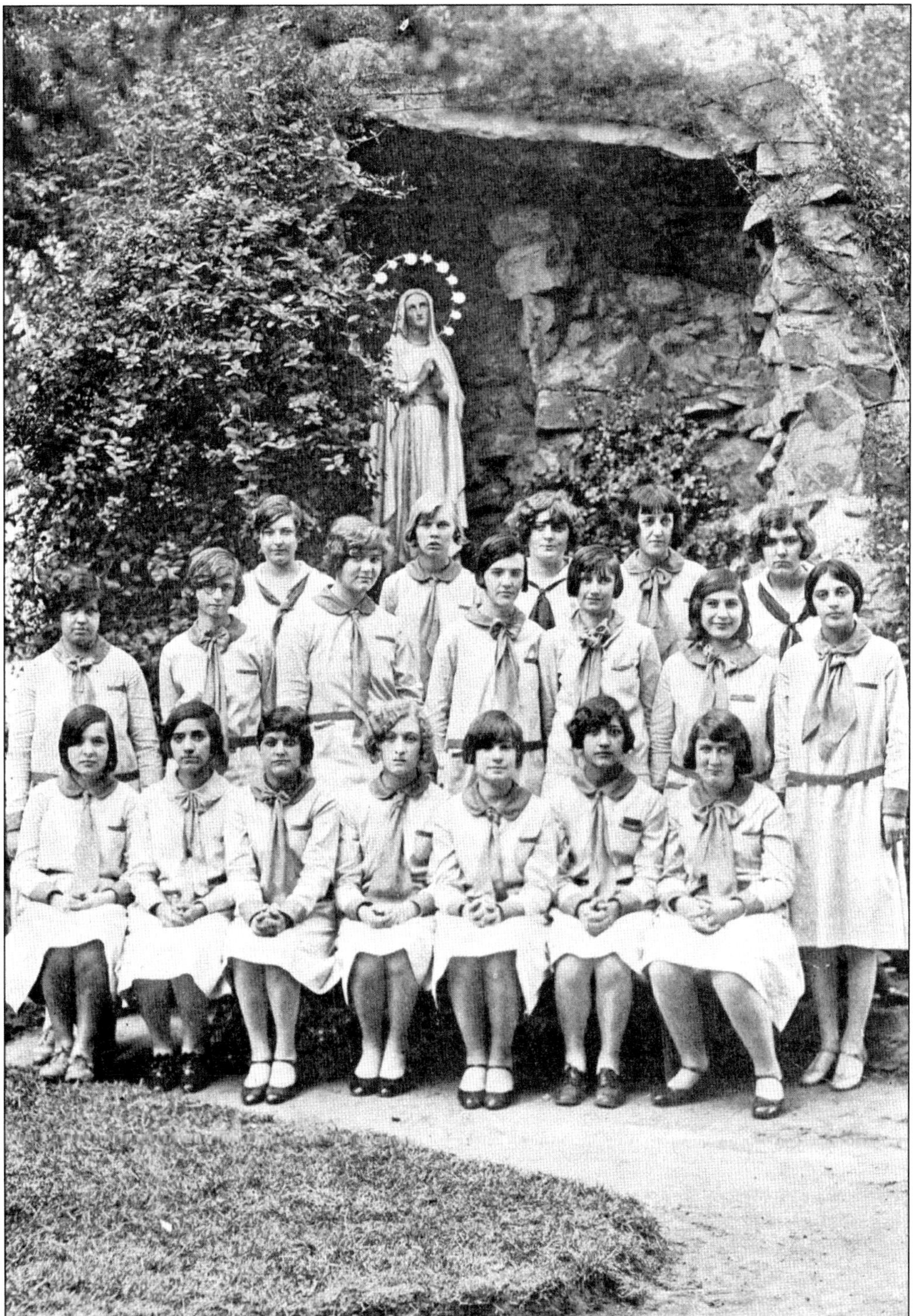

St. Joseph's Academy, incorporated in 1875, had been in the business of graduating healthy, refined, and capable young women since the late 1860s, 50 years before this class of 1931 poses on campus before the "Grotto of Our Lady of Lourdes" for the 1928 yearbook. (SPL.)

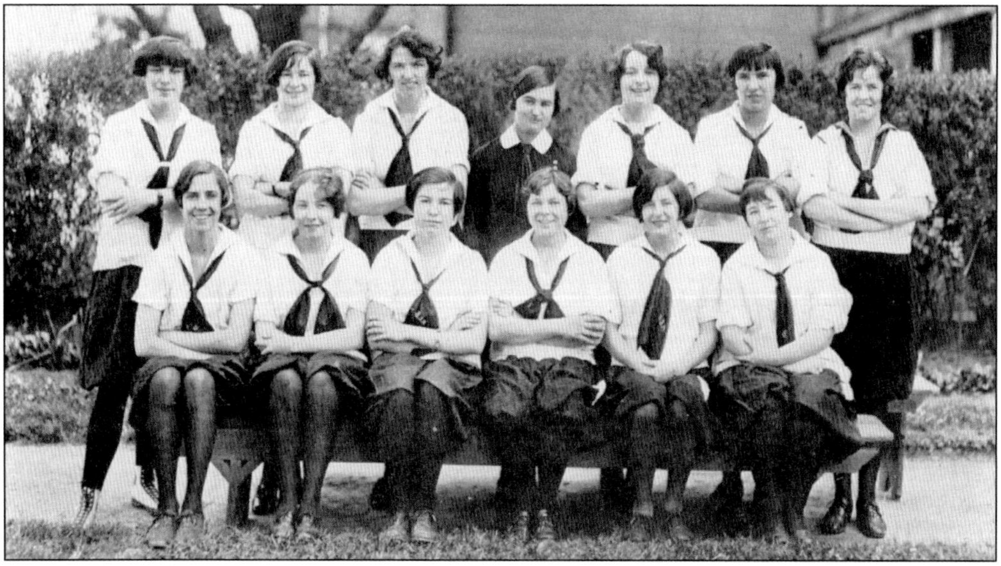

Many of the students that took lessons or resided at the site came from large families with working-class backgrounds and middle-class expectations. Elsie Carmody, the last lass standing on the right, had a father who was a spring-maker for the Southern Pacific Railroad, a brother who was a firefighter for the city, two brothers who sold real estate and hardware for large local firms, and a sister employed as a typist at the state controller's office. (SPL.)

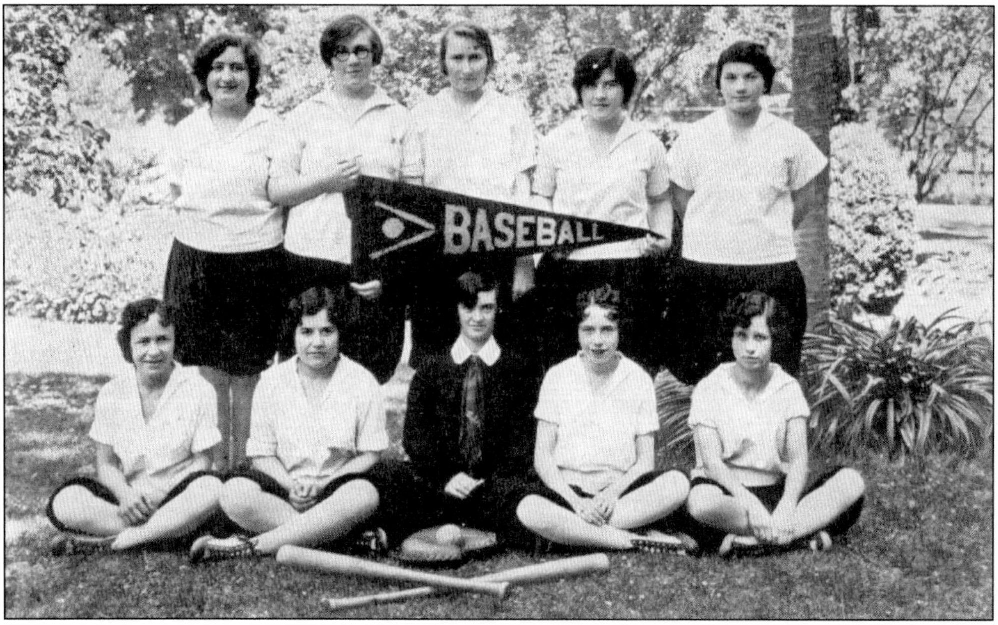

The senior baseball team of St. Joseph's Academy poses 80 years ago bare-legged, equipment on display, in the landscaped gardens of the grounds that covered one square block of Alkali Flat. Those who can be identified are Edith Pinaglia, (second row, far left) born in 1912 and one of three sisters who attended the academy; teammates Marie McLoughlin and Elizabeth Bennett (second and fourth from left, respectively, in the second row); and team leaders Ila Anderson and Claire Calley (first row, third and fourth from left respectively), both born in 1911, sitting cross-legged beneath the pennant won for baseball under their guidance. (SPL.)

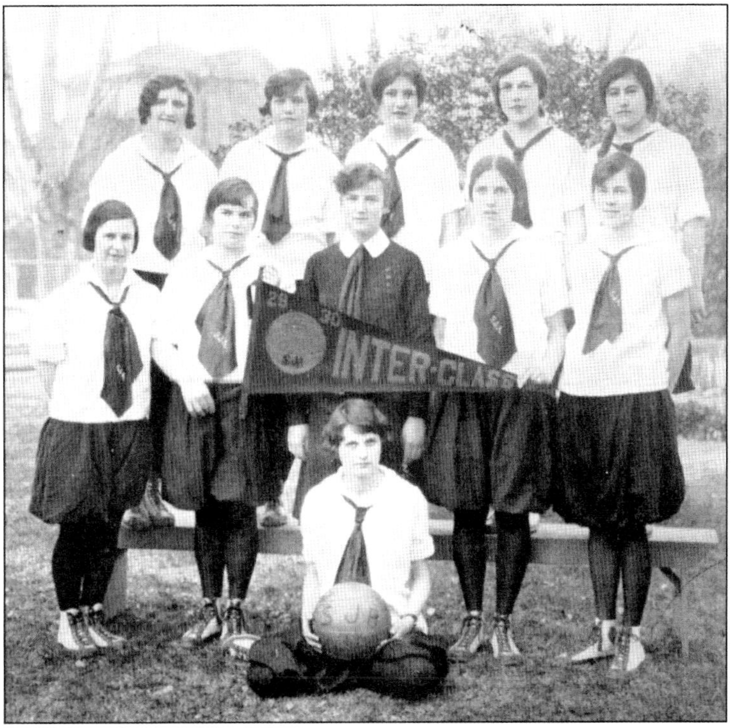

The interclass pennant in basketball went to the juniors of St. Joseph's Academy, class of 1930, who pose in their best athletic outfits. Bounded by a residential district adjacent to industry and close to a growing downtown midway through its century of service, a historian noted, "The school is beautifully situated and every precaution is taken to insure a healthy environment for the girls . . . the graduates rank among the most accomplished and intellectual women of the state." (SPL.)

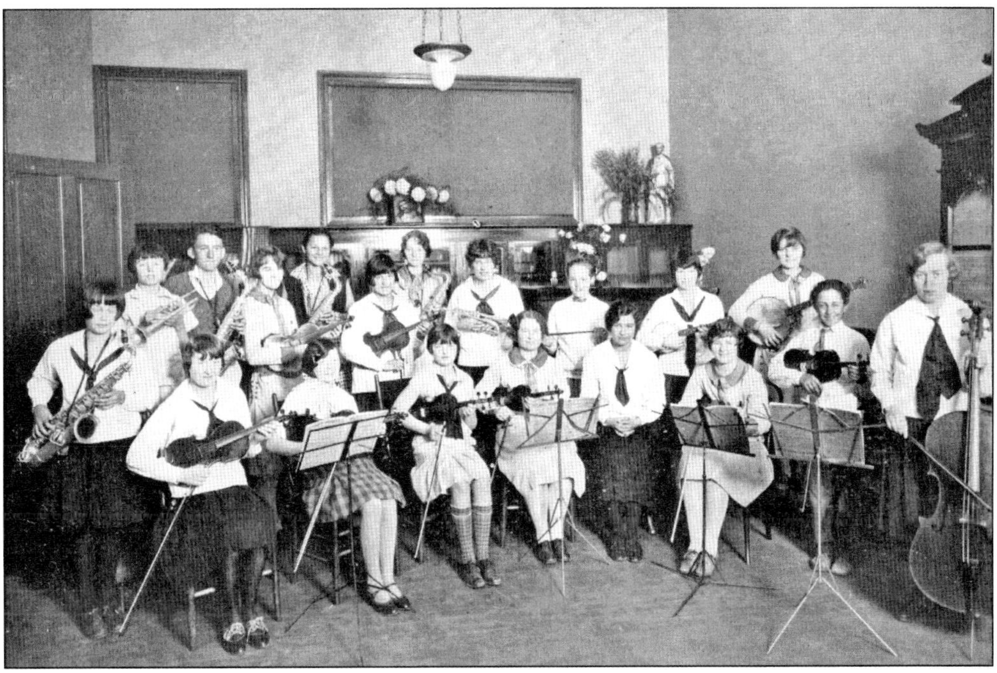

Music was a long-standing tradition at St. Joseph Academy, and this picture of their orchestra appeared in *Echoes of SJA*, the school's yearbook for 1927. St. Joseph Convent's first superior, Rev. Mother Mary Vincent Phelan, studied music in Europe and headed a department that instilled a love and skill for instruments and sounds—at a price. In 1895, tuition per quarter was $60, but charges for private music lessons ran from $1 a visit to $18 for four months of organ practice. (SPL.)

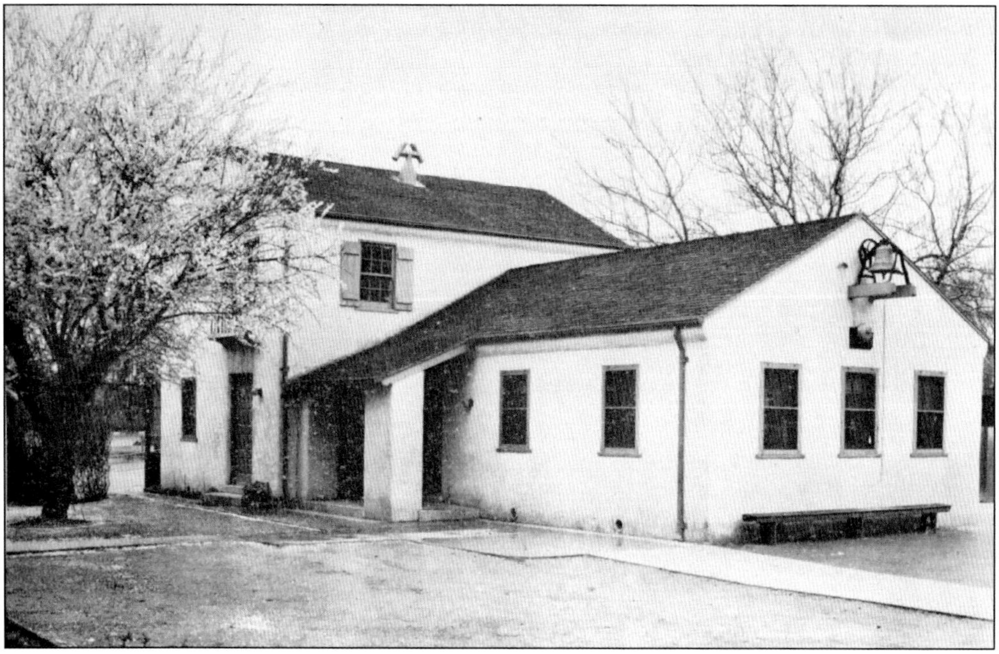

The 1928 yearbook for St. Joseph Academy refers to this building on the grounds as "The Lodge," where lunches were eaten and school-day parties were held. The bell with an attached pull rope hearkened back to the earlier days of the convent and school, before electricity came to town. (SPL.)

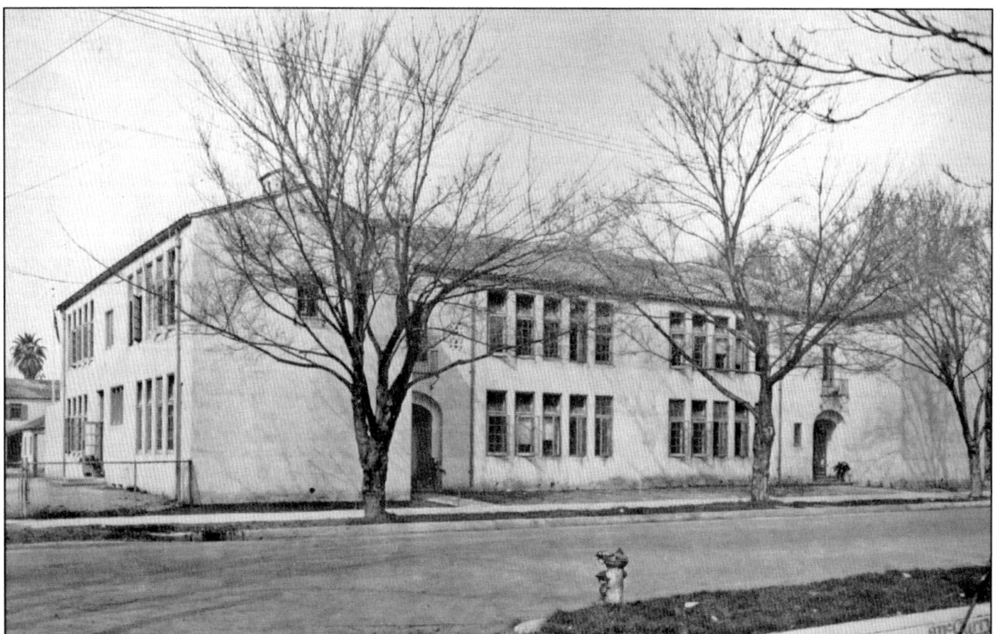

The new school building at the corner of Ninth and F Streets opened in the fall of 1926 at a cost of $65,000 and housed the parochial eight grades and St. Joseph's Academy High School. The library and business department stayed in the old structure until early in the 1950s, when a concrete convent went up on the old site. (SPL.)

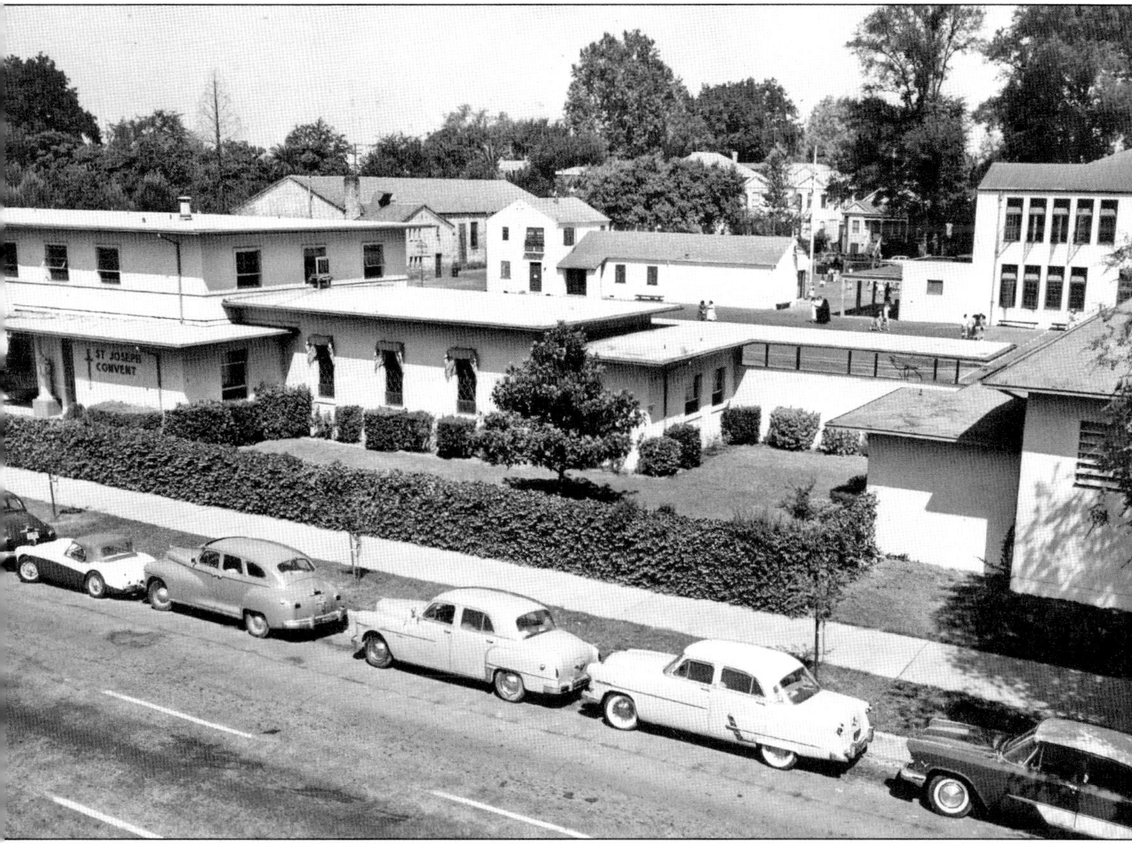

The new convent at Eighth and G Streets and much of the square block St. Joseph's Academy school grounds are visible in this shot taken in the late 1950s from G Street looking northeast. Adjacent to the convent is the chapel and a block of classrooms that face Ninth Street. The two-story building in the upper right is the new St. Joseph's Parochial School constructed in 1926, and the buildings next to the flagpole house the kitchen and cafeteria. (CSH.)

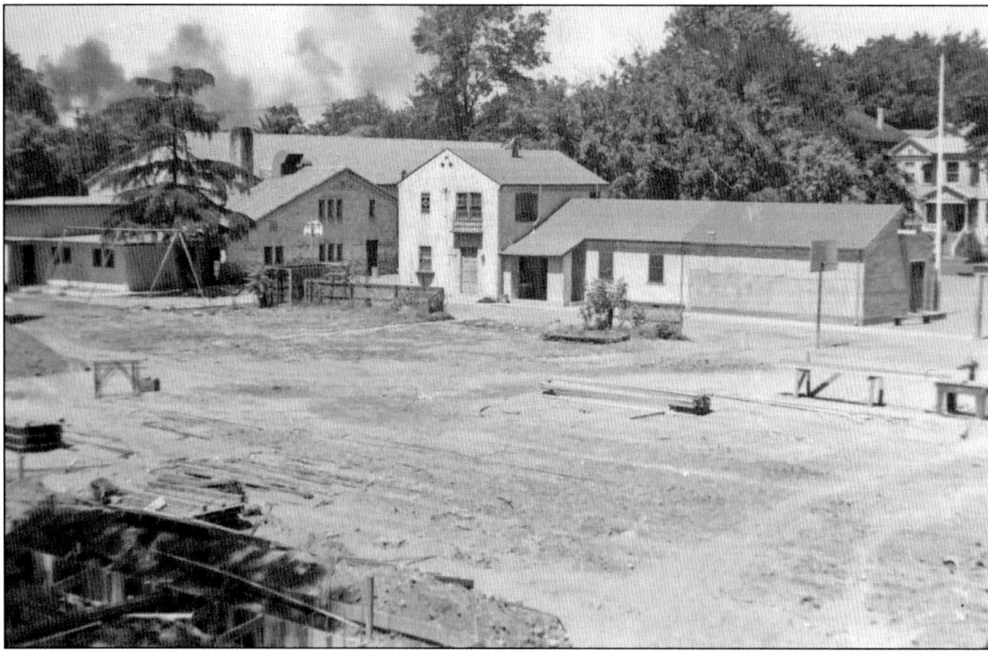

By August 1950, construction on the new St. Joseph's Convent was still at ground level, offering an unobstructed look at the vacant playing fields and the school cafeteria with the old bell used in days gone by above the entrance. The gymnasium and auditorium on the left face Eighth Street, and beyond the cafeteria building some of the stately homes still standing on F Street are visible. (CSH.)

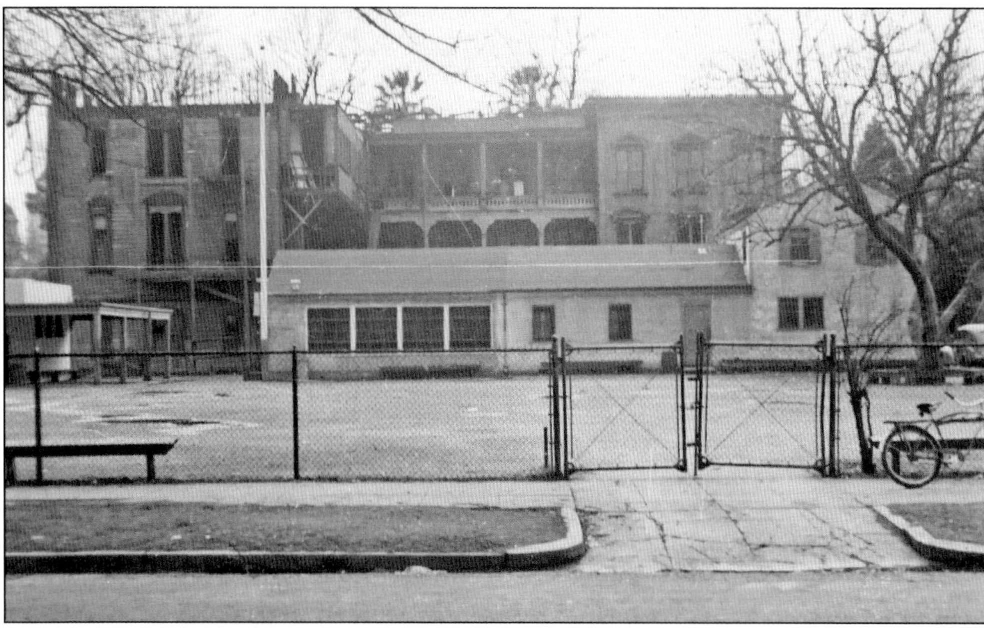

St. Joseph's Academy and Convent underwent extensive renovation at different stages of its century-plus tenure in Sacramento. This shot taken from F Street, before the old school structure was razed, shows the venerable group of buildings that housed the dining rooms, kitchen, chapel, dormitory, classrooms, and recreation hall on its creaky three stories for generations. (CSH.)

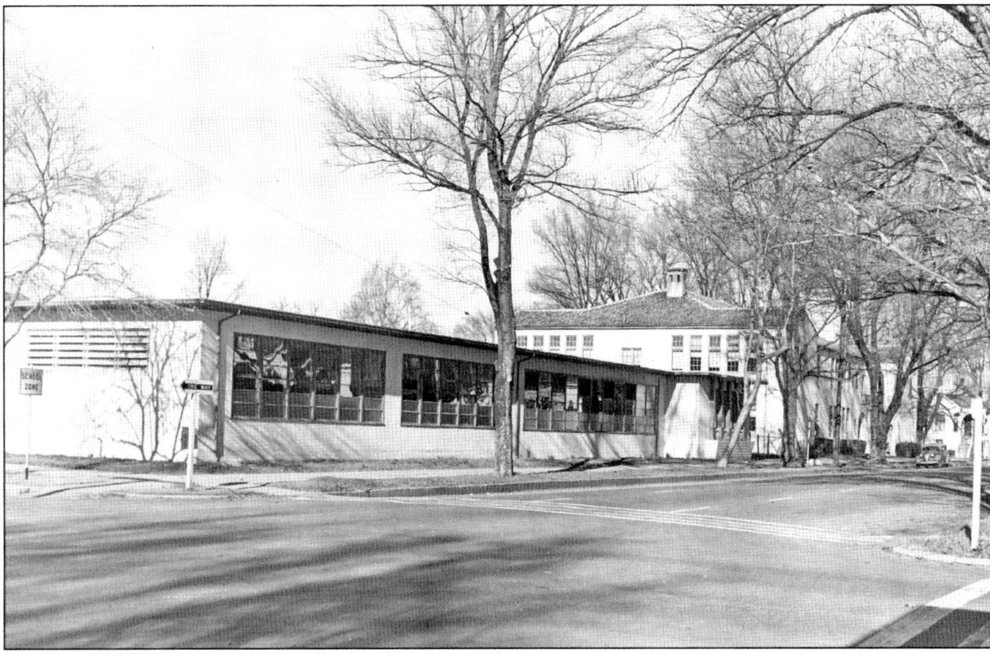

A row of empty classrooms and St. Joseph's Parochial School face a nearly deserted Ninth Street on the last day of 1950. When the parochial school first opened in 1926, Mrs. Ella McClatchy donated a set of copies of famous paintings collected during her travels in Europe to St. Joseph's Academy, and they hung in the entrance hall of the school for years. (CSH.)

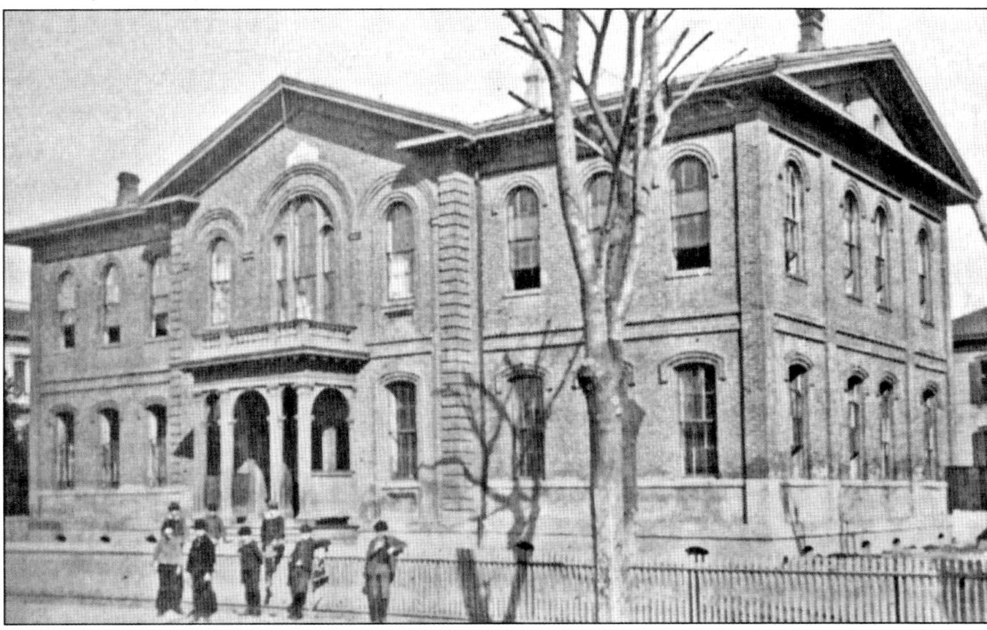

Located at Thirteenth and G Streets, Washington School was built in 1869 at a cost of $13,720 to replace two wooden structures felled by arson and to meet the needs of the city's burgeoning northern wards. In 1919, the school's name and pupils relocated to Seventeenth and E Streets, and its use—as a continuation school, training center for the Army Signal Corps, and headquarters for the American Red Cross—continued well into the 20th century. (SPL.)

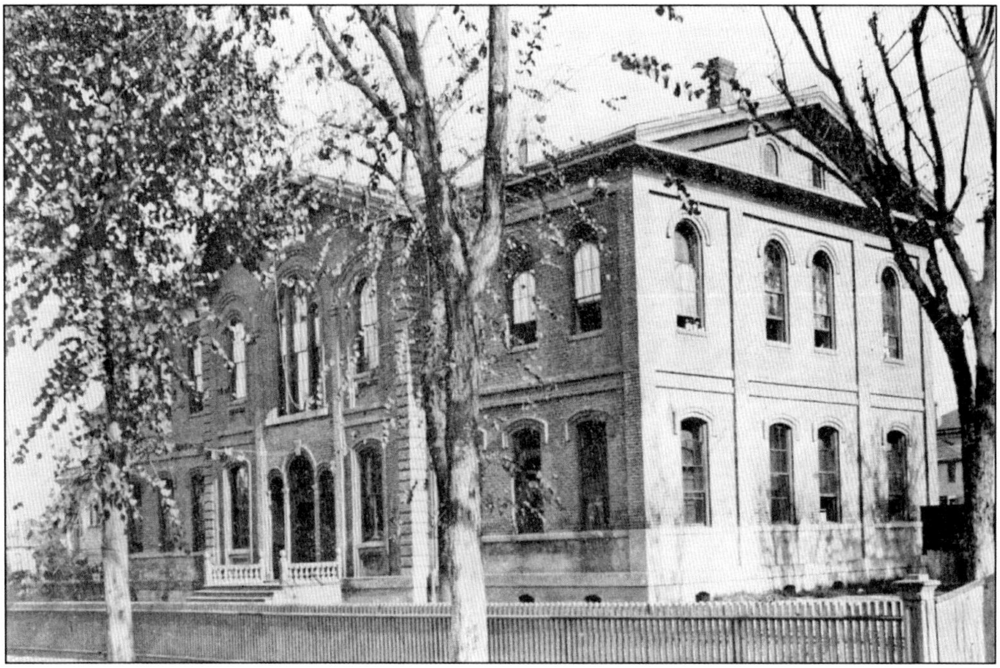

The second public school to be added to the Alkali neighborhood, shown here in 1895, was the Union Free School in 1864. Built at a cost of just over $10,000, the two-story brick schoolhouse at Seventh and G Streets was meant to replace Primary School No. 5, which had been set ablaze "by an incendiary" in August 1863. Also know as Primary School No. 1, it was closed in 1903–1904. (SPL.)

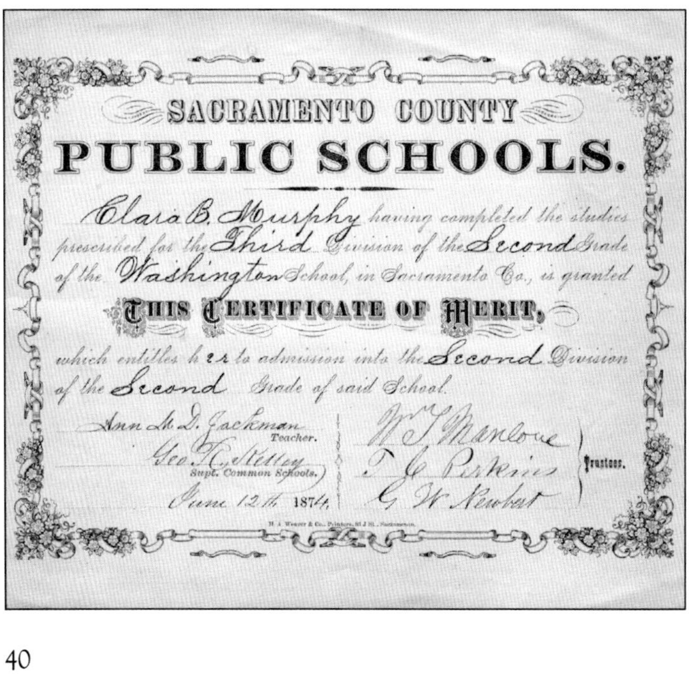

SACRAMENTO COUNTY

PUBLIC SCHOOLS.

Clara B. Murphy having completed the studies prescribed for the Third Division of the Second Grade of the Washington School, in Sacramento Co., is granted

THIS CERTIFICATE OF MERIT,

which entitles her to admission into the Second Division of the Second Grade of said School.

Ann M. D. Jackman, Teacher.
Geo. H. Stelley, Supt. Common Schools.
June 12th 1874

W. T. Manlove
T. C. Perkins
G. W. Newbert
Trustees.

This document made official Clara Murphy's 1874 graduation from the third division of the second grade at the Alkali's Washington School. Clara was one of seven children who lived on Seventh Street, between G and H Streets. Her father was a blacksmith for the Central Pacific Railroad who, by 1880, took his family eastward to Brighton (near today's Sacramento State University) to claim a piece of that area's emerging hops industry. (SPL.)

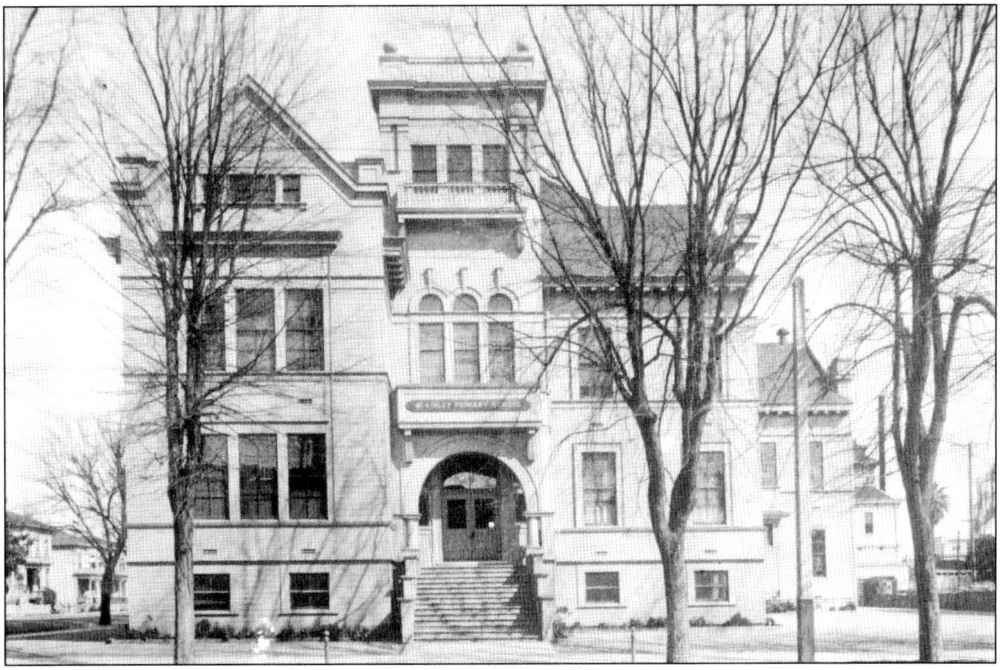

McKinley Primary School on Seventh and G Streets, built just before the turn of the century, led a less-than-charmed existence. In its four short decades, an arsonist tried to burn it down in 1908, it was condemned in 1913, a smallpox scare shut its doors in 1925, and ebbing enrollment, spurred by the Depression, effectively ended its role as a public school in 1932. Yet another fire sent Civilian Conservation Corps workers fleeing out its doors in 1935. (CSH.)

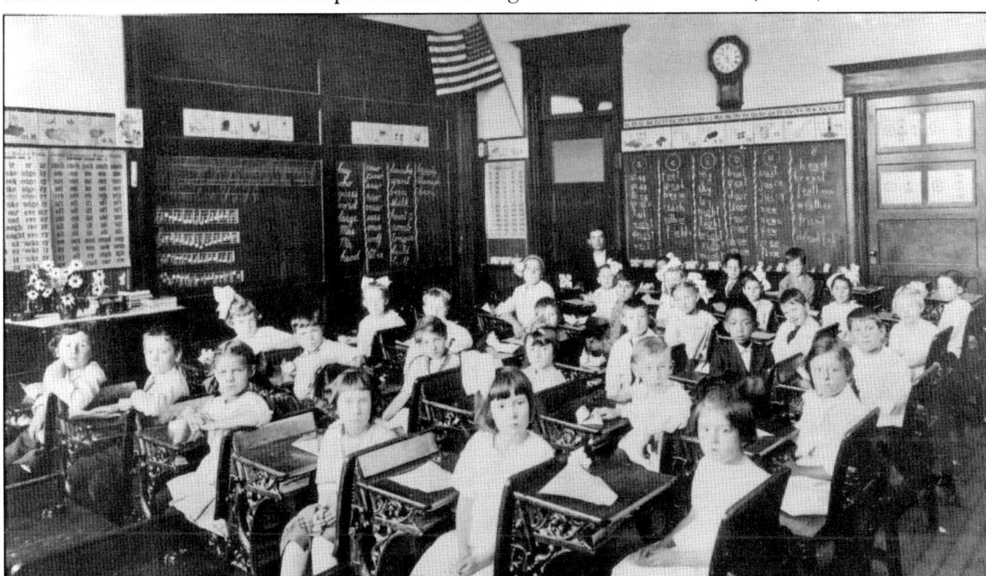

Serious, but beguiling, eyes look toward the camera in this 1914 photograph from McKinley School, which replaced the venerable Union School that was closed down just a decade earlier. With the growth of industry within and around the Alkali in the first two decades of the century, by 1921 the school's enrollment swelled to being one of the largest in the city at nearly 700 pupils. (SPL.)

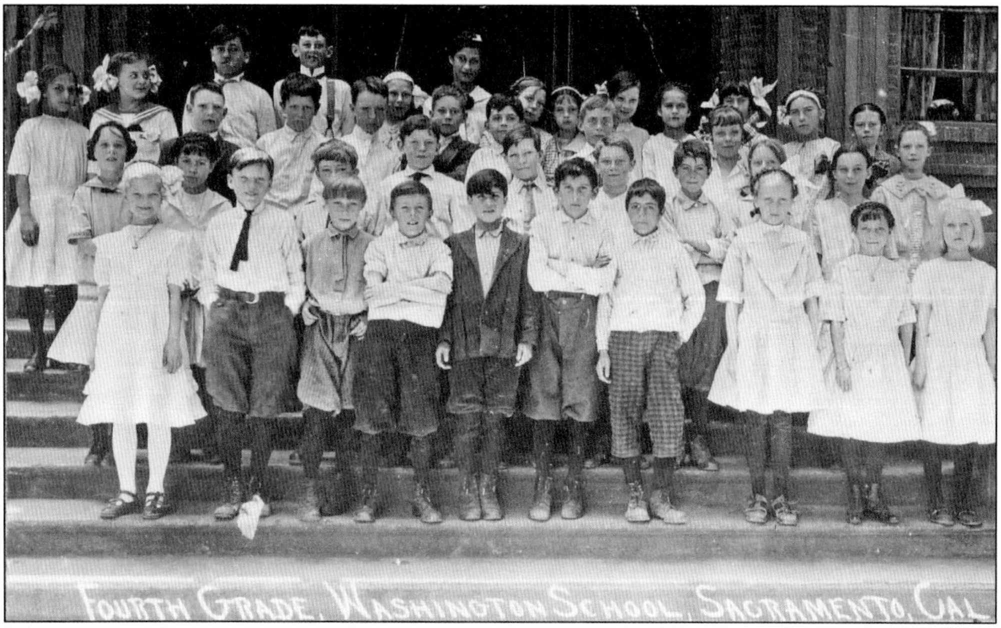

The novelty of a rare photograph is not lost on this group of fourth graders at the northern entrance to the Alkali's Washington Primary School around 1915. In December of the same year, first through fifth graders regaled family members with a winter festival, crooning "Rainy Days," "Mother Goose," and an Italian folk song. Instrumental accompaniment was provided by the school's own "Pumpkin Band." (CSH.)

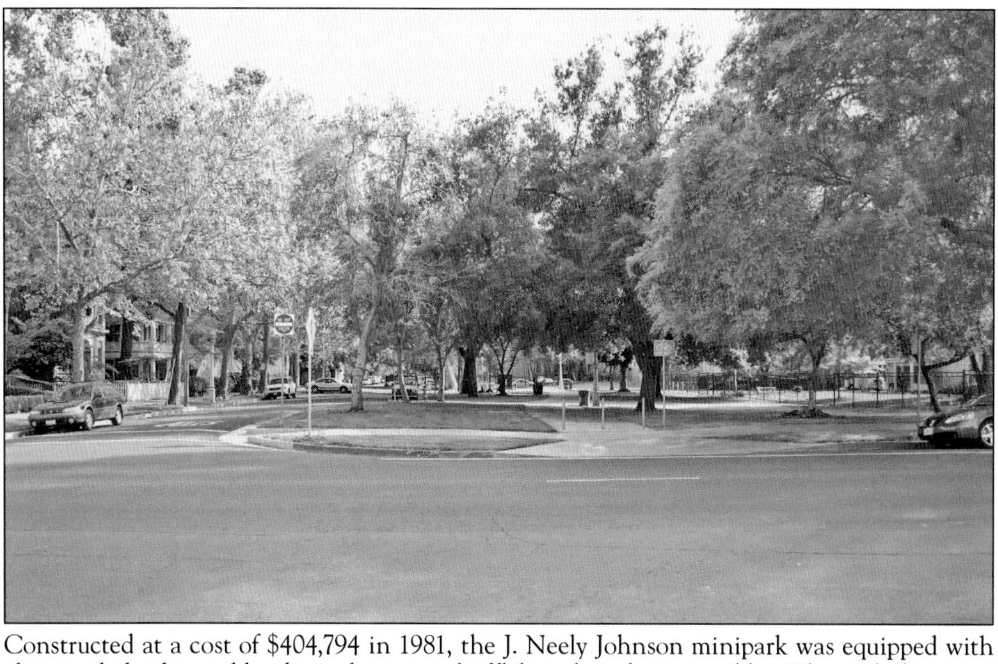

Constructed at a cost of $404,794 in 1981, the J. Neely Johnson minipark was equipped with chess and checkers tables, horseshoe pits, shuffleboard, and picnic tables. The park, however, soon became the nexus of tensions between residents and elements of the area's homeless and drug-dealing population. In the mid-1980s, several amenities, including tables, were removed in the hopes of dissuading criminal activity and loitering. (SPL.)

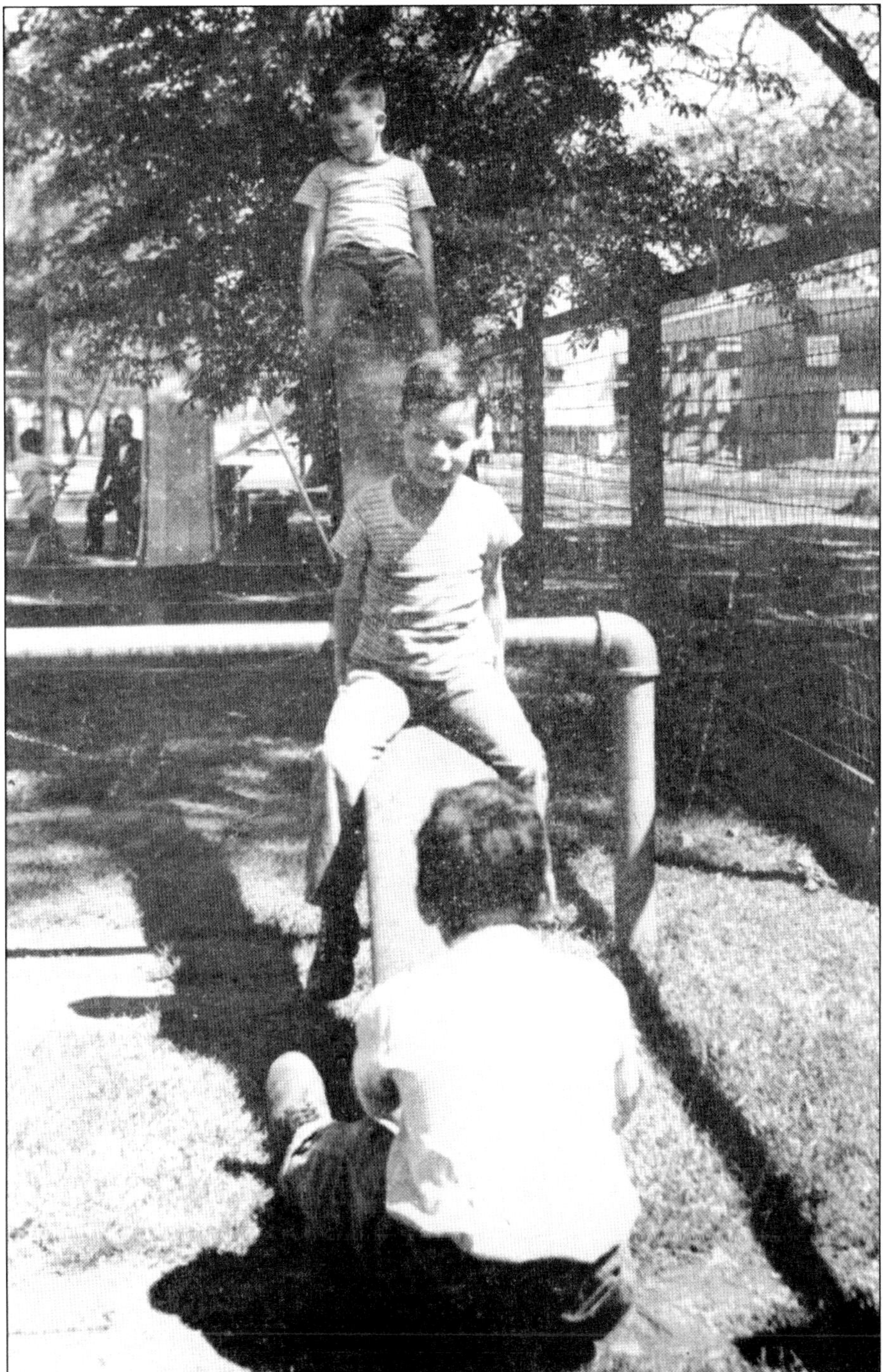

Alkali Park and playfield provided recreation facilities for neighborhood children in this industrial area beginning in the late 1930s. One of the original 2.5-acre public squares set aside for public recreation by John A. Sutter Jr. in 1849—the plot at the edge of Alkali Flat—became a right-of-way for the Central Pacific Railroad in 1863. It remained an unused parcel of land for decades. The park later became a haven for transients and alcoholics. (SPL.)

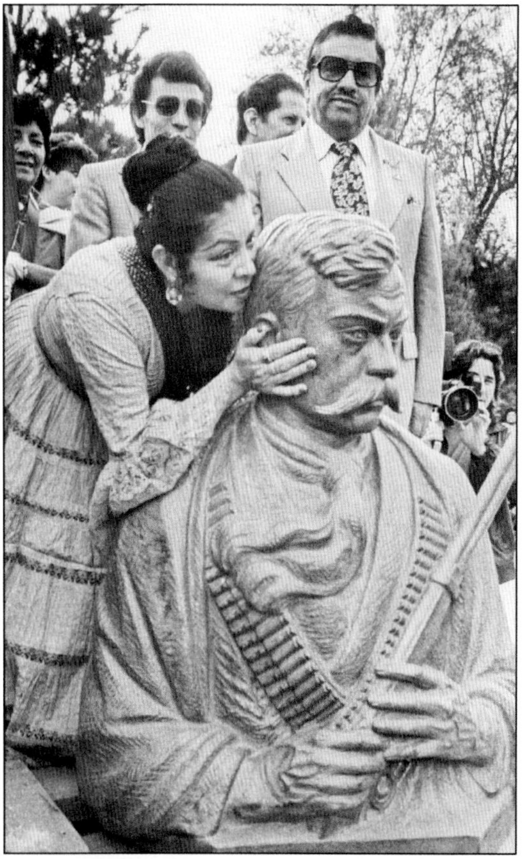

By 1970, thirty-seven percent of Alkali Flat's population was Hispanic, making it the district's largest minority. The appearance of iconic symbols like Mexican revolutionary Emiliano Zapata would follow as Zapata Park, at 905 E Street, saw the unveiling of the folk legend's bust. Created in a Mexico City foundry, the bronze is seen here in the tender embrace of Zapata's granddaughter, Maria Elena Zapata, during dedication ceremonies on November 20, 1981. (CSH.)

This rooftop view captured dedication ceremonies at Emiliano Zapata Park on August 11, 1975. The park's establishment was cosponsored by the Alkali Flat Project Area Committee and the Sacramento Housing and Redevelopment Agency. (CSH.)

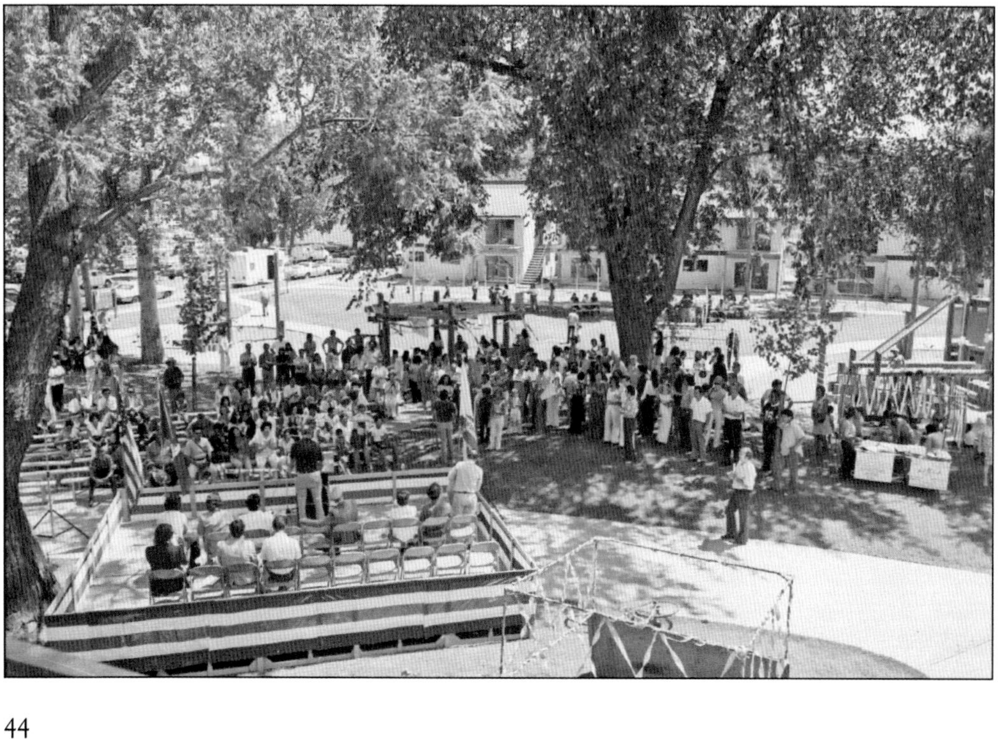

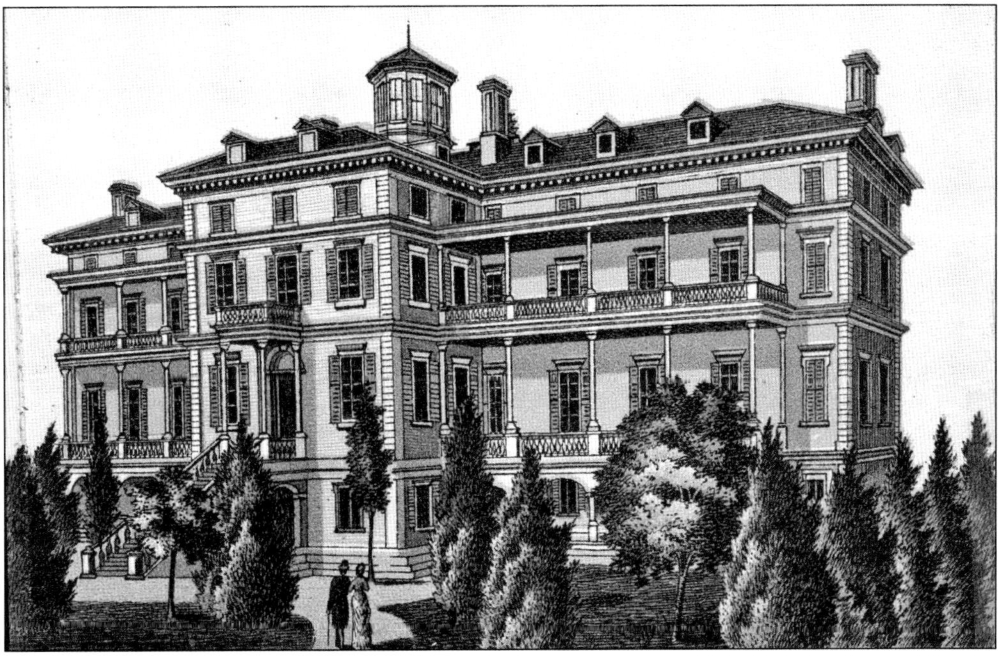

Built in 1869 at the corner of Thirteenth and C Streets at a cost of $64,000, the Central Pacific Railroad Hospital, depicted here in 1887, was a result of the company's desire to fill a health-care and morale vacuum for its employees, many of whom were migrants, solitary, and without sufficient funds to acquire proper care. (SPL.)

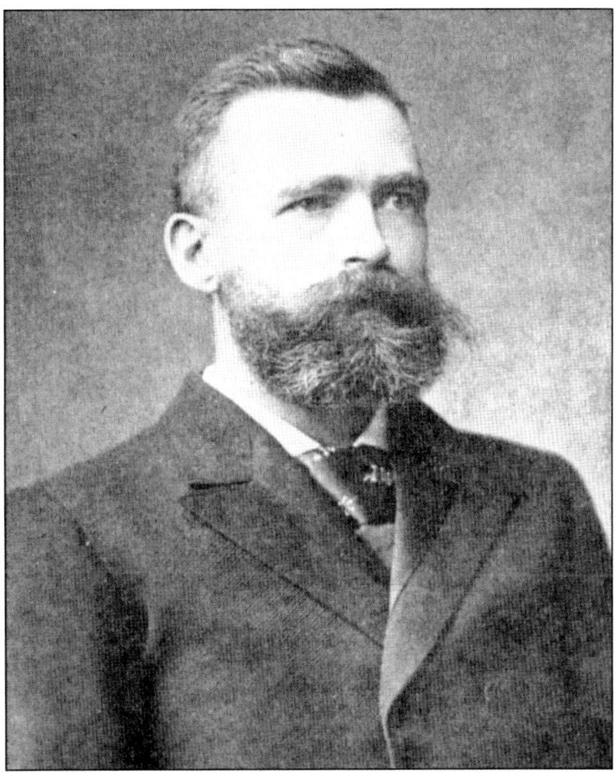

Pictured here in 1890, Thomas W. Huntington, MD, was a surgeon at the Central Pacific Hospital from 1882 until his death in 1929 and was one of the best medical talents in the early American West. His adherence to the principles of English physician Joseph Lister and the early use of antiseptics during patient recovery were groundbreaking. Overnight, and through the employment of such methods, Central Pacific deaths from infection from traumatic accidents dropped from between 30 to 40 percent to 5 to 7 percent. (SPL.)

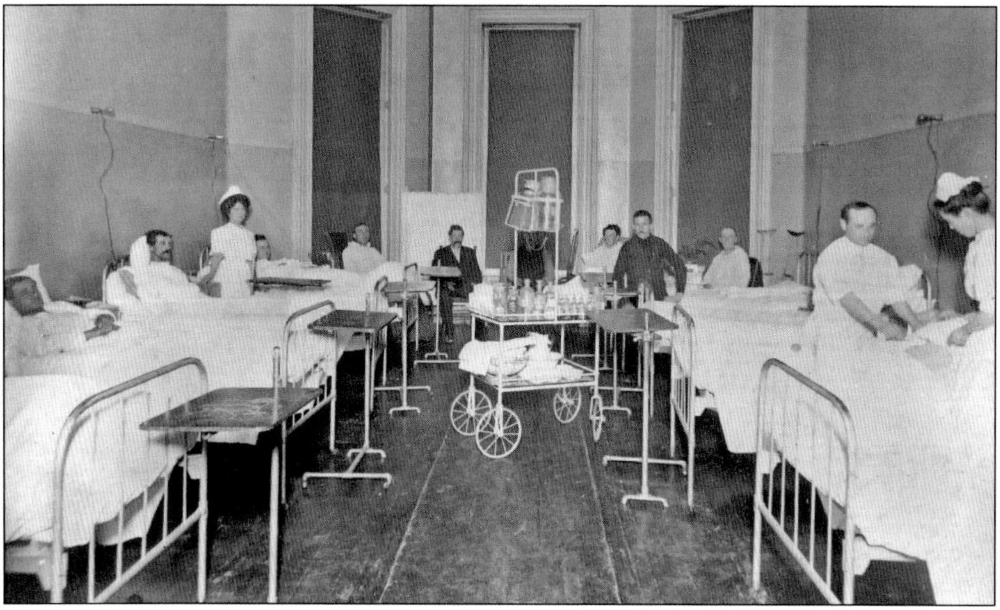

The Central Pacific Railroad Hospital was reputed to be one of the best hospitals on the West Coast. Pictured here around 1900 is one of the facility's six wards. Each one could accommodate up to 18 patients comfortably, while at its greatest capacity the hospital was designed to hold 125. (CSL.)

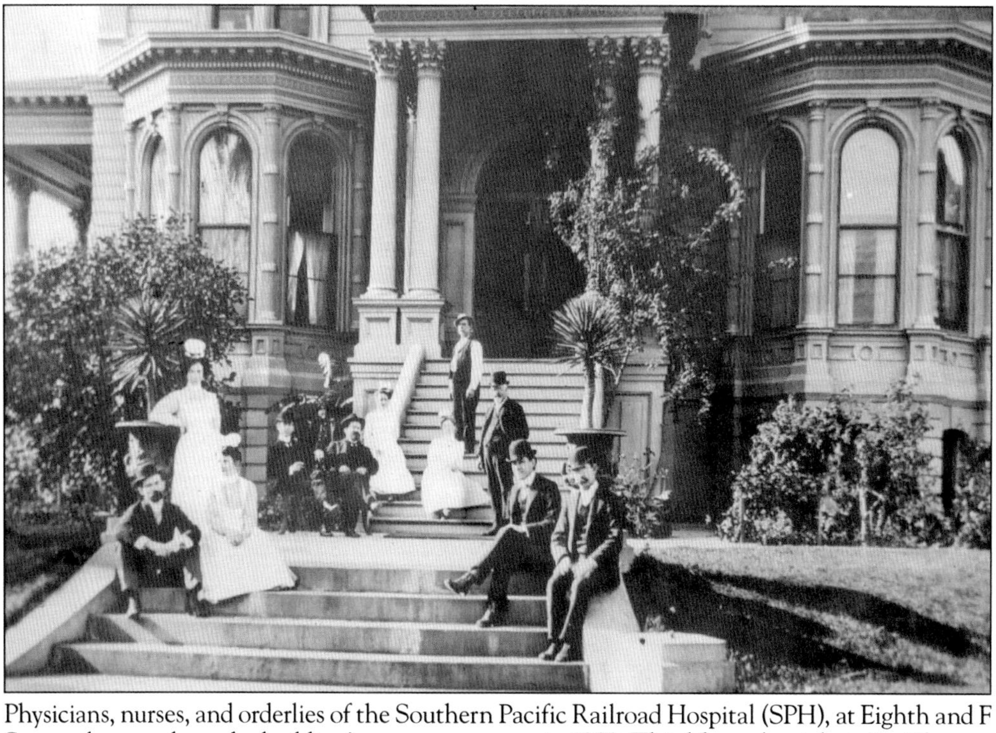

Physicians, nurses, and orderlies of the Southern Pacific Railroad Hospital (SPH), at Eighth and F Streets, lounge about the building's eastern entrance in 1902. Third from the right is Dr. Thomas Ross who, at the time of the photograph, was superintendant of the SPH and president of both the Sacramento City Board of Health and the California Medical Society. Just four years after this photograph was taken, Ross passed away from a stroke. (CSH.)

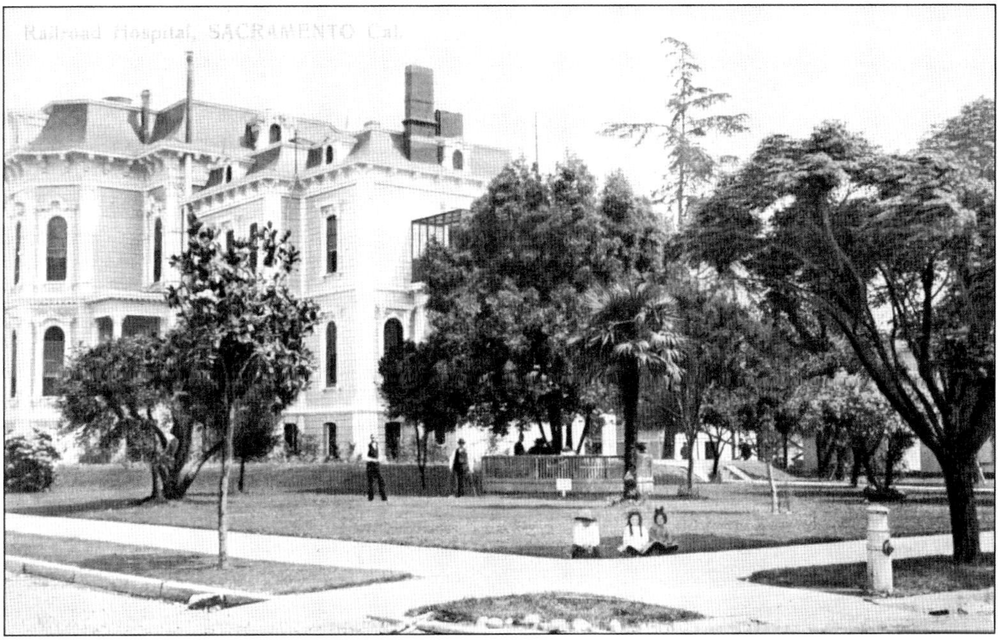

What was once the palatial home of railroad mogul Charles Crocker became the company hospital of the Southern Pacific Railroad in 1900. By 1906, the three-story structure, including a basement, could accommodate up to 55 patients and was touted as a refreshing alternative to other hospitals with its "home-like character," stated the January 27, 1906, *Sacramento Union*. (SPL.)

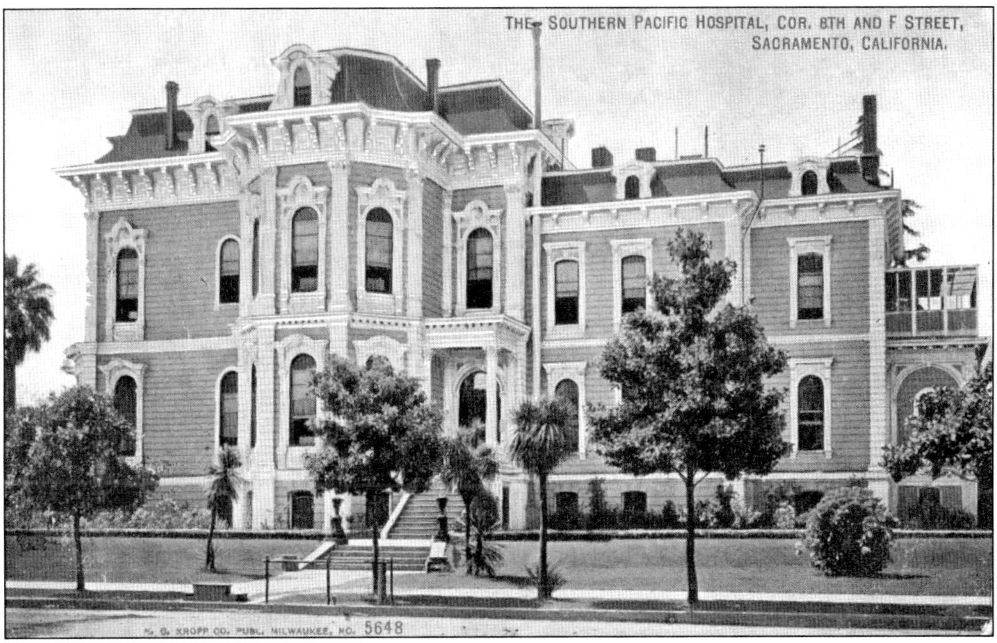

The would-be Southern Pacific Railroad Hospital was built in 1870. Seen here looking south from F Street, the hospital, having outgrown its walls in 1911, took up new residence at Second and H Streets. The house was leveled in the fall of 1915 after falling into disrepair and becoming the home of several rat nests and standing "covered by masses of vines," observed the October 19, 1915, *Sacramento Bee*. (SPL.)

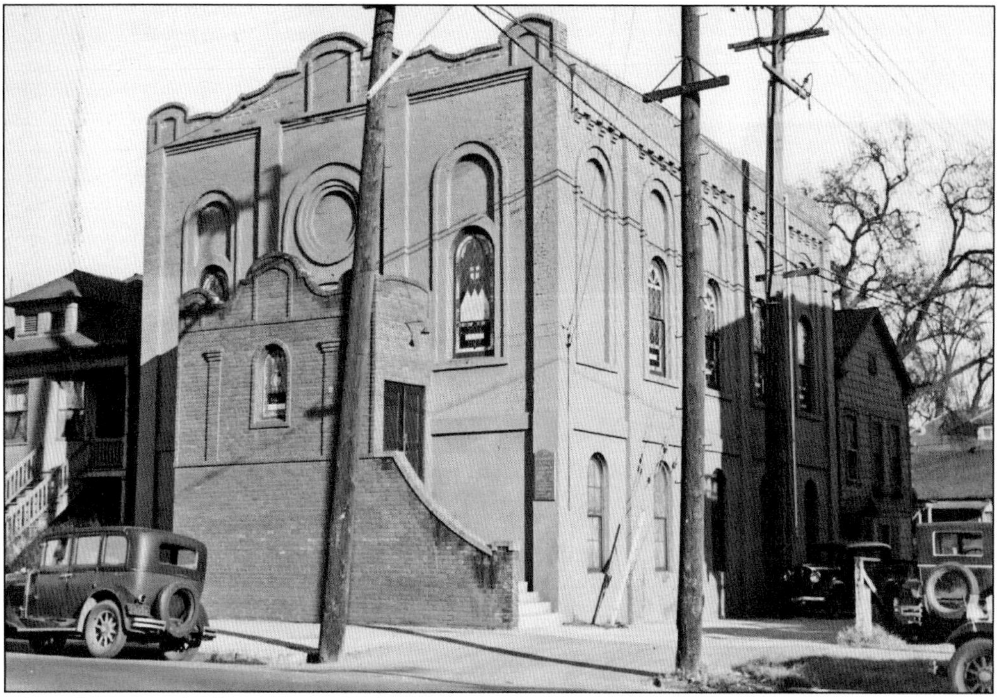

The African Methodist Episcopal Church, the first African American religious congregation on the Pacific Coast, was established in Sacramento in the summer of 1850 at the I Street residence of Daniel Blue. Months later, a lot between G and H Streets and Seventh and Eighth Streets was purchased for a sum of $250,000 for the construction of a more formal place of congregation. Pictured here during the 1920s is the church's third rendition at 715 Seventh Street. (CSH.)

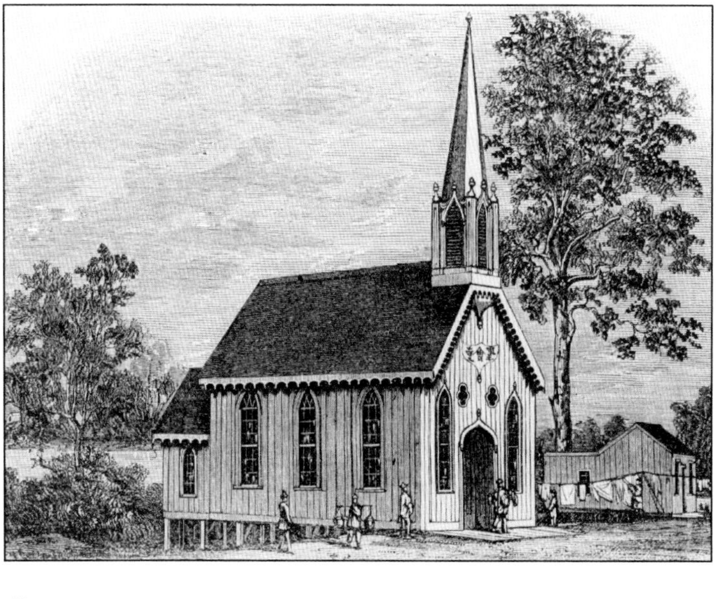

Simply known as the Chinese Chapel, the lakeside structure, situated on Sixth Street between H and G Streets, was built in June 1855 by the Rev. J. Lewis Shuck, a Southern Baptist minister and missionary whose charge it was to convert the city's Chinese population to Christianity. With the outbreak of the Civil War, and his flock peaking at a mere 16 members, Shuck left for South Carolina. (CSL.)

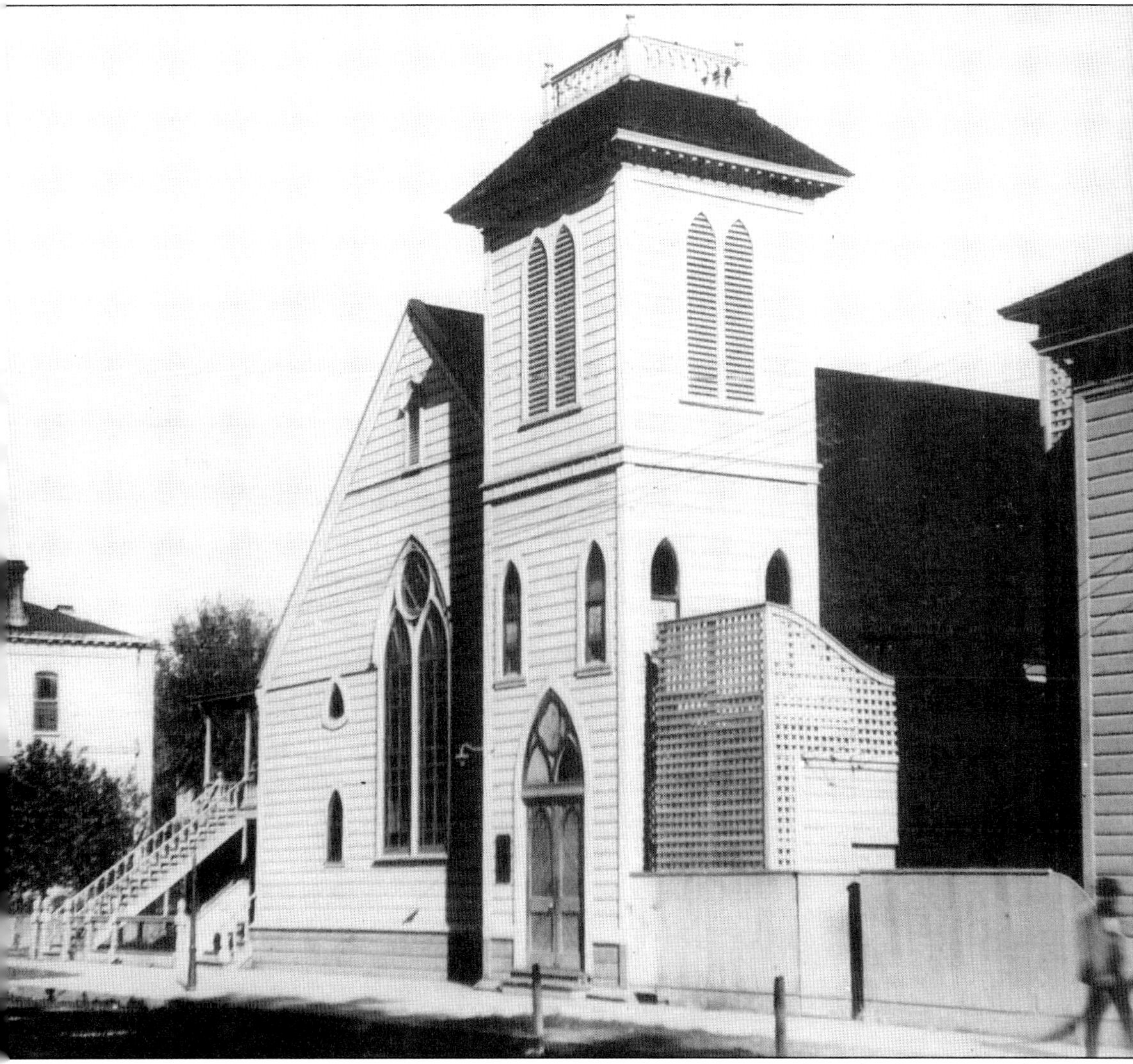

On the outer edge of the Alkali at Eleventh and H Streets was the Central Methodist Episcopal Church, pictured here in 1901. It originally rested at Sixth and H Streets, where it stood from 1856 to 1869. In 1869, flooding forced it to higher ground, when water supposedly rose 18 inches above the church's pews. It was razed in 1924 to make room for the Sacramento Northern depot. (CSH.)

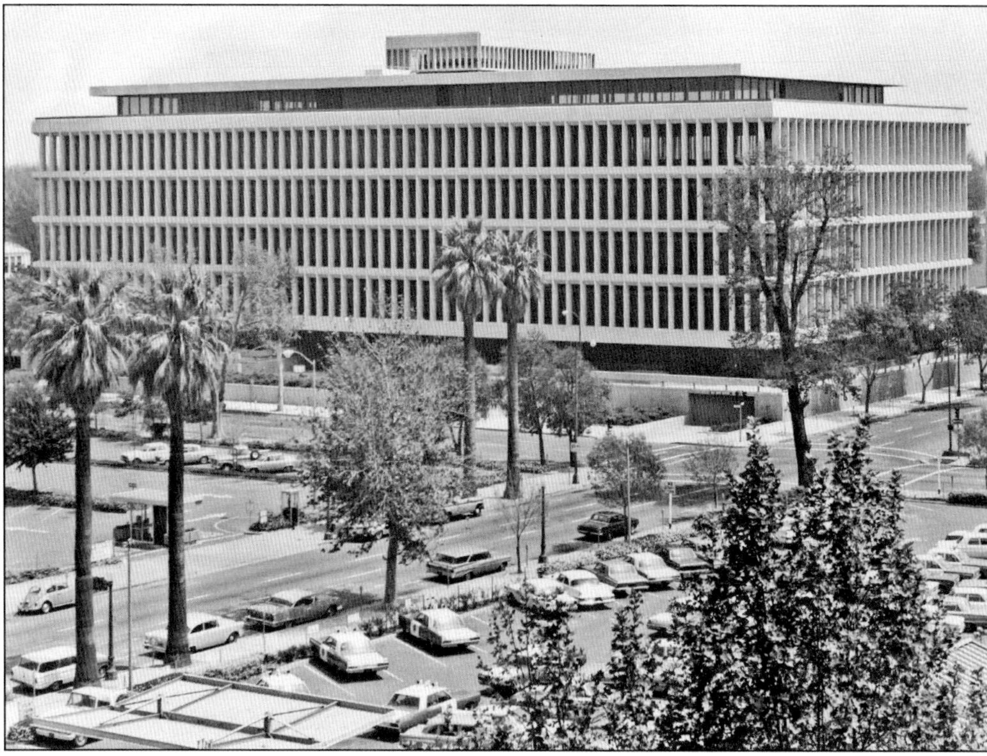

Perhaps the most frequented public building in Alkali Flat, the Gordon D. Schaber Downtown Courthouse at Ninth and H Streets was opened in October 1965, primarily as a hall of justice and more secondarily as a Cold War bomb shelter. The six-story and nearly 300,000-square-foot structure, with its 44 courtrooms, was completed at a cost of $8.8 million. (CSH.)

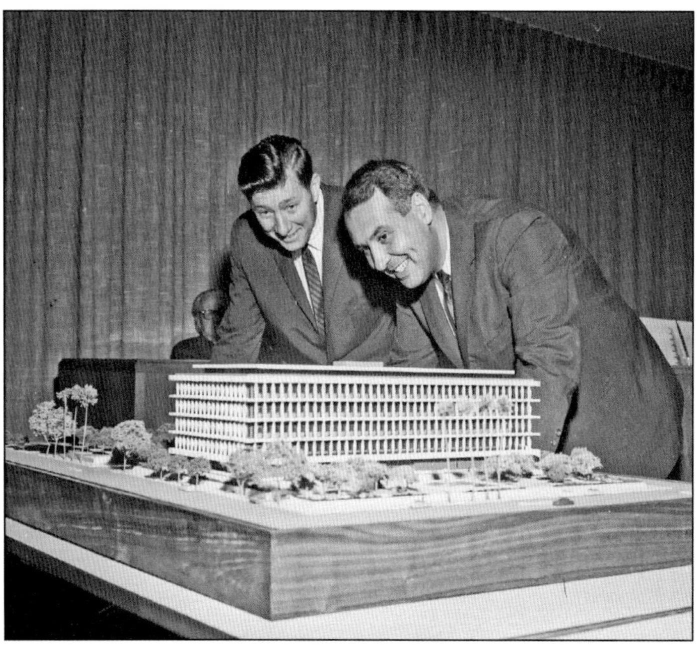

Giddy amidst the glow of things to come is architect Daniel Nacht (left) and Sacramento County supervisor Fred Barbaria in January 1960. The downtown courthouse was the fourth superior court building since the county's founding in 1850. Barbaria was also a proponent of preserving the previous courthouse, which rested on Seventh and I Streets. Demolished in 1970, he called it "one of the finest things assembled in downtown Sacramento." (CSH.)

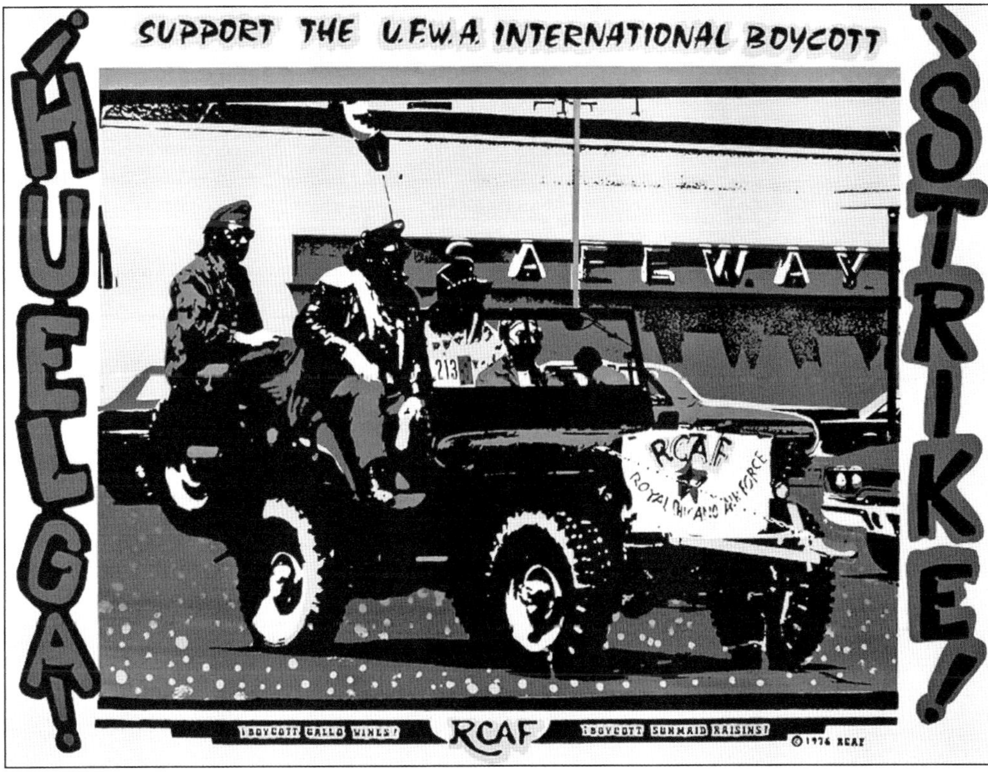

The Royal Chicano Air Force (RCAF) proved to be one of Sacramento's, and the nation's, most influential art cooperatives during the 1960s, 1970s, and 1980s. Founded in 1969, and germinating from the Alkali, the group's art helped promote the Chicano struggle for civil rights, labor organizing, and self-definition. This print captures four RCAF members in trademark garb, boycotting a Safeway store, very likely in Woodland. (CSUS.)

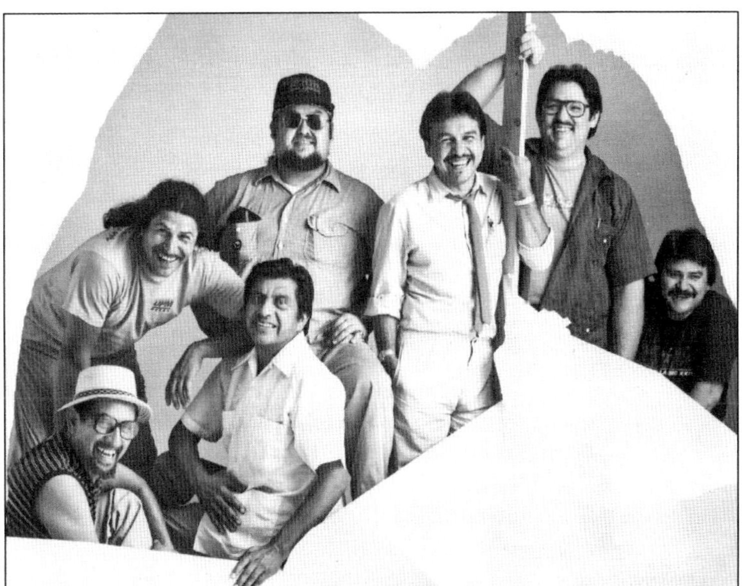

This photograph of the RCAF was taken in 1984 to promote the group's poster art. Entitled "Winging It: an In-Flight Retrospect of RCAF Posters," the showing was held at the Alkali's Galeria Posada on Twelfth and F Streets. Members, from left to right, are Jose Montoya, Juanishi Orosco, Esteban Villa, Ricardo Favela, Rudy Quellar, Louie Gonzales, and Armando Cid. (CSH.)

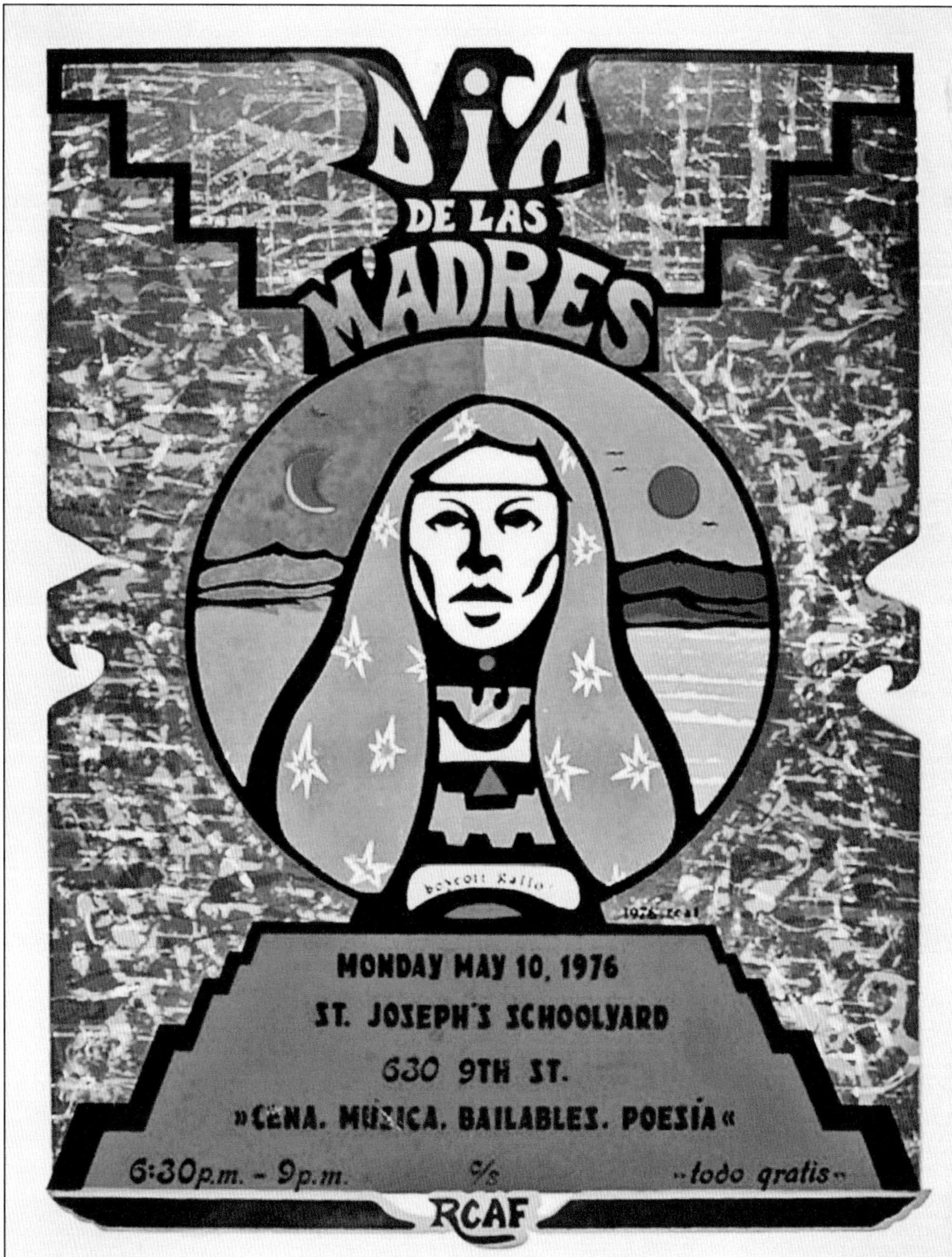

This exquisite poster by the RCAF's Ricardo Favela offers a composite of imagery far beyond the overt message of a Mother's Day 1976 dinner dance at St. Joseph's School at Ninth and G Streets. Representing the United Farm Workers, familiar symbols and "unifiers" of the Chicano liberation movement—the Virgin of Guadalupe and the eagle—are blended with subtle encouragement to boycott the Gallo Winery. (CSUS.)

The bilingual *Alkali Review* was indicative of the Alkali's strong Spanish-speaking population. This June 1974 issue presents stories appealing to the development of the Plano de Alkali Apartments and legal and nutritional services to seniors. By 1970, eighty percent of Alkali's housing stock was comprised of rentals, while one third of its residents were considered elderly. (CSH.)

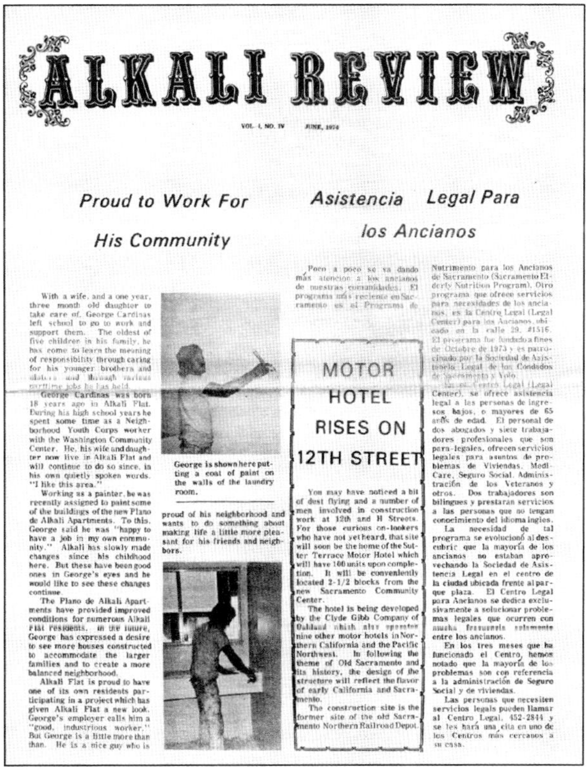

ALKALI REVIEW

VOL. I, NO. IV JUNE, 1974

Proud to Work For His Community

With a wife, and a one year, three month old daughter to take care of, George Cardinas left school to go to work and support them. The oldest of five children in his family, he has come to learn the meaning of responsibility through caring for his younger brothers and sisters and through various parttime jobs he has held.

George Cardinas was born 18 years ago in Alkali Flat. During his high school years he spent some time as a Neighborhood Youth Corps worker with the Washington Community Center. He, his wife and daughter now live in Alkali Flat and will continue to do so since, in his own quietly spoken words, "I like this area."

Working as a painter, he was recently assigned to paint some of the buildings of the new Plano de Alkali Apartments. To this, George said he was "happy to have a job in my own community." Alkali has slowly made changes since his childhood here. But these have been good ones in George's eyes and he would like to see these changes continue.

The Plano de Alkali Apartments have provided improved conditions for numerous Alkali Flat residents. In the future, George has expressed a desire to see more houses constructed to accommodate the larger families and to create a more balanced neighborhood.

Alkali Flat is proud to have one of its own residents participating in a project which has given Alkali Flat a new look. George's employer calls him a "good, industrious worker." But George is a little more than than. He is a nice guy who is proud of his neighborhood and wants to do something about making life a little more pleasant for his friends and neighbors.

George is shown here putting a coat of paint on the walls of the laundry room.

Asistencia Legal Para los Ancianos

Poco a poco se va dando más atencion a los ancianos de nuestras comunidades. El programa más reciente en Sacramento es el Programa de Nutrimento para los Ancianos de Sacramento (Sacramento Elderly Nutrition Program). Otro programa que ofrece servicios para necesidades de los ancianos, es la Centro Legal (Legal Center) para los Ancianos, ubicado en la calle 29, #1516. El programa fue fundado a fines de Octubre de 1973 y es patrocinado por la Sociedad de Asistencia Legal de los Condados de Sacramento y Yolo.

[illegible] Centro Legal (Legal Center), se ofrece asistencia legal a las personas de ingresos bajos, o mayores de 65 años de edad. El personal de dos abogados y siete trabajadores profesionales que son para-legales, ofrecen servicios legales para asuntos de problemas de Viviendas, Medi-Care, Seguro Social, Administración de los Veteranos y otros. Dos trabajadores son bilingues y prestaran servicios a las personas que no tengan conocimiento del idioma ingles.

La necesidad de tal programa se evolucionó al descubrir que la mayoría de los ancianos no estaban aprovechando la Sociedad de Asistencia Legal en el centro de la ciudad ubicada frente al parque plaza. El Centro Legal para Ancianos se dedica exclusivamente a solucionar problemas legales que ocurren con mucha frecuencia solamente entre los ancianos.

En los tres meses que ha funcionado el Centro, hemos notado que la mayoría de los problemas son con referencia a la administración de Seguro Social y de viviendas.

Las personas que necesiten servicios legals pueden llamar al Centro Legal, 452-2844 y se les hará una cita en uno de los Centros más cercanos a su casa.

MOTOR HOTEL RISES ON 12TH STREET

You may have noticed a bit of dust flying and a number of men involved in construction work at 12th and H Streets. For those curious on-lookers who have not yet heard, that site will soon be the home of the Sutter Terrace Motor Hotel which will have 100 units upon completion. It will be conveniently located 2-1/2 blocks from the new Sacramento Community Center.

The hotel is being developed by the Clyde Gibb Company of Oakland which also operates nine other motor hotels in Northern California and the Pacific Northwest. In following the theme of Old Sacramento and its history, the design of the structure will reflect the flavor of early California and Sacramento.

The construction site is the former site of the old Sacramento Northern Railroad Depot.

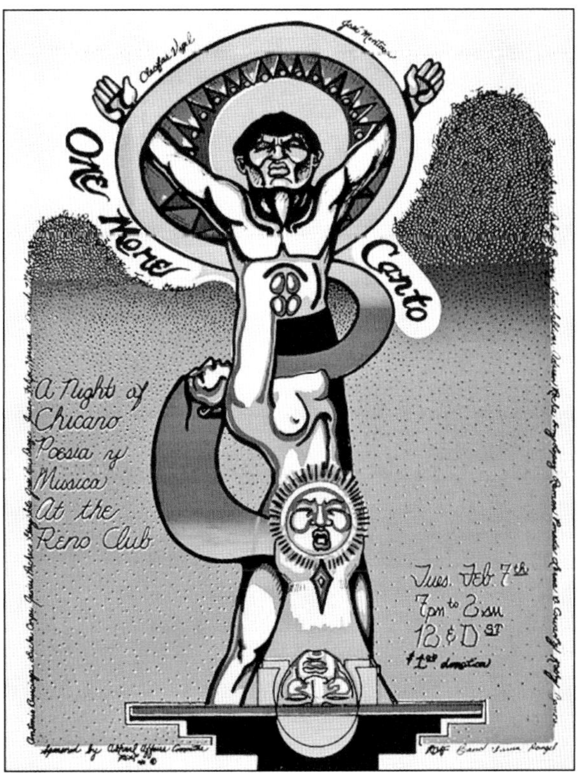

Club Artistico Reno at 415 Twelfth Street served as a cultural hothouse for Alkali Latinos for over 25 years. Over that span, three Spanish-language movies were filmed there, and its stage was graced by Latin American singers and actors alike. The club was razed in the spring of 1987 for redevelopment. This RCAF poster, crafted by Juanishi Orozco, promotes a music and poetry event at the Reno. (CSUS.)

With an eye on exposing the city to Mexican and Native American culture, in the spring of 1971 local college students founded La Raza Bookstore at 1228 F Street. La Raza also housed various Latino political and cultural organizations, including the Cesar Chavez–led United Farm Workers. Redevelopment forced the bookstore from the heart of the Alkali in 1986. This image was created by RCAF artists Louie Gonzalez and Dave Contreras. (CSUS.)

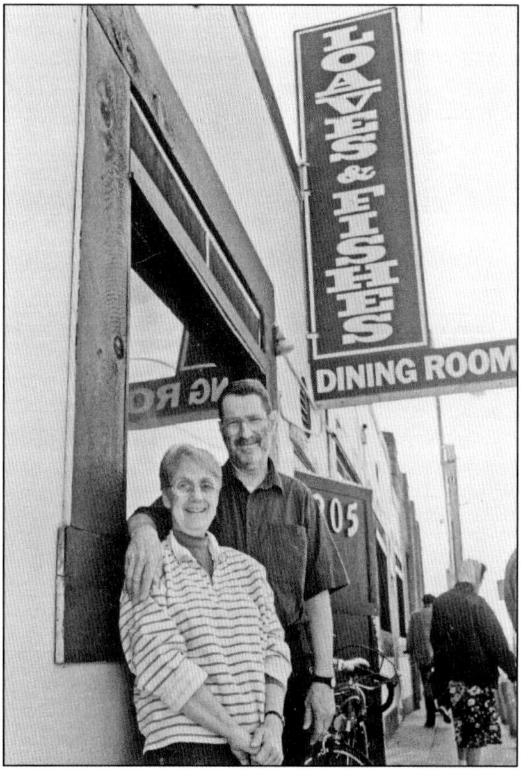

Chris and Dan Delany, cofounders of Loaves and Fishes, a faith-based private charity providing food and shelter to those in need, are pictured here in 1985. The facility, set in what had been a tavern, opened in August 1983 on North Twelfth Street with 75 seats and a monthly budget of $1,500. As of 2009, the facility faced an ominous 14 percent increase in the area's homeless population compared to the figure in 2007. (CSH.)

Three

Alkali Industry

by James Scott and Tom Tolley

The Alkali's earliest industry came from expatriates and their ability to conjure bottled spirits. Thanks to an enterprising group of Chinese, a rice and bean distillery was set up on Seventh and E Streets in 1854, only to be then upstaged by German brewing ventures at the Ohio Brewery in 1855 and then by the City Brewery in 1856. By 1858, both breweries were together producing roughly 1,300 gallons of lager beer per week. The area's most revered industrial presence—the Central Pacific Railroad (Southern Pacific after 1884)—appeared in 1868 on a 30-acre expanse along the old channel of the American River, later stretching into 20 acres of China Slough landfill. By 1889, SPR had produced upwards to 1,500 jobs, and between 1872 and 1937, the shops built some 200 locomotives. By 1925, SPR's workforce had grown to 3,396 with a payroll topping $5 million. By the spring of 1914, after $100,000 and almost 15 months of construction, the Phoenix Milling Company had a state-of-the-art facility at Twelfth and D Streets. In 1919, it would be sold to the Globe Milling Company of San Francisco but remain a memorial to the Alkali's industrial heritage for decades to come, simply known as the Globe Mills. Little did a young Dane named Carl Hansen realize when he stepped upon the ocean liner *St. Paul* in 1900 that his efforts would make Alkali Flat the epicenter of dairy food production in Sacramento. Another immigrant, Raul Mercado, brought a love for the Mexican staple of tortillas from his native Guadalajara, Mexico, to the Alkali and three western states in 1954 and beyond. Smaller, less conspicuous industry found a friendly home in the Alkali as well: Meister and Sons, arguably Sacramento's original automaker, made a brief home for itself at Ninth and D Streets, while Burnett and Sons, a planning and milling company, and the city's second-oldest operating business, made its move to the area in 1932.

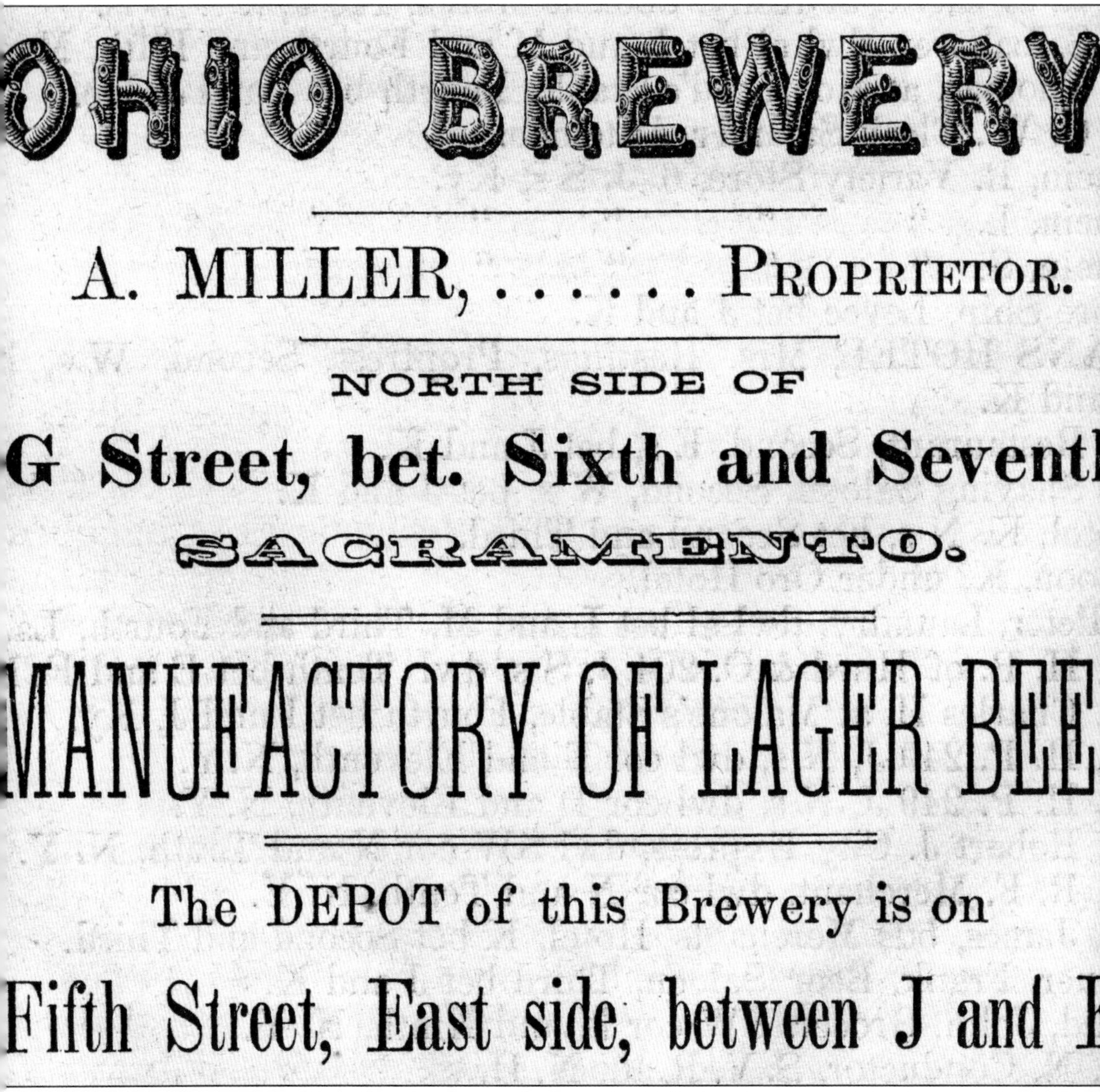

Pictured is an Ohio Brewery advertisement from the 1857 City Directory. The brewery, located at Seventh and G Streets, was one of the first signs of industry in Alkali Flat and one of the first breweries in the city to produce lager-style beers. By 1858, demand pushed lager production at the Ohio Brewery to 500 gallons a week. In 1860, for a cost of $22,000, the brewery's owner and native Swabian, Anton Miller, added a 32-foot by 82-foot beer hall to the already three-story facility, which also contained a cellar, a saloon, and living quarters for Miller and his family. (SPL.)

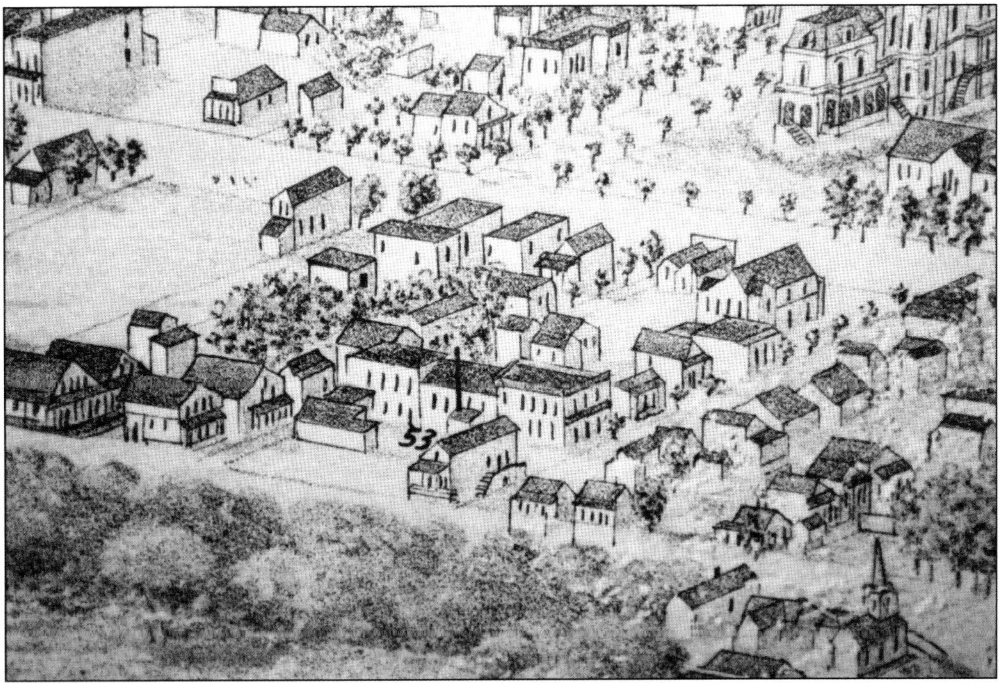

This cropping of Koch's 1870 *Bird's Eye View of the City of Sacramento* represents the only known image of the Ohio Brewery, here identified as number 53 and resting on the shores of China Slough. The brewery was founded in 1855–1856 and, as of 1857, was distributing much of its beer through its own depot on Fifth Street, between J and K Streets. The Chinese Chapel sits in the lower right corner. (SPL.)

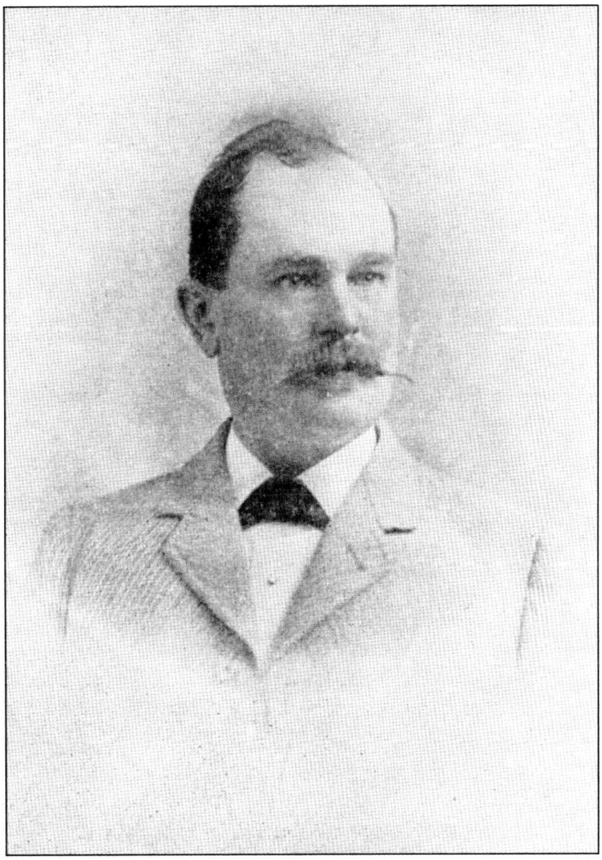

Sacramento's most successful brewing legacy in Alkali Flat came about when an 18-year-old Swiss émigré named Frank Ruhstaller became foreman at the City Brewery in 1865. After stints with the Pacific and Sutterville Breweries, he purchased the City Brewery in 1881. He soon started his own brewing label and, in 1897, became the majority shareholder in the once-competing Buffalo Brewery. (SPL.)

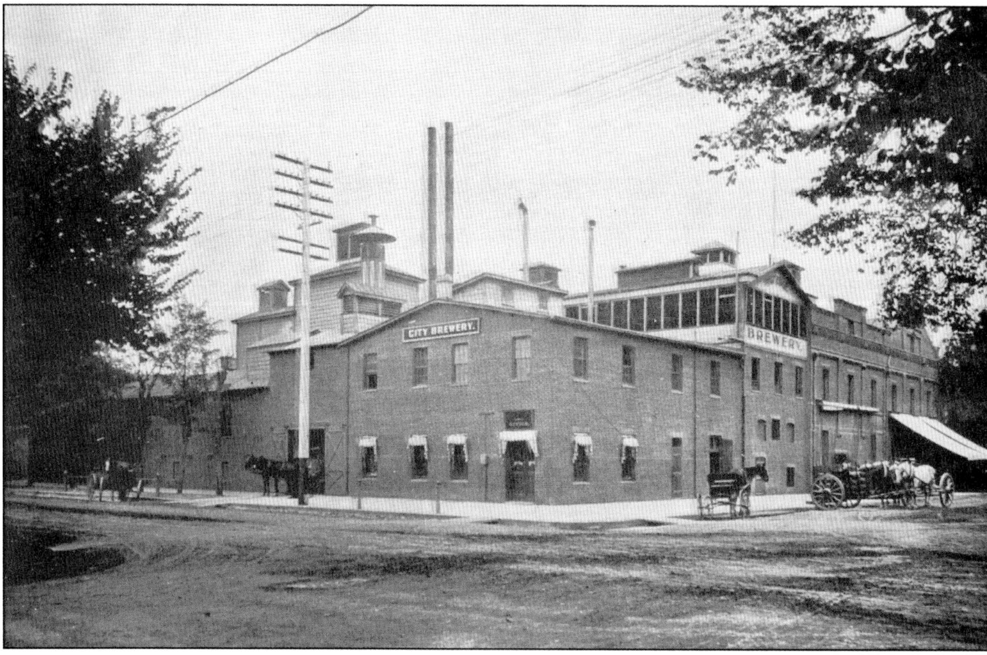

Resting around 1900 at the northeast corner of Twelfth and H Streets, the City Brewery was established in 1856 by German expatriates Wilhelm Borchers and Benedict Hilbert. The two-story structure was made of brick, occupied a lot measuring some 80 by 160 feet, and possessed a 40-foot by 80-foot cellar for cooling its lager-style beer. (SPL.)

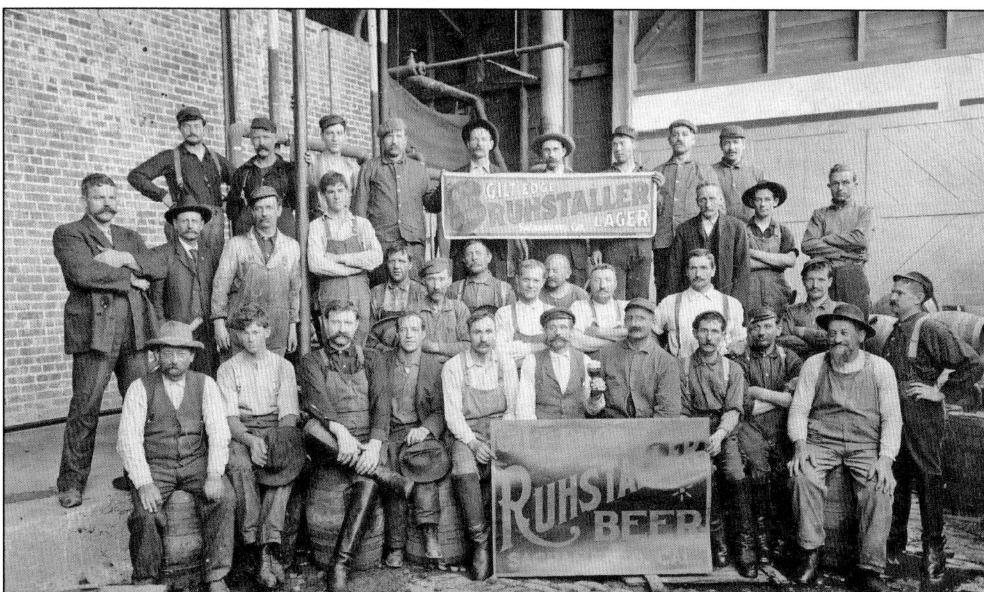

By 1915, the City Brewery had grown to occupy nearly an entire city block with its facilities. The complex and its hearty denizens had gotten so noisy that Alkali residents like Fannie Goddard of 1227 H Street found it a nuisance and sued for $5,000 in damages. She also told the *Sacramento Bee* in March 1912 that the brewery's crew used "obscene and common swearing and cursing which assails the site and hearing of my family and visitors." (CSH.)

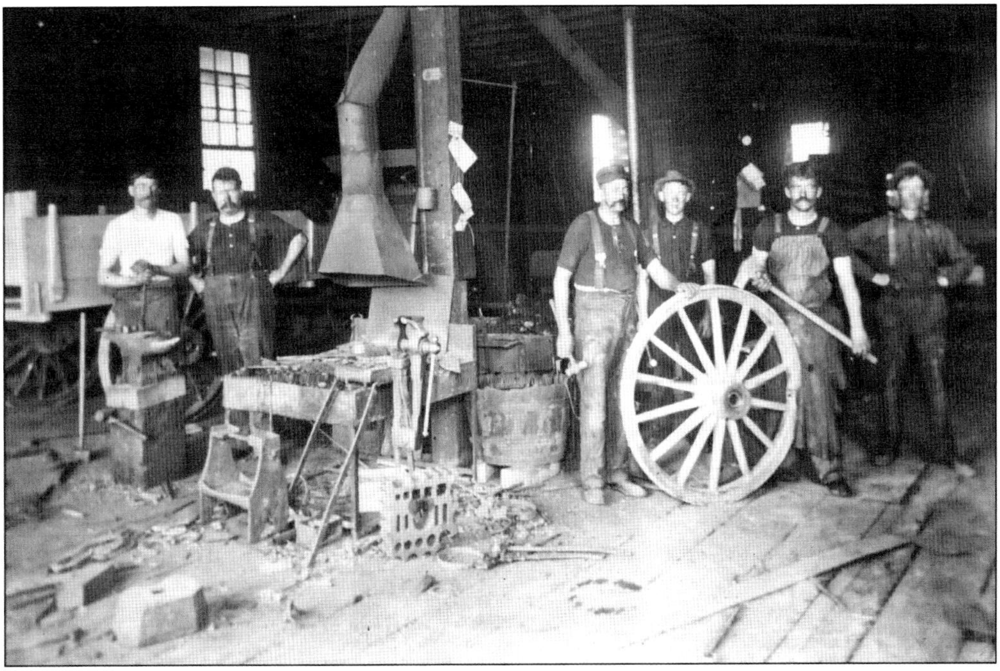

A 1902 interior view of Bennett's Blacksmithing Shop, located at Twelfth and D Streets, is shown here. Its founder, Henry Bennett, emigrated from Ontario, Canada, to Sacramento in 1875. By 1882, he had opened his shop, making him one of the Alkali's only blacksmiths for the next 60 years. Pictured from left to right are "Swede," William Carmichael, Henry Bennett, "Dutch," William "Box Car Billie" Henderson, and Walter Bennett. (CSH.)

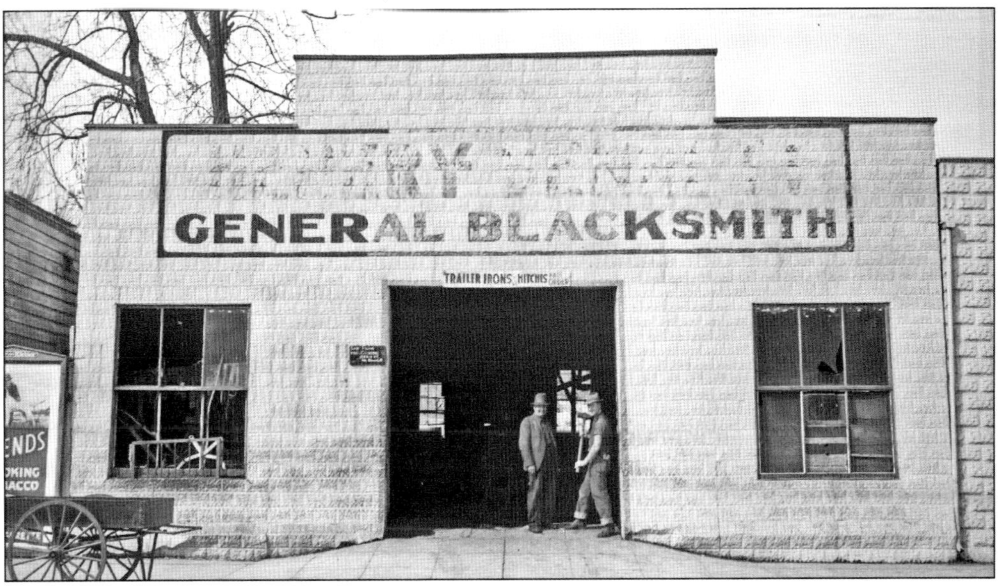

Pictured here in 1941 are Walter Bennett and an employee at the Twelfth and D General Blacksmith Shop. With the death of his father in 1931, Walter took full control of the family business but changed the establishment's name. When the business opened in 1882, it was one of 21 blacksmithing shops in the city; by the time of this photograph, the number was down to 5. (CSH.)

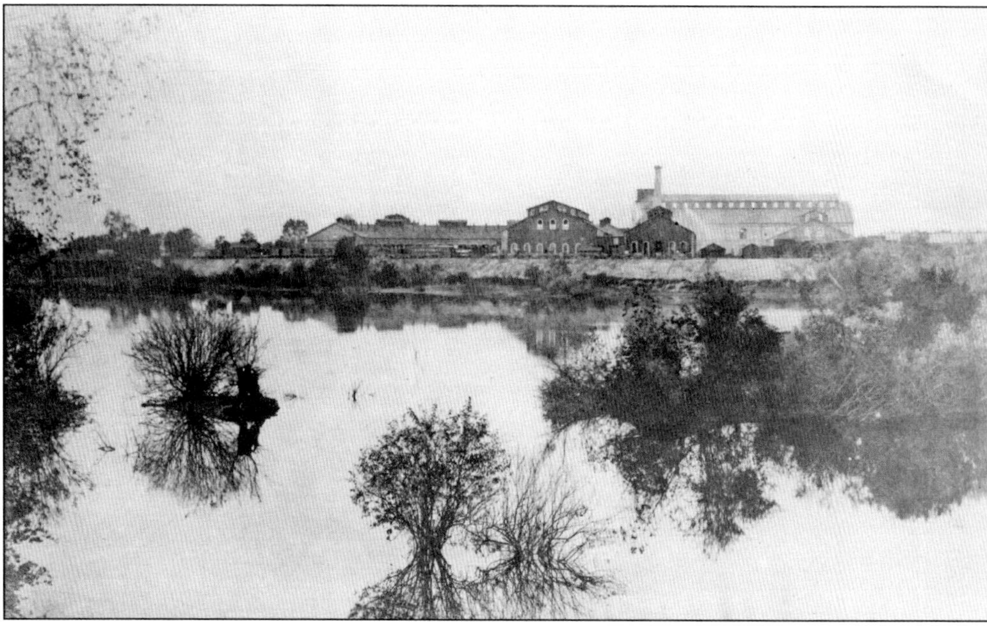

This 1869 view of the Central Pacific rail yards comes from the southern edge of the China Slough, revealing, from left to right, the car building shop, the blacksmith shop, and the car shop. The distant stack reached 92 feet above the elevation of the shops and was comprised of no less than 600,000 bricks. (CSH.)

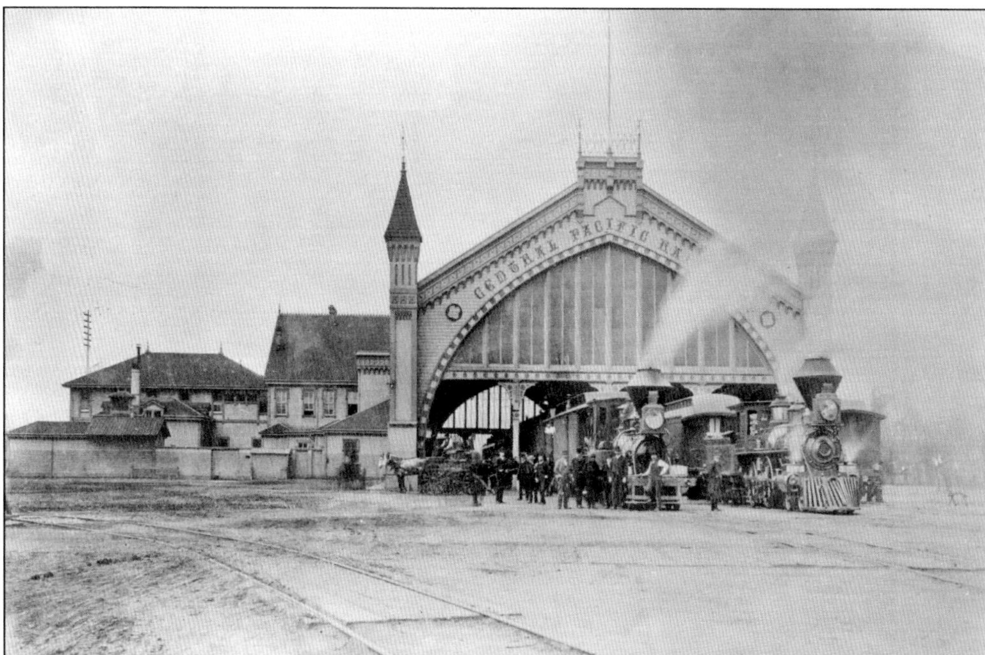

Shown in 1887 is the three-track Central Pacific depot also commonly known as the "Arcade Station." One of the most modern stations of its day, the gothic-style garage with its signature twin spires was built in 1879 almost entirely of wood and boasted a 150-seat dining room. The Arcade was third in the line of CP/SP depots and was replaced in 1925. (CSH.)

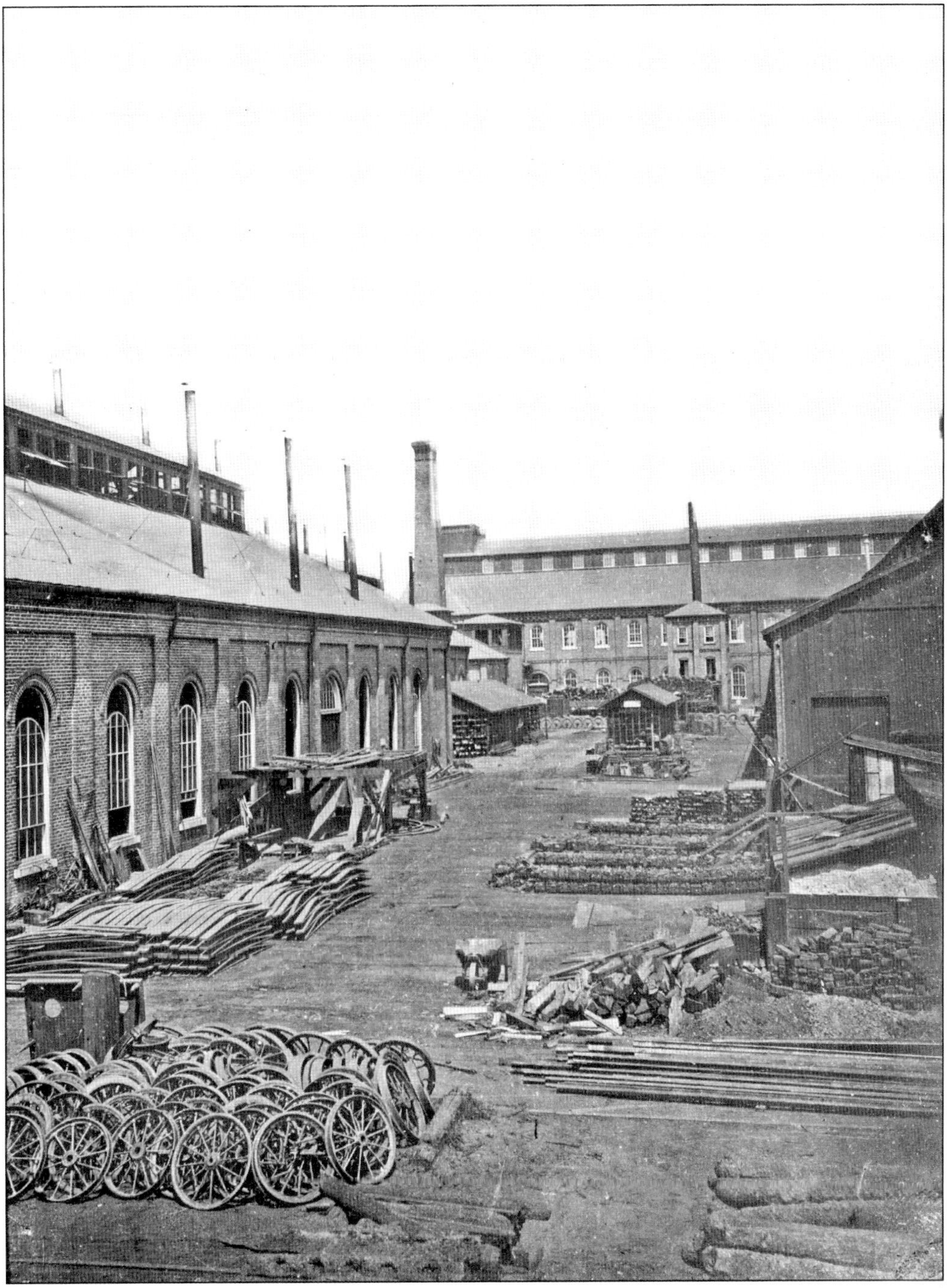

Here is a view between blacksmith and car-building shops in 1872, the same year that Central Pacific turned out its first eight-wheel locomotive. Straight ahead is the yard's sawmill and cabinet shop. What was nothing more than a shed, with a forge and a few tools in 1863, had grown into one of the world's largest rail yards by the mid-20th century. (CSH.)

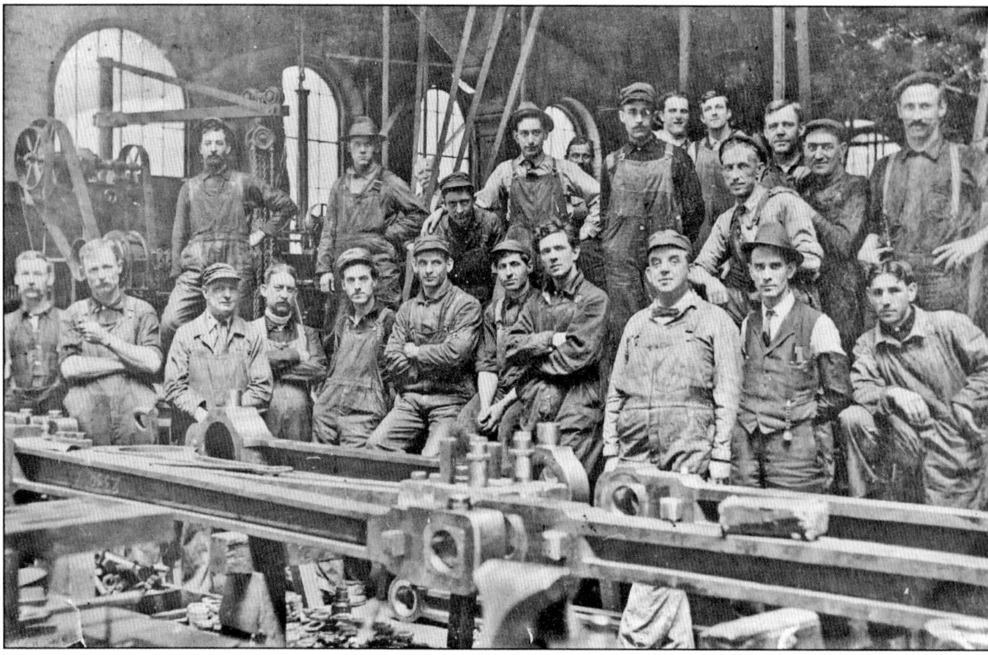

Italian workers in the Southern Pacific locomotive shop take a moment's pause for this photograph, taken in 1925. By 1930, Italians made up the largest European-born ethnicity in Sacramento, numbering well over 2,000. Moreover, at the time of this photograph, SP's car shops were the second-biggest producer in Sacramento's manufacturing sector at nearly $9 million, just behind canning and preserving. (CSH.)

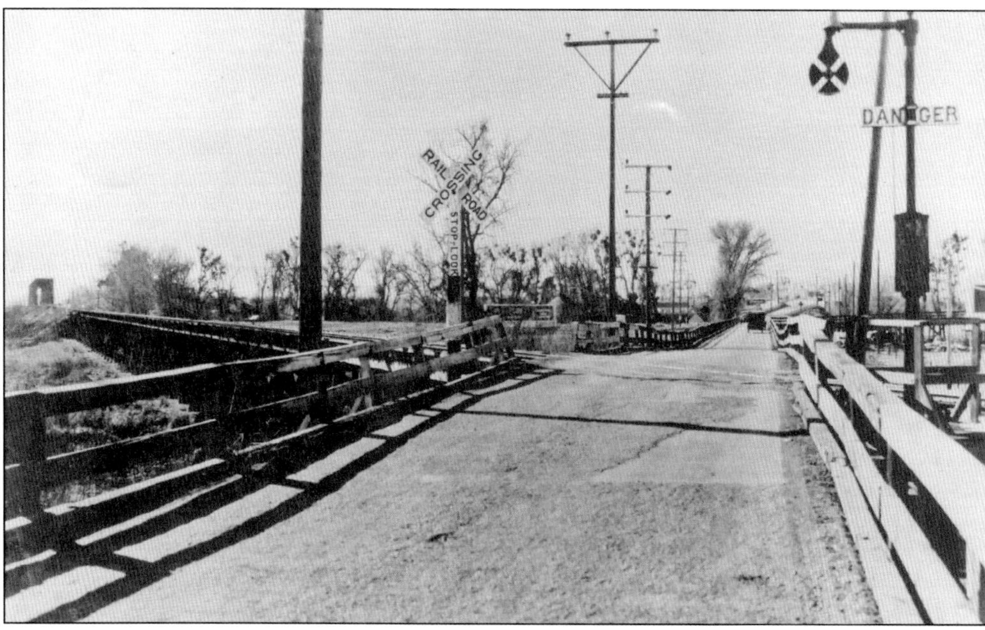

At the turn of the 20th century, Sacramento's lifeblood industry, the railroad, was killing people. Subsequent outrage seemed to pique in 1908–1910, at which time pleas for safer crossing grades from both public and private citizens filled local papers. Pictured here is one of the more notorious, where Twelfth Street met the B Street Levee. (CSH.)

In 1870, German expatriate August Meister brought his love of transportation to Sacramento, where his award-winning A. A. Meister and Sons carriage factory would become a city fixture well into the 20th century. For 12 of those years, the company was situated at Ninth and D Streets, where it reinvented itself in 1906 and began to build both automobiles and carriages. Heartbreak hit Meister when, in March 1919, a fire, starting in the upholstery and trimming shop, destroyed the plant at a cost of $500,000. Seven firefighters were injured and 400 birds at a next-door aviary were killed. In June 1924, the company went on to rebuild on Sixteenth and B Streets. (At right, CSH; below, SPL.)

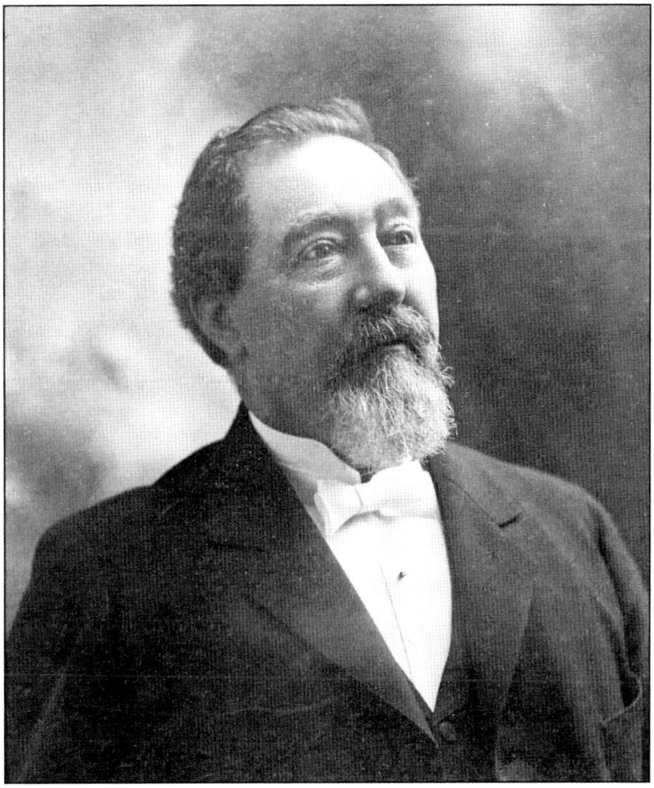

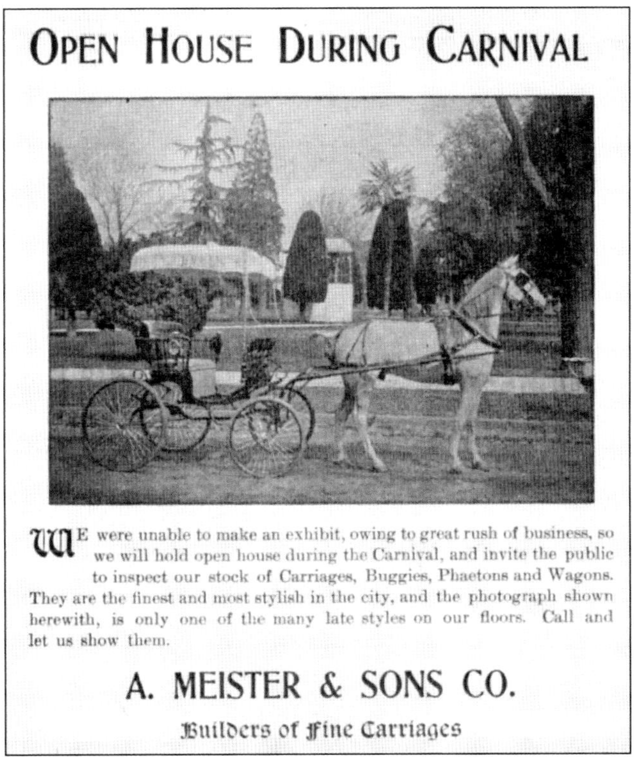

OPEN HOUSE DURING CARNIVAL

WE were unable to make an exhibit, owing to great rush of business, so we will hold open house during the Carnival, and invite the public to inspect our stock of Carriages, Buggies, Phaetons and Wagons. They are the finest and most stylish in the city, and the photograph shown herewith, is only one of the many late styles on our floors. Call and let us show them.

A. MEISTER & SONS CO.

Builders of Fine Carriages

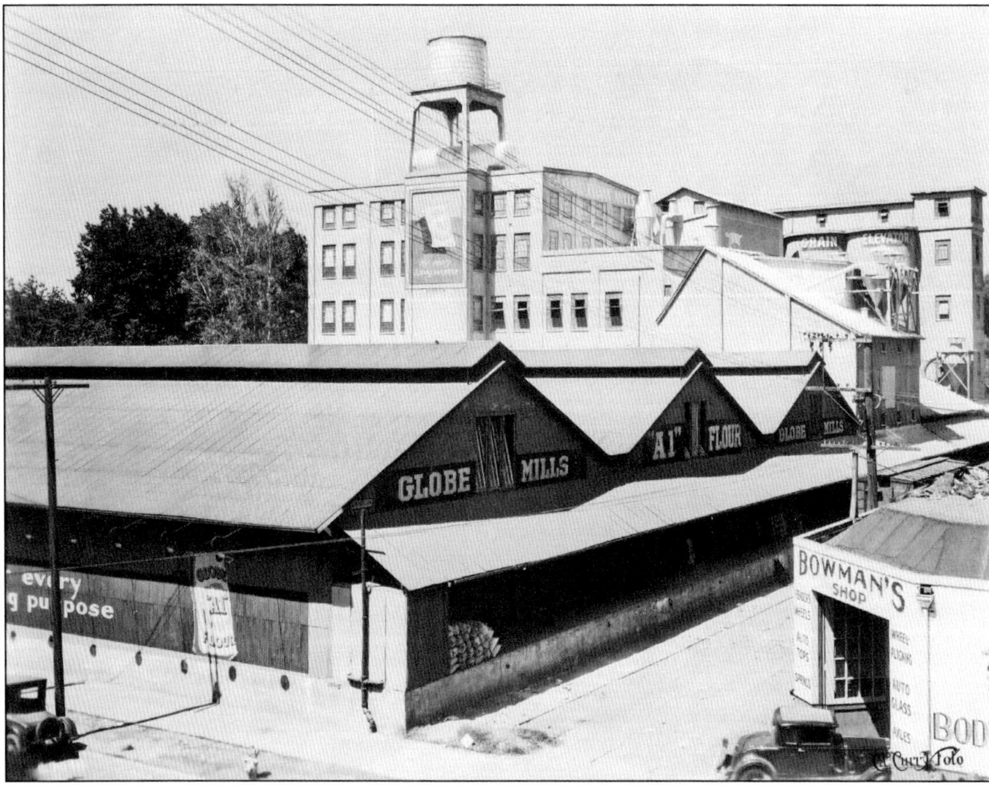

Pictured here in 1933, at Twelfth and C Streets, is the five-story-high Globe Mills, perhaps the highest profile of Sacramento's four flour feeds. By this time, the city's grain industry, drawing off nearly 73,000 acres of Sacramento County grain stands, was producing well over $3 million a year in grain stuffs. Just prior to the Great Depression, Sacramento's roughly 200 mill workers could rely on a gainful wage of between $4 and $4.25 an hour. (CSL.)

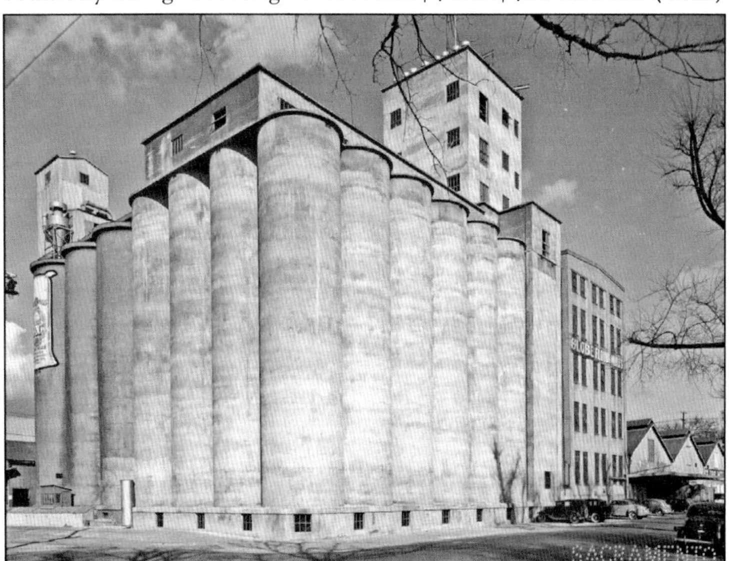

This March 1942 photograph shows a recently modernized Globe Mills building. Its renovation—started in August 1941—came via the federal government's wartime plan to increase grain storage capacity and overcome nationwide shortages. At completion, the building's 46 signature silos measured 125 feet in height and, at capacity, could hold up to 500,000 bushels of grain. (SPL.)

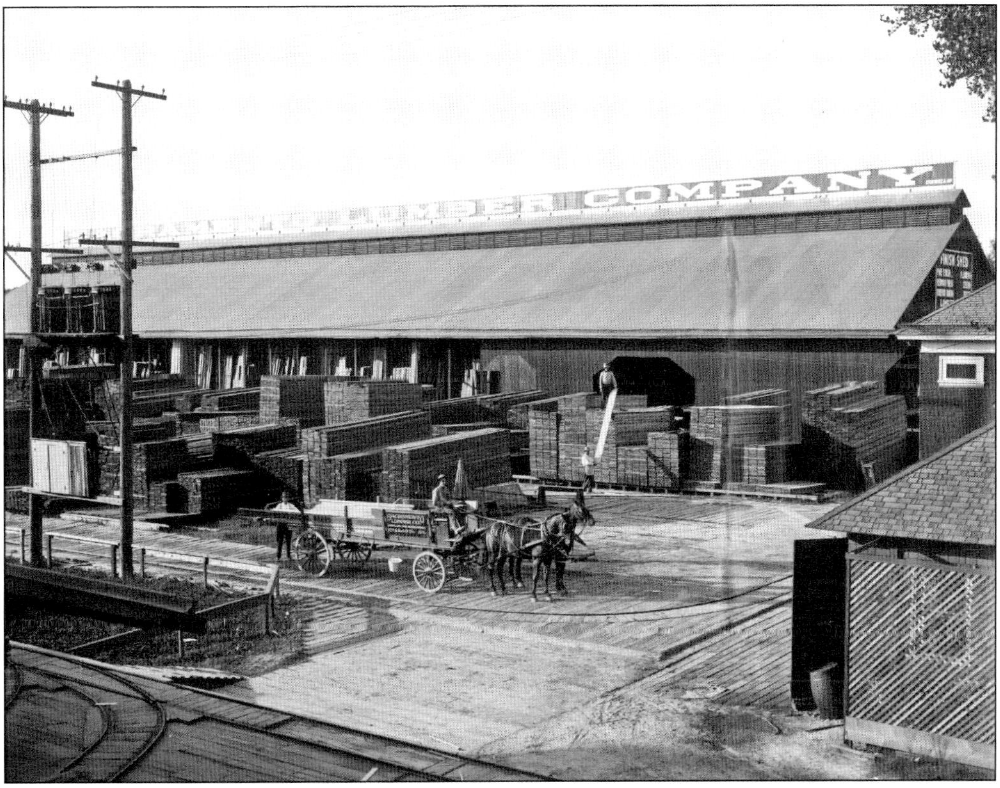

In 1913, the Sacramento Lumber Company and its 50 employees opened at Twelfth and B Streets, where a proximity to the Sacramento River and Southern Pacific facilities kept handling costs low and profit margins wide. Pictured here are two modes of transport within the mill: a horse-drawn wagon and, as evidenced by tracks, narrow-gauge engines. (CSH.)

Myrtle H. Thomas sits on the front left fender of a Kane and Trainor Ice Company delivery truck sometime around 1912. The Kane and Trainor Ice Company began in 1901 and moved to 517 Sixth Street before Isaac Trainor took his company to Ninth and C Streets around 1914. Sitting in the cab of the truck are, from left to right, Sue Bell, Myrtle Simpson Chamberlain, and Gertrude Neeley. (CSH.)

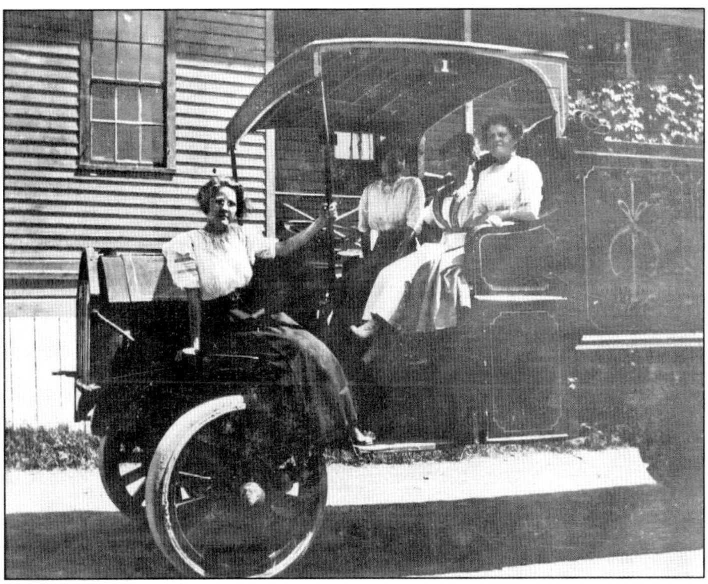

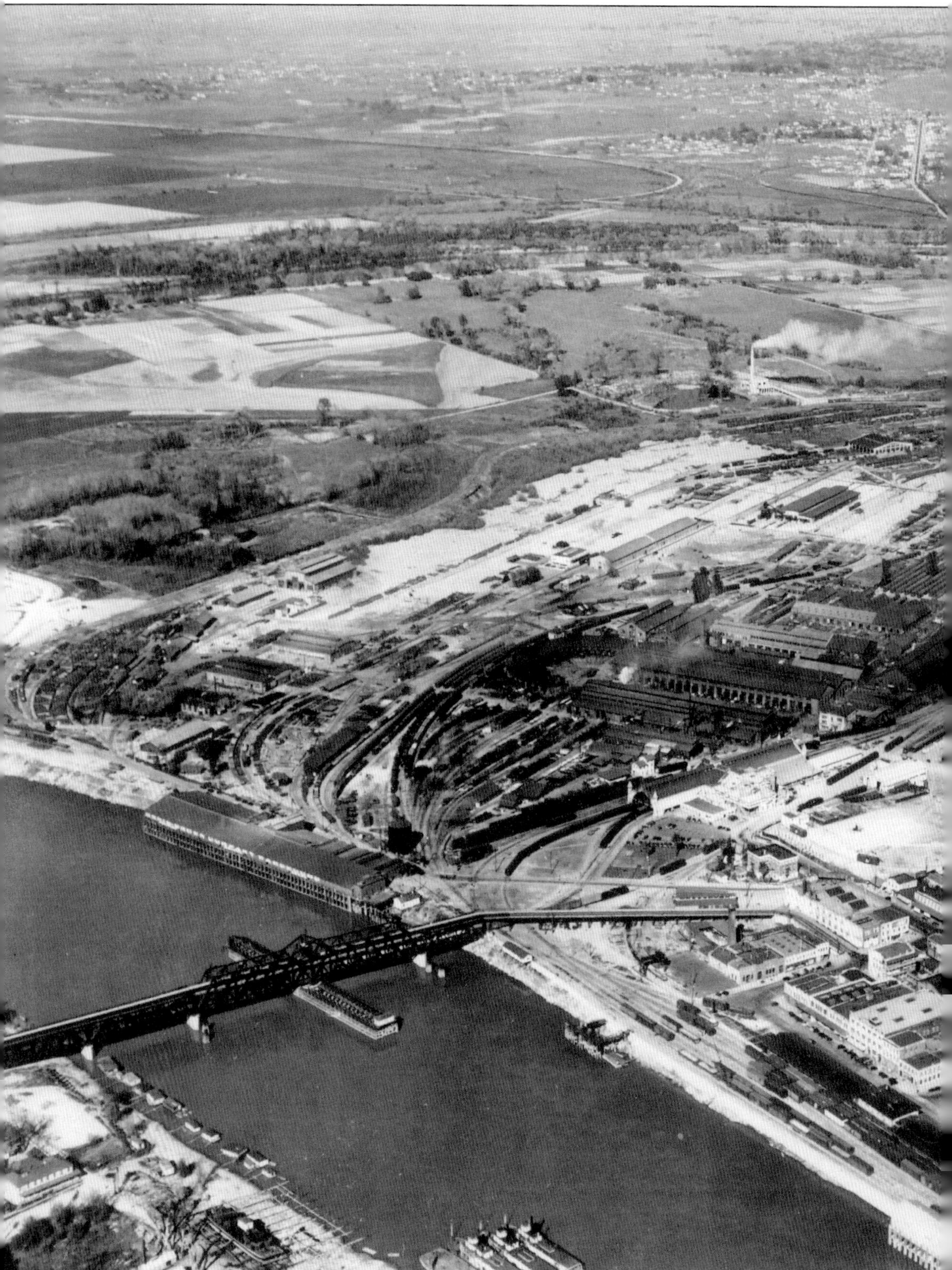

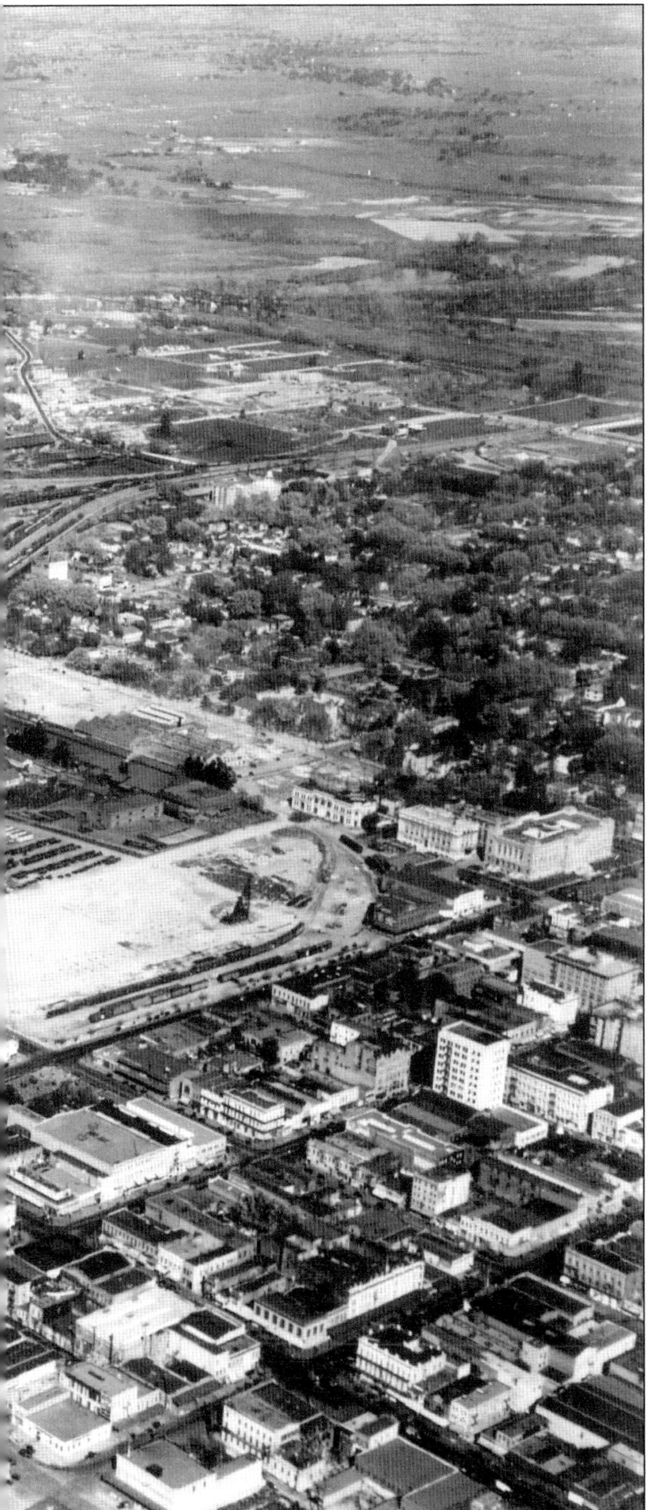

This 1925 aerial shot provides a choice view of Alkali Flat amidst the coverage of oak, cottonwood, box elder, and ash and its relation to the immensity of the encroaching Southern Pacific rail yards and burgeoning tracts north of B Street and the American River. Hard at work is a smoke-belching city incinerator in the photograph's upper middle section, while Globe Mills, the Sacramento Lumber Company's warehouse, and the Twelfth Street Bridge all sit prominently to the upper portion of the photograph. To the far left is the city's water filtration plant. With the exception of the SP shops, all of these structures were less than a decade old. They represent what the *Sacramento Bee*, just a few years later, coined the city's "great industrial future," and one in which the Alkali would hold prominence. (CSH.)

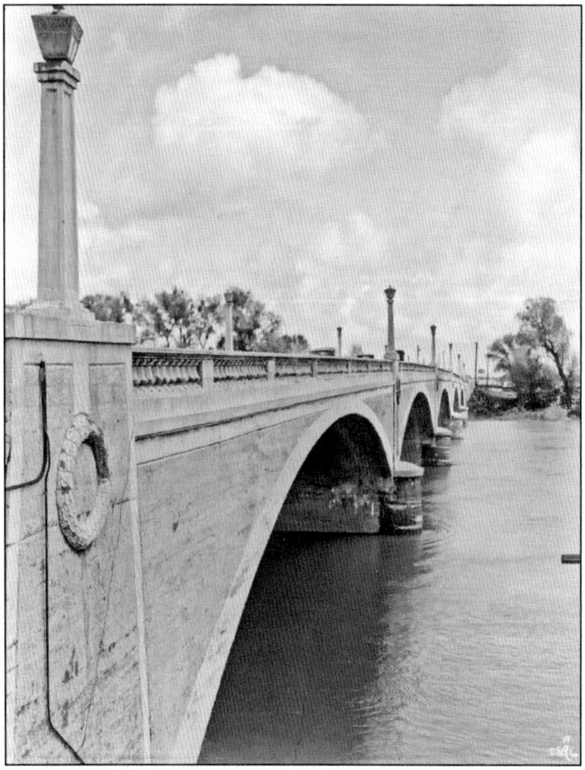

This photograph of the Twelfth Street Bridge was taken in 1920. When completed in 1915, under the design of county surveyor Frank Miller, the bridge and its five Romanesque arches gave Sacramentans a reason to travel through the Alkali. Known as a "Luten Arch" bridge, it spanned 600 feet, bank to bank, and was illuminated by 12 high-powered electric lights. It was built by Ross Construction at a cost of $120,000. (CSH.)

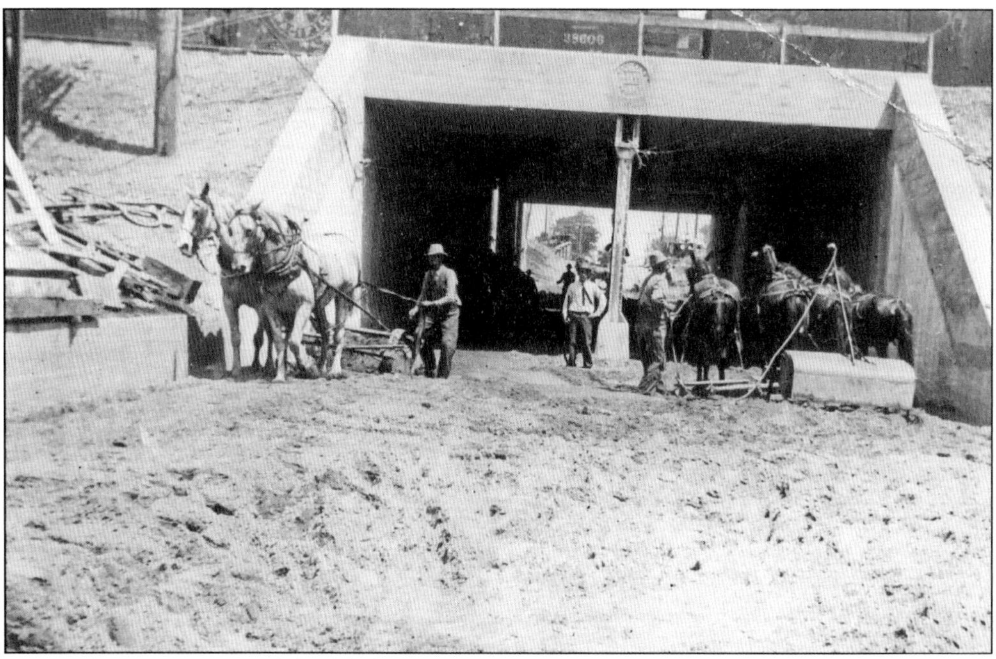

One of the more meaningful public/private works projects in Alkali Flat was the Twelfth Street "subway," which replaced the dangerous grade crossing in 1913. With the help of 50 men, several mules, Fresno scrapers, 400 piles, and 7,000 sacks of cement, the project was completed in six months. The underpass cost the city $10,000 and Southern Pacific $30,000. (CSH.)

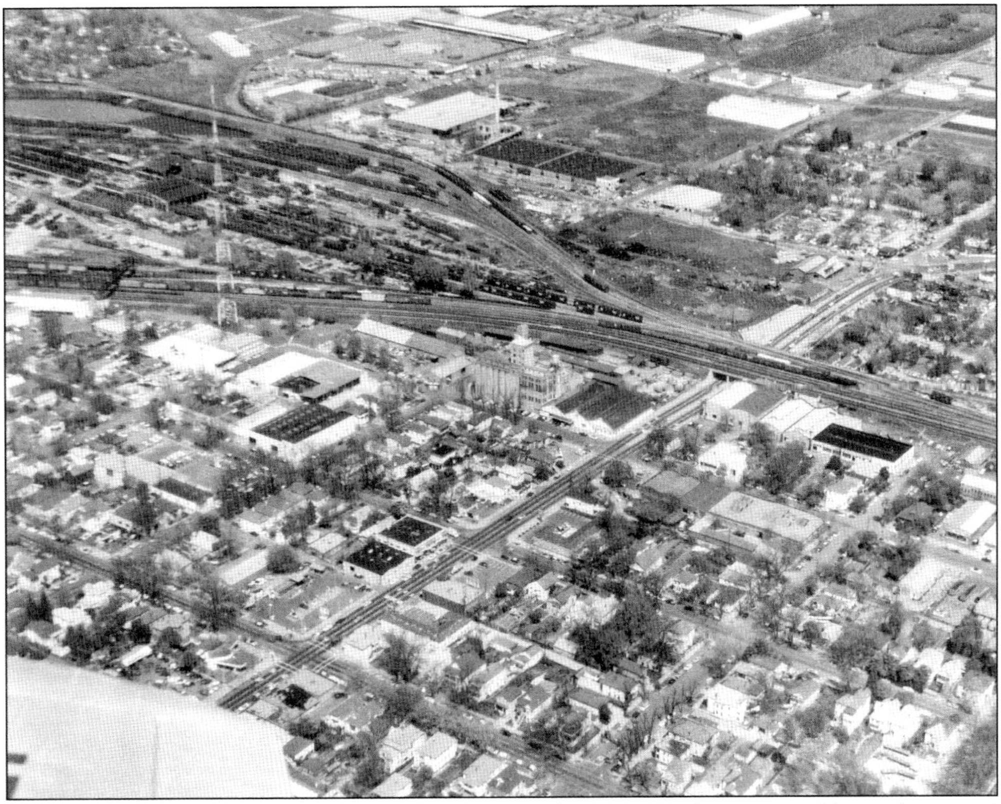

Alkali flat from about E to Thirteenth Streets and points northeast is visible in this aerial photograph taken by KCRA-TV's Harry Sweet in 1960. The station's transmission tower stands against the huge Southern Pacific yards, shops, boxcars, and full trains awaiting loads or departure. Burnett and Sons Lumber, Globe Mills, and the blocks taken by Crystal Cream and Butter to the left represent the area's largest industry. (KCRA-TV, Sacramento.)

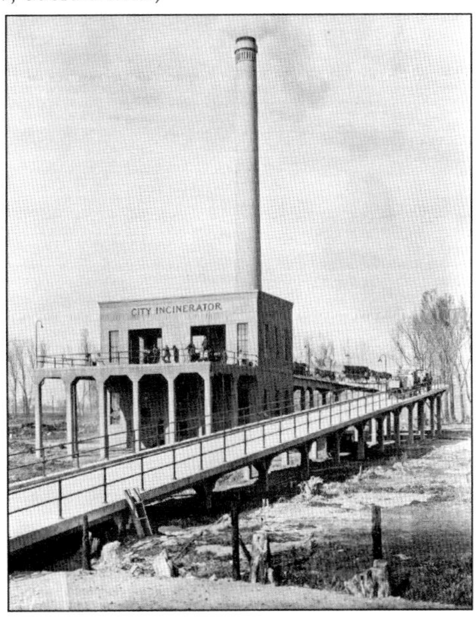

Built in 1924 for a cost of $215,000, the city incinerator, with its location near the B Street Levee, stood—and still stands—as a symbol of the city's post–World War I growth. The incinerator formed a linchpin for the industrial development of what was called "No Man's Land"—the area between Sacramento and the incorporated town of North Sacramento. At its height, the incinerator was burning 130 tons of waste daily. (CSL.)

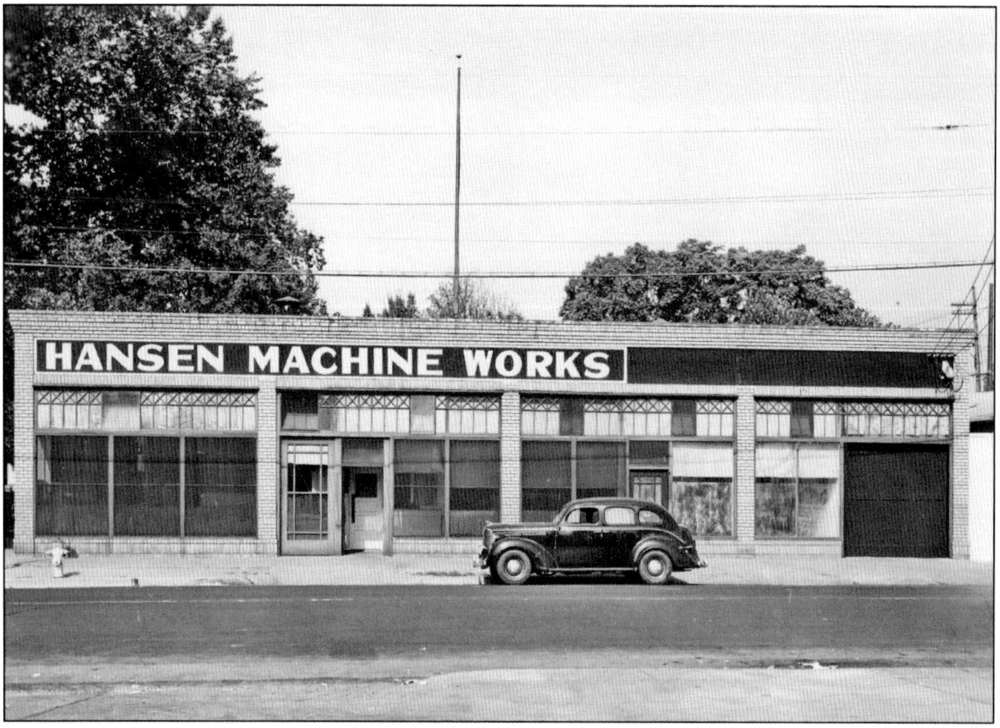

Waldemar Hansen was in his 20s when he left Illinois for Sacramento to take a position as a machinist. By 1925, he had broken out on his own, opening Hansen's Machine Works on 728 Twelfth Street. Pictured here in 1935, the business flourished in its attention to crankshaft cylinders and other machinery and stood as an anchor of skilled industry in the Alkali until mid-1970s. (SPL.)

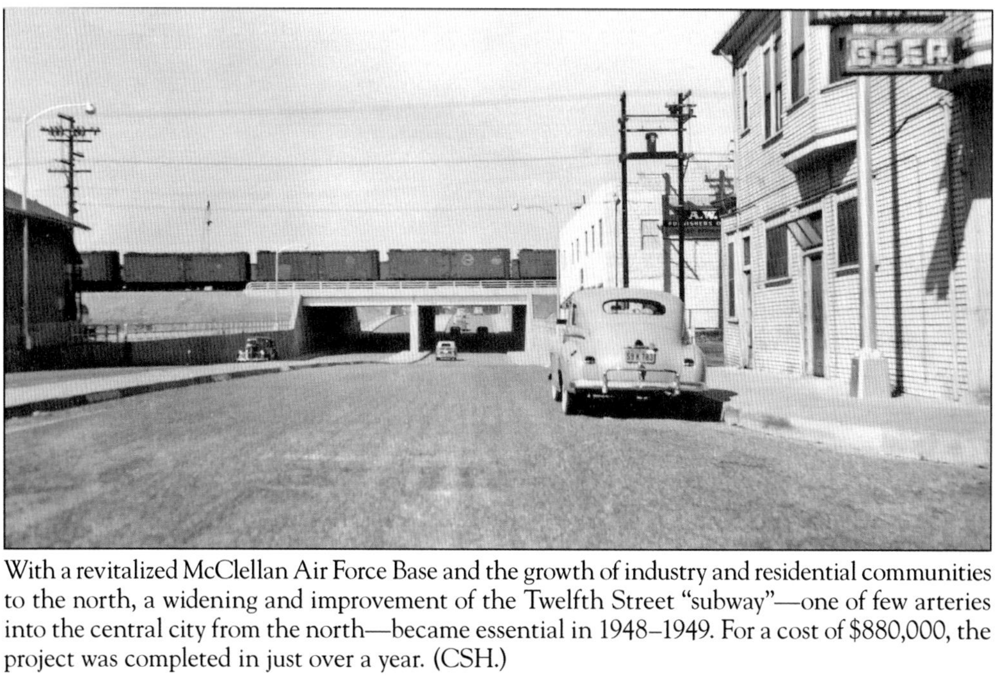

With a revitalized McClellan Air Force Base and the growth of industry and residential communities to the north, a widening and improvement of the Twelfth Street "subway"—one of few arteries into the central city from the north—became essential in 1948–1949. For a cost of $880,000, the project was completed in just over a year. (CSH.)

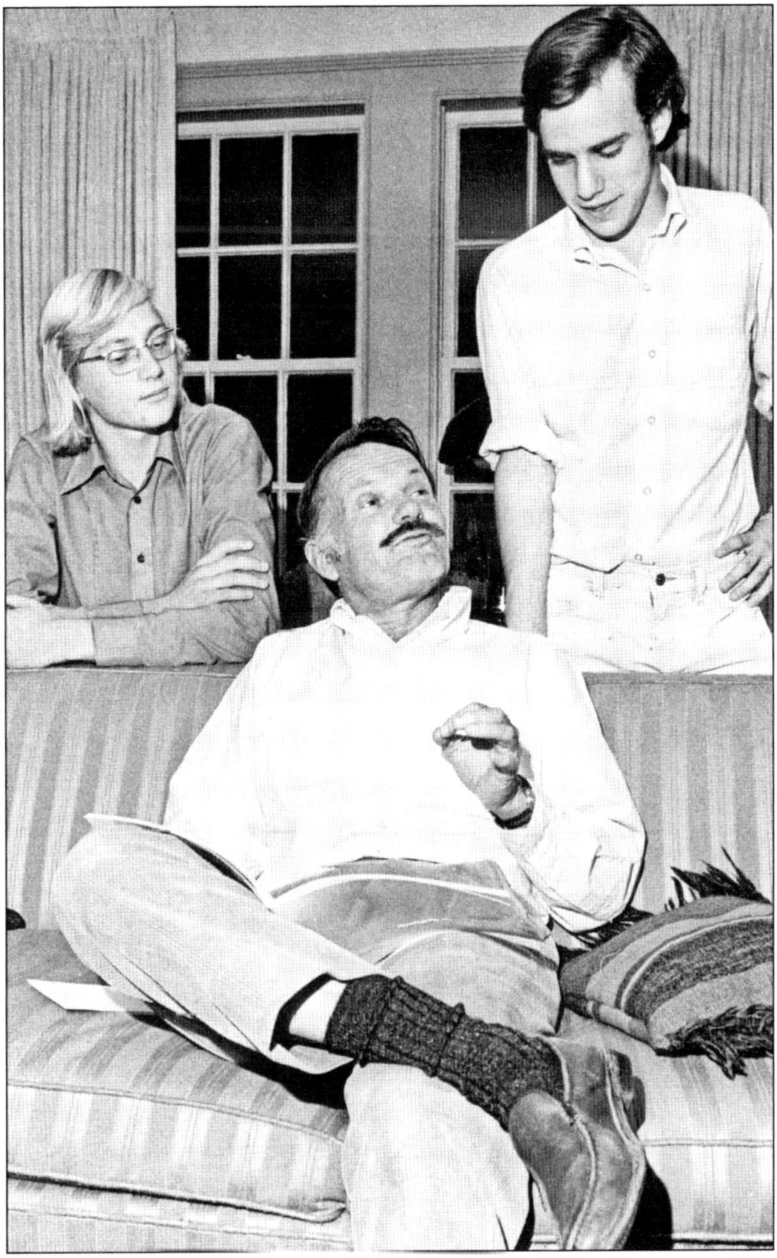

Following the surge of industry to the northerly sections of Alkali Flat, Burnett and Sons, perhaps the oldest planning and milling company in the city, moved to its current Eleventh and C Streets location from Twelfth and J Streets in 1932. The company was founded by Philetus Burnett in 1869, but its highest-profile operator is the founder's great-great grandson, R. Burnett Miller. Miller's career has also seen stints as a member of the 11th Armored Division during the Battle of the Bulge in 1944–1945, Sacramento city councilman (1972–1977), mayor of Sacramento (1982–1983), and president of the Crocker Art Museum Association. Miller is pictured here (center) in November 1973 discussing his city council (3rd District) victory over then political neophyte Phil Angelides who, at the time, was a 20-year-old attending Harvard University. Standing to the right is Miller's son and current company vice president, Fitz. (CSH.)

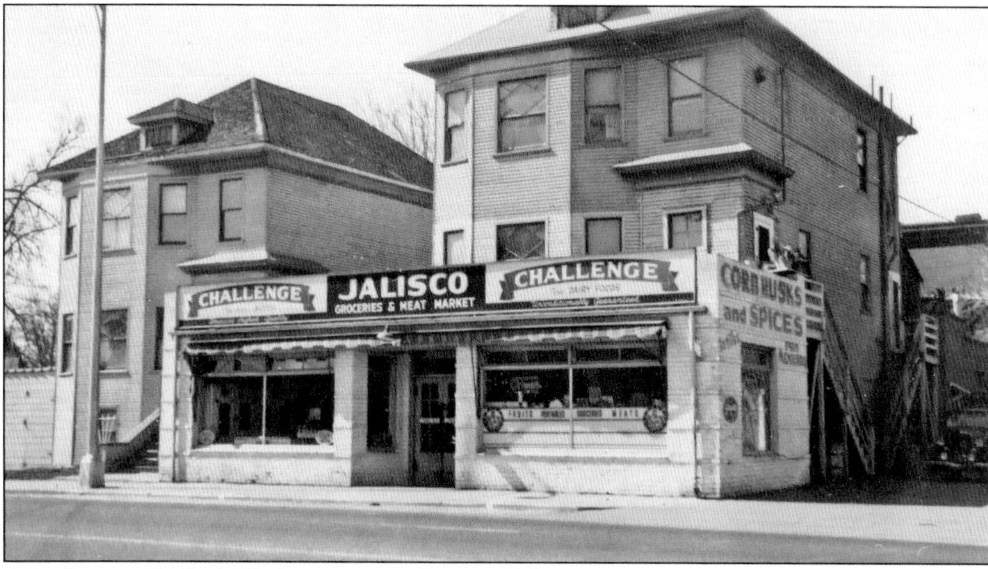

A harbinger of Alkali Flat's increasing diversity, Jalisco Mexican Grocery, seen here in 1950 at 318 Twelfth Street, experienced considerable growth after being purchased by Raul Mercado in 1957 and converted into Jalisco Tortillas, Inc. Up to the mid-1980s, Jalisco distinguished itself as one of the state's top producers of tortillas, at its height shipping units throughout Northern California, Nevada, and Oregon. During his tenure with Jalisco, Mercado served as president of the Sacramento Hispanic Chamber of Commerce and was recognized in 1987 for his contributions to community life by the California Human Development Corporation. Pictured below in 1983 is Jalisco worker Juan Gutierrez. (Above, CSH; below, Craig Lee.)

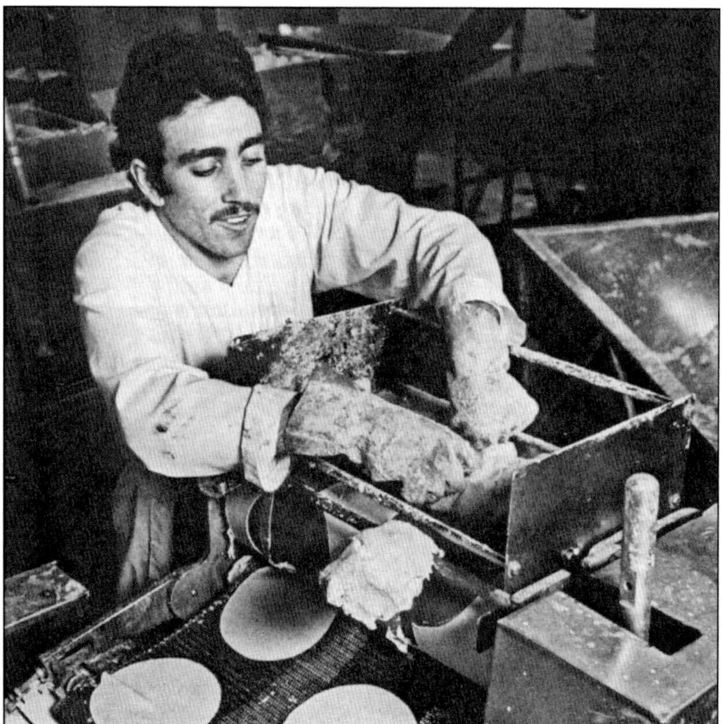

Great Dane Carl Hansen fulfilled his portion of the American dream in Northern California, a turn-of-the-century immigrant who processed hard work and innate skill into the Sacramento Valley's premiere dairy producer, Crystal Cream and Butter. Born in 1876, Hansen and his wife, Gerda, purchased the company and its large grounds at 1013 D Street in 1921. (CSH.)

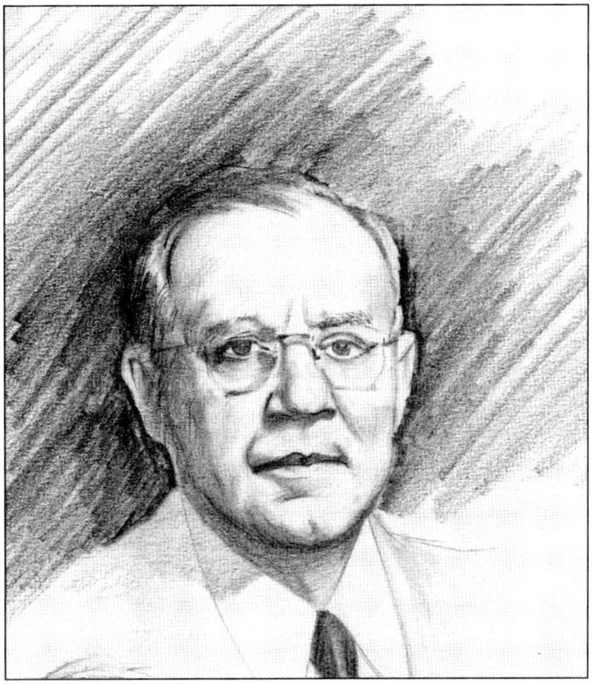

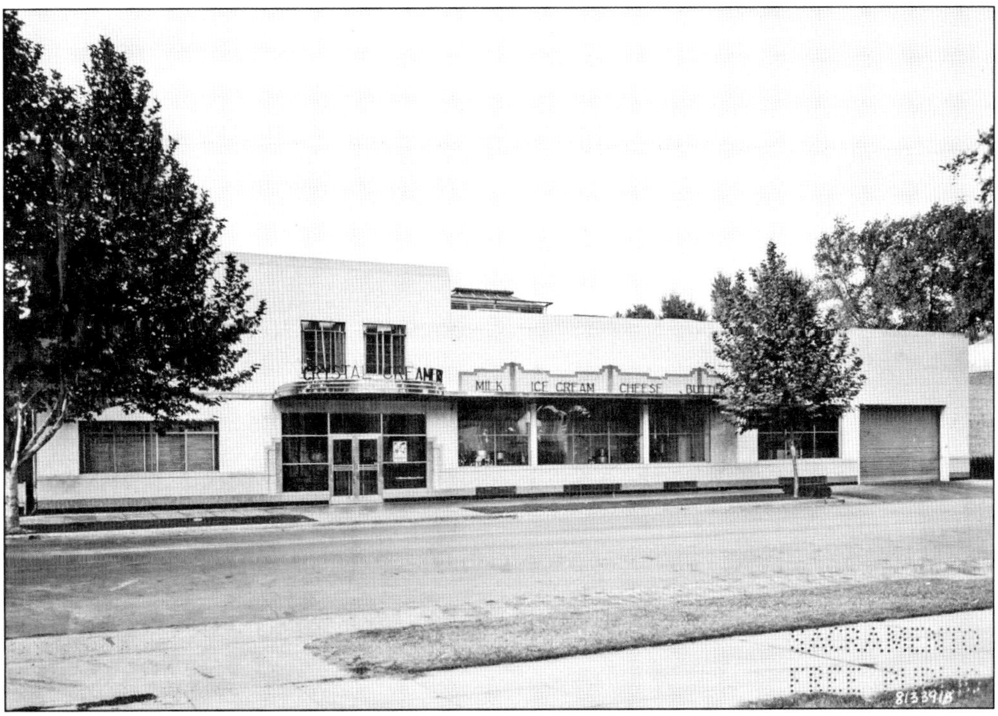

For over 90 years, the Crystal Cream and Butter Company office at 1013 D Street headquartered a 537,000-square-foot complex that manufactured and processed dozens of products in all shapes, sizes, and flavors. Many of the products' labels bore the dairymaid in a full, flowered skirt that symbolized the firm for over 50 years. Until the company's sale, Sacramento's oldest residential neighborhood hosted the area's largest dairy manufacturer. (SPL.)

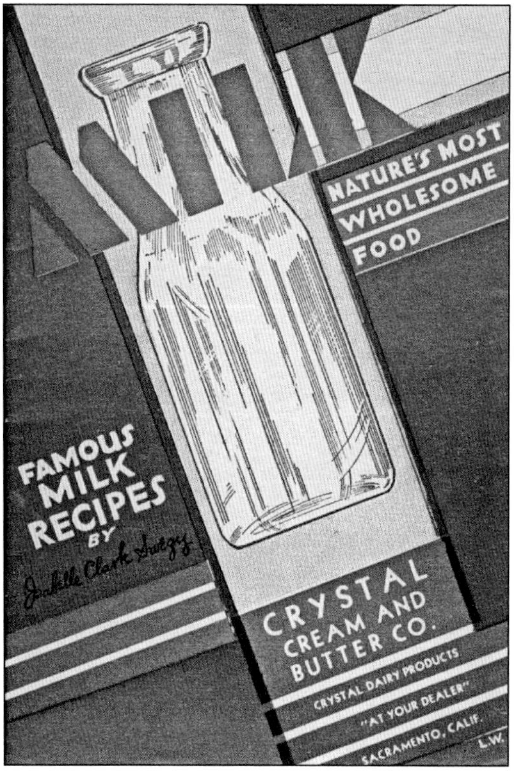

Within a few years of Crystal Cream and Butter Company's purchase by the Hansen family in 1921, the dynamic dairy had added bottled milk, the first available in the Sacramento Valley. In 1931, they offered the first locally produced ice cream and the following year arranged to publish a 32-page booklet of recipes that relied heavily on dairy products and claimed to be the first complete guide to the use of milk ever published. (SPL.)

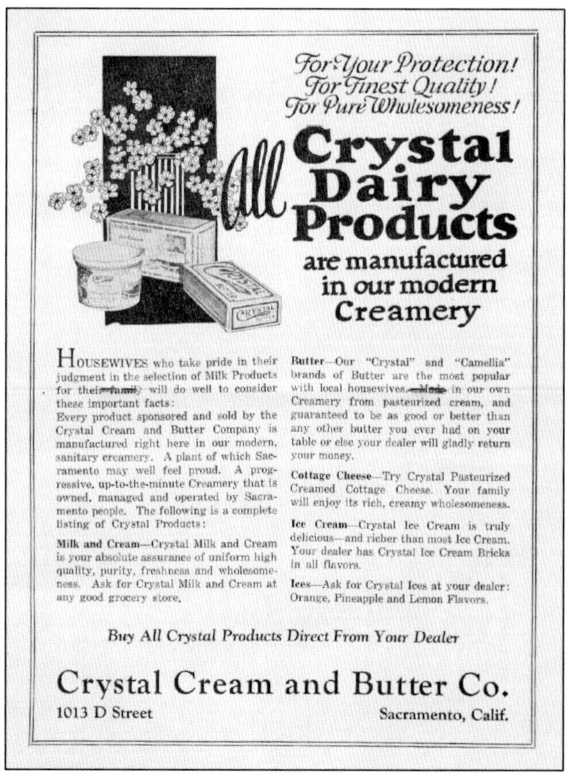

Back in 1932, quality was what Crystal dairy products said set them apart, and the firm at 1013 D Street backed that standard for another 75 years. When the Hansens purchased the concern in 1921, they expanded their line, created their own products, and kept local dairy farms connected. Before closing down their plant and offices in Alkali Flat in 2007, the company could still boast that collecting whole milk directly from Sacramento Valley farms and processing it themselves placed their product on porches and store shelves within 24 hours. (SPL.)

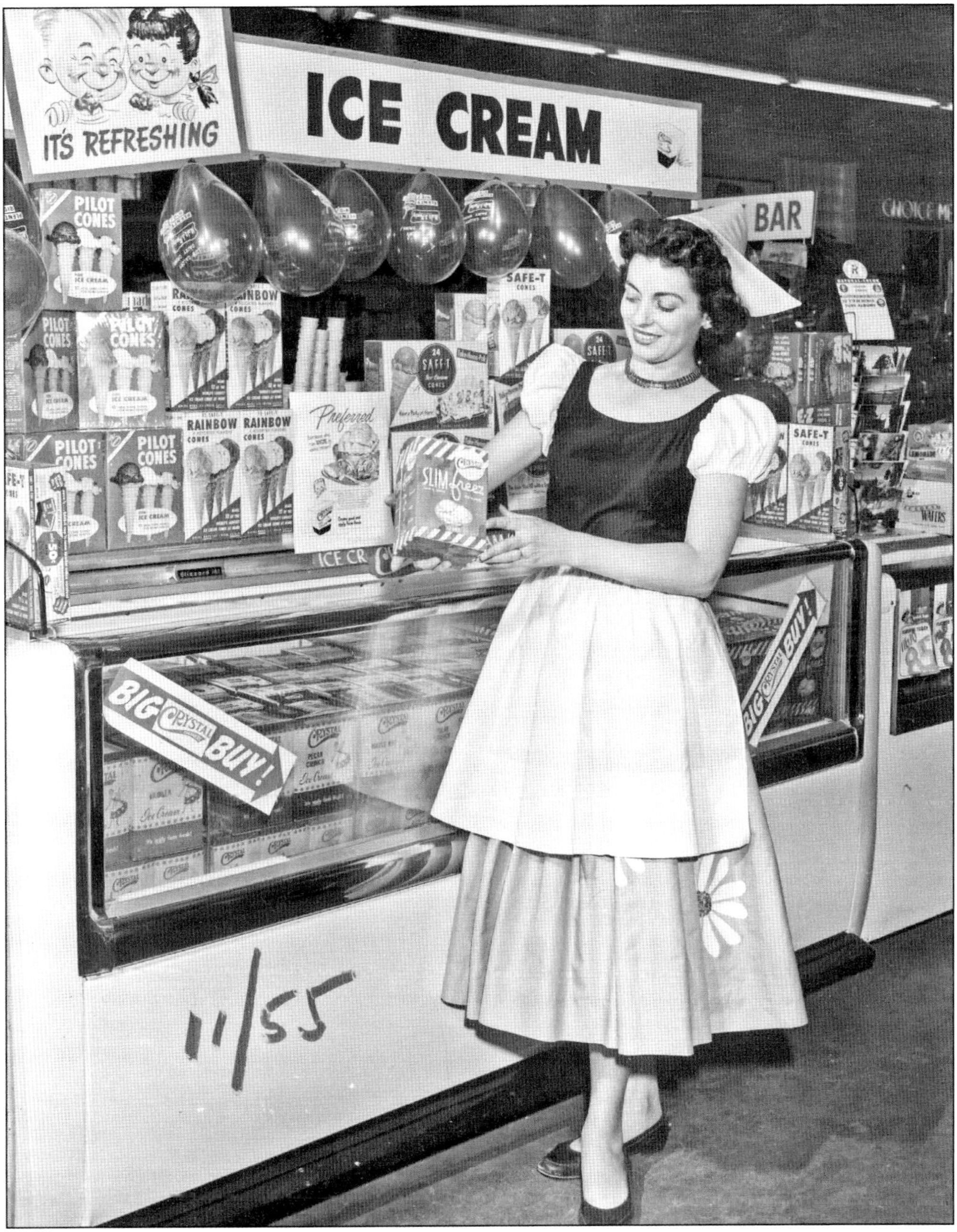

In 1952, Crystal Cream and Butter led the Sacramento Valley in store sales of butter and ice cream but lagged behind competitors for the cottage cheese market. By the time owner Carl Hansen passed away in 1957, the company led most competitors in home and delivery sales and had added new products to their line, including an orange soft drink and bottled hot sauce. Busy store displays and personal appearances by costumed company representatives boosted sales and promoted product image. (CSH.)

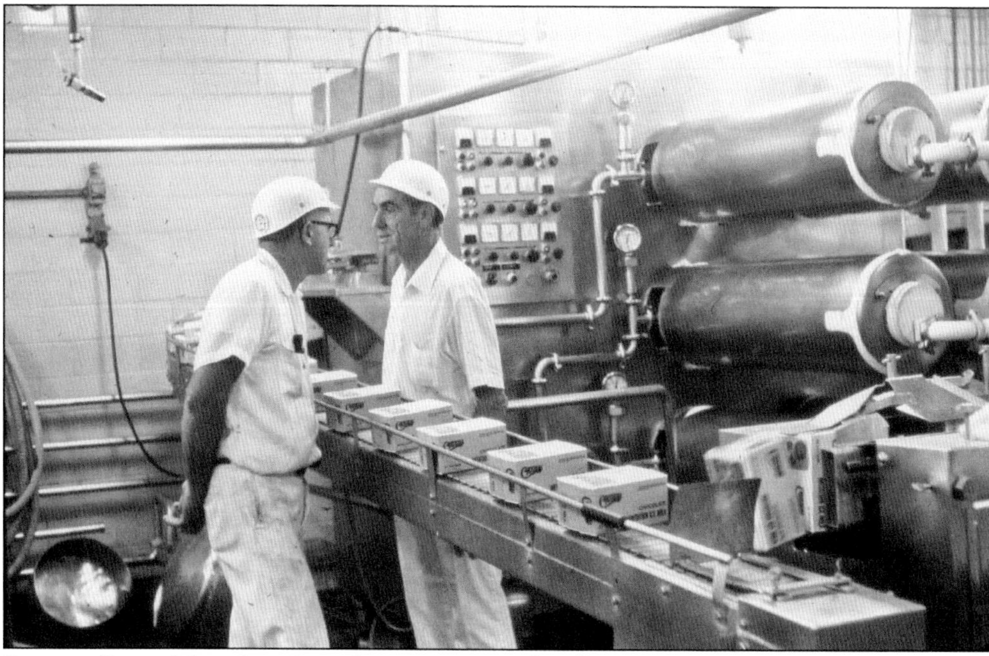

Frozen gallons of chocolate Crystal imitation ice milk roll past two plant workers engaged in what must have been a difficult conversation. This photograph from 1976 shows how the product was mixed in large drums before being piped down to waiting cartons. Crystal Dairy was the first local company to produce and package ice cream and fruit-flavored ices back in 1931. (Tom Myers.)

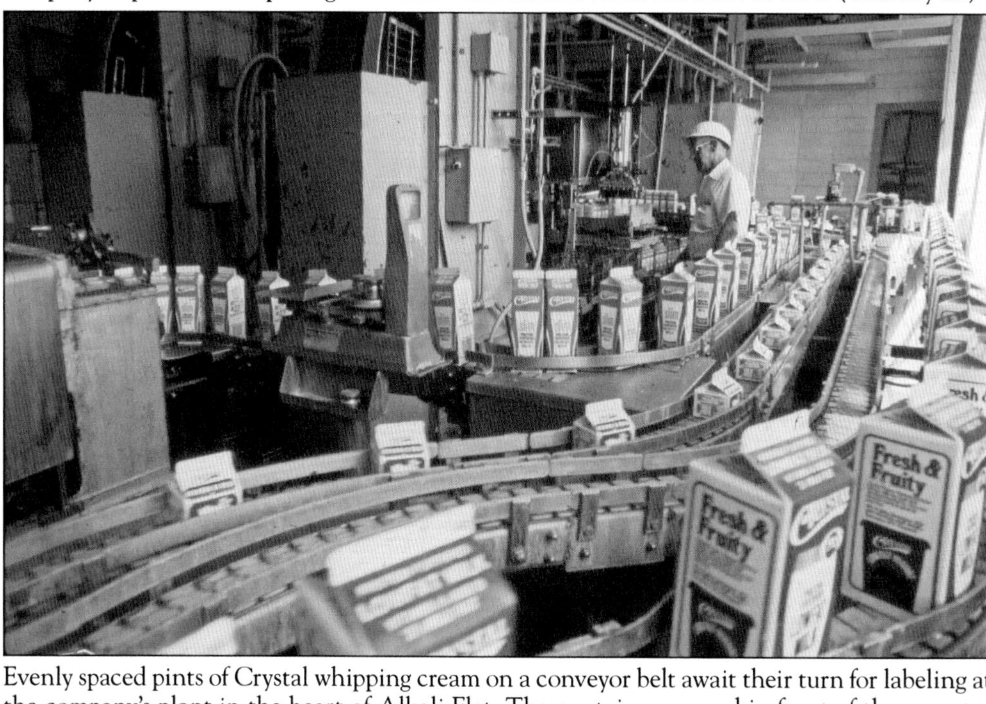

Evenly spaced pints of Crystal whipping cream on a conveyor belt await their turn for labeling at the company's plant in the heart of Alkali Flat. The containers passed in front of the operator at the rate of 85 cartons per minute and when properly stamped and approved moved on to the shipping area. (Tom Myers.)

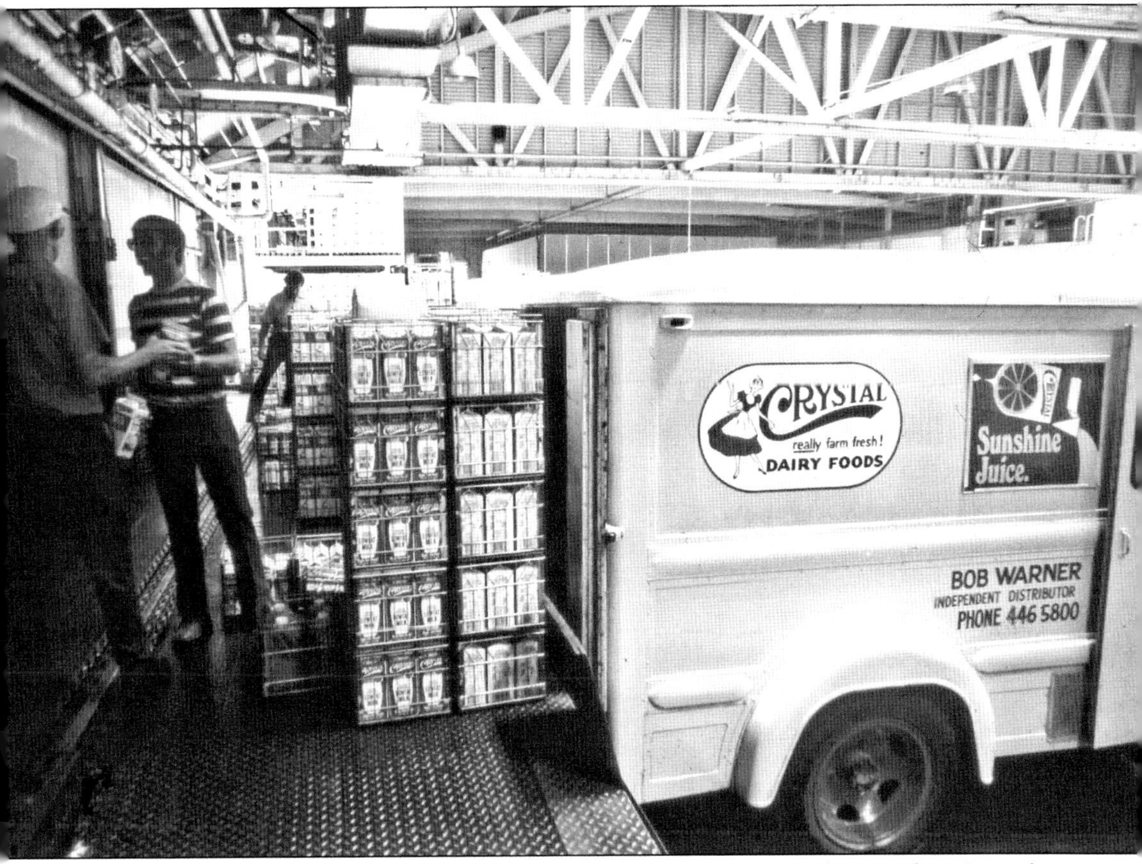

Crystal Cream and Butter Company's best-selling product was butter until 1948 when Crystal milk hit the No. 1 spot in store receipts, but by 1962 they led the pasture in store and home sales of all dairy products. During that decade, Crystal owned the largest fleet of home-delivery trucks in the country. (Tom Myers.)

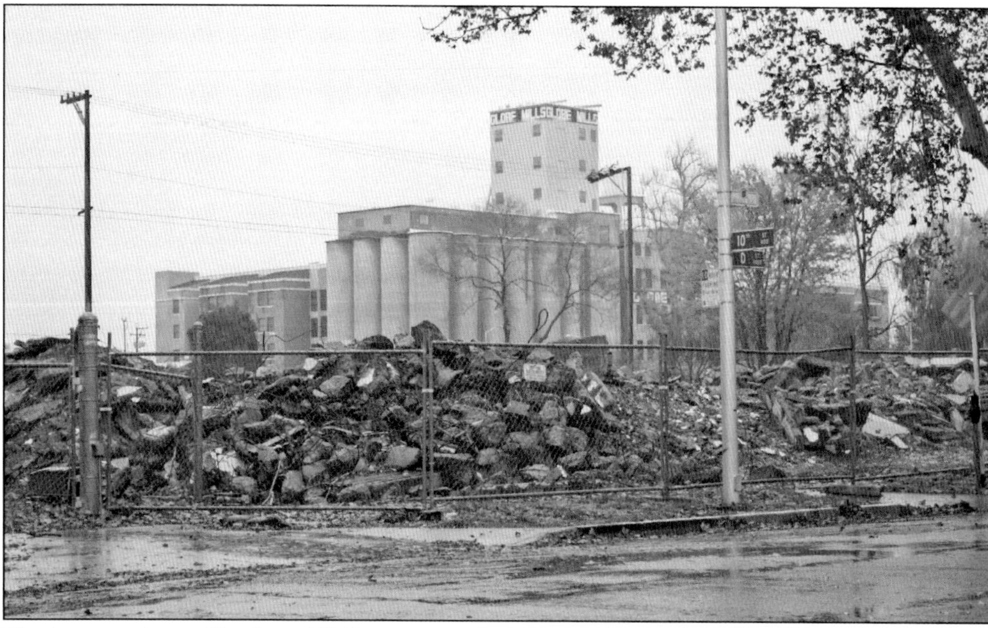

The intersection at Tenth and D Streets was at one time alive with traffic, the carts and wagons bringing milk to Crystal Cream and Butter Company eventually giving way to trucks. Neighboring Globe Mills, built in 1913 shortly after Crystal first set up operation at 1013 D Street, lives on as a residential and office property. (SPL.)

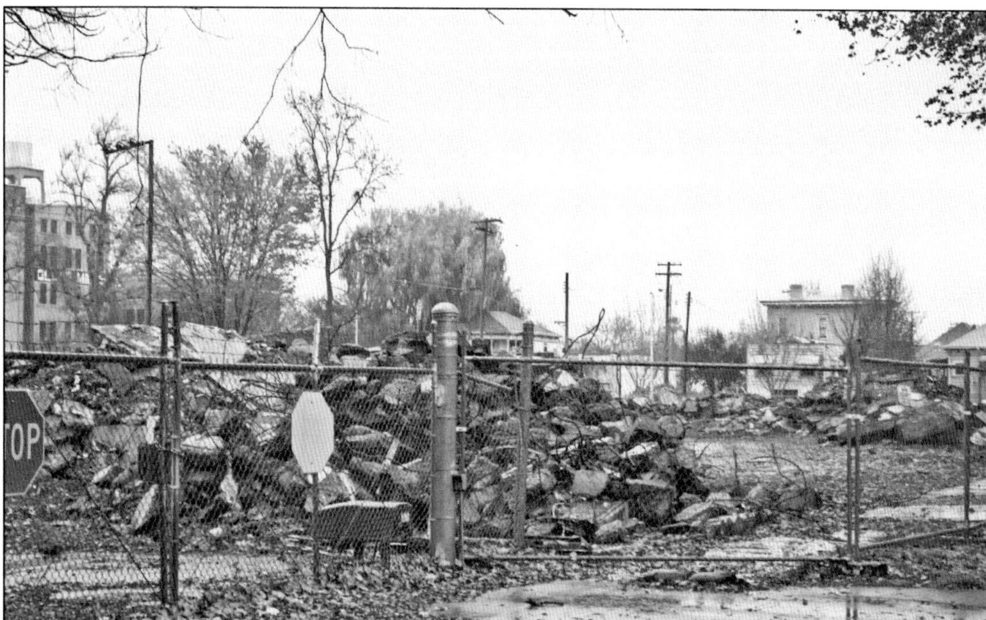

Alkali Flat's identity as an industrial area changed drastically over the years, but the messy demise of Crystal Cream and Butter Company brought to a close an association that had long benefitted the neighborhood. The enormous complex, including the processing plant and blocks of buildings, were demolished in late 2008 and with it went nearly a century of commerce and goodwill. (SPL.)

Four

Alkali Media, Mechanics, and Merchants by James Scott and Tom Tolley

Double-decker busses once rolled down Twelfth Street, an accidental swabby named "Skipper Stu" broadcasted a kid's show from Ninth and D Streets, and pumping gas at Twelfth and C Streets was a guy who squatted behind the plate for the St. Louis Cardinals in 1924. These flashes of novelty represent but a tincture of the Alkali Flat story and are par for a neighborhood that has been around for over 150 years. Courtesy of a rehabilitated dairy truck barn, transmission from the Alkali's own media outlet, KCRA, started on September 3, 1955, going public from the California State Fair, where visitors could see themselves on television. Owner Ewing C. "Gene" Kelly began his local empire with radio station KCRA-AM, which broadcasted from Eleventh and J Streets, and with the cooperation of the Hansen family used existing structures on Crystal Cream property to front the 573-foot antenna tower that beamed news and current shows to the Sacramento Valley. By 1955, there were over 57,000 television receivers in the valley, and the small station at Ninth and D Streets instantly became a large part of the lives of more than 60 percent of the Sacramento Valley's families. Along with road improvements and the 1914–1915 construction of the Twelfth Street Bridge, the Alkali sat directly between the nascent communities above the American River and Sacramento's city center. Accordingly, service stations and auto-body garages would sprout up along the Alkali's main drag, Twelfth Street, standing at the ready throughout the 20th century to serve Desoto-driving solon and bracero alike. Also along the Twelfth Street corridor one could find havens to sample exotic foods from south of the border, a friendly place to get a haircut and straight shave, a corner store to grab canned tomatoes for the evening's cannelloni, and a laundry for laborers to get any number of industrial substances off and out of their clothes.

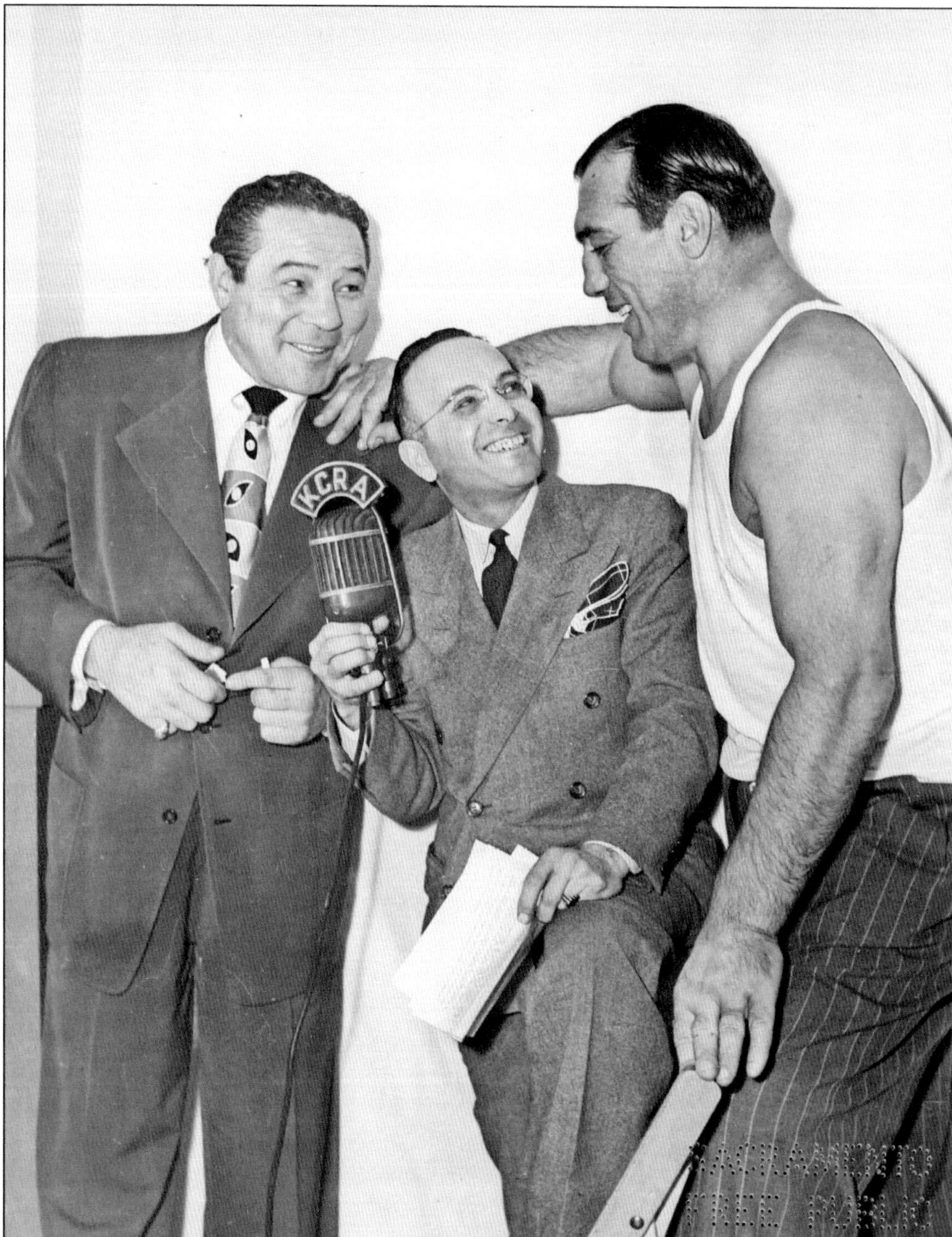

Radio sportscaster William "Steve" George wears a leery smile and clutches his microphone just a bit tighter while sandwiched between former world heavyweight boxing champions Max Baer (on the left) and Primo Carnera during a broadcast for KCRA-Radio around 1950. Baer earned international recognition when he scored knockouts against Germany's Max Schmeling in 1933 and the towering Carnera in 1934. He was always popular in Sacramento, where he lived until his passing in 1959. (SPL.)

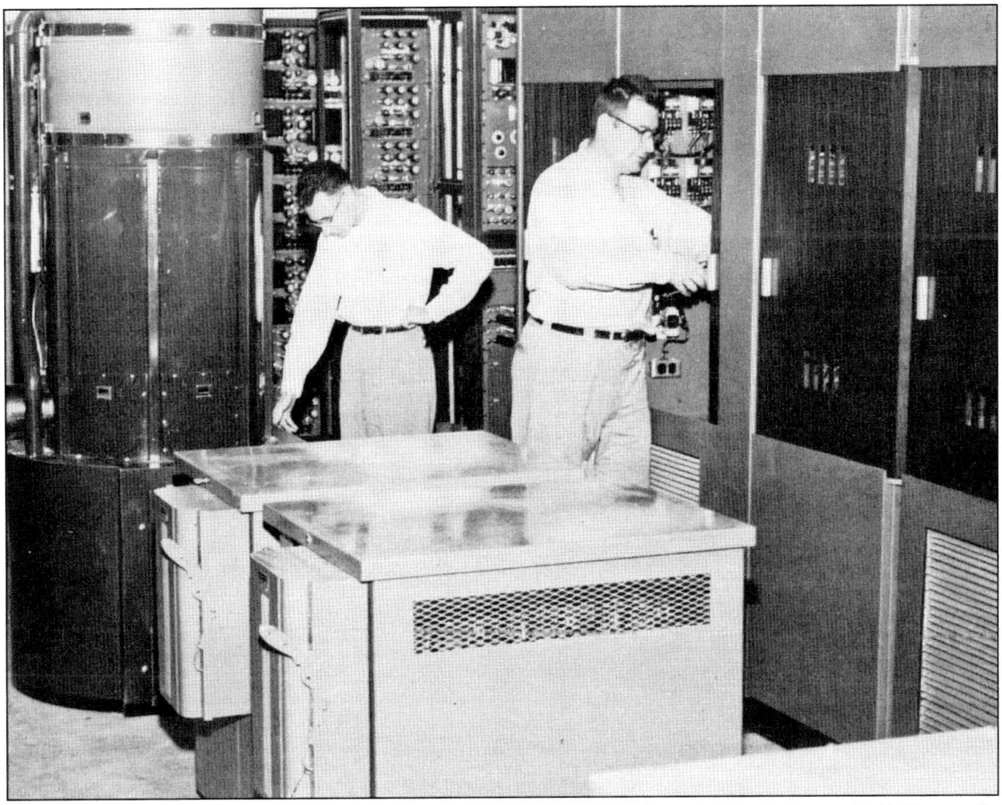

KCRA-TV's chief engineer, Herb Hartman (on the left), and assisting engineer, Bill Karpisek, were largely responsible for building the station and gathering the engineering and technical staff that made Channel 3 first in broadcasting in the Sacramento Valley. Hartman worked for KCRA-Radio before owner Ewing Kelly entrusted him with the television facility, and Karpisek was with him when the station debuted in September 1955. (SPL.)

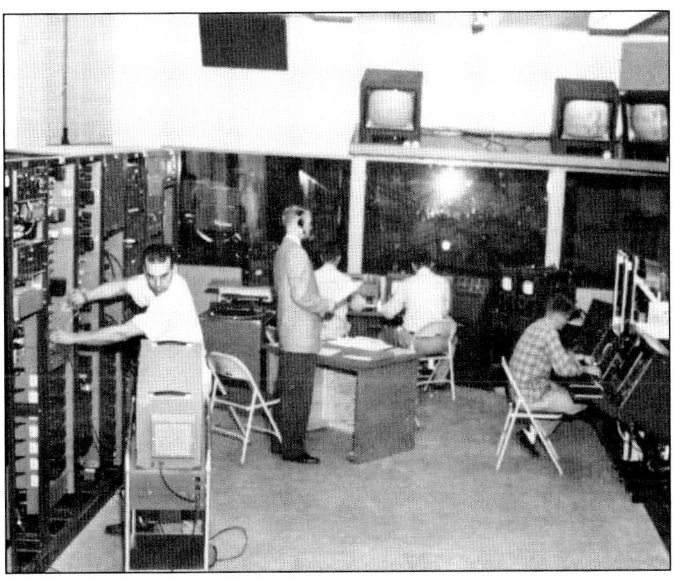

Television broadcasting was only a decade old in the mid-1950s, and the KCRA-TV studio looks spare and primitive by today's standards in this shot from 1956. To the left, carefully watching the monitor while making the necessary adjustments, is Frank Eberhart, and the station's first "Captain Sacto," Fred Wade, takes his cues from the screens positioned near the ceiling. Bob Worthylake is at the control board to the right, while two unknown engineers work behind Wade. (SPL.)

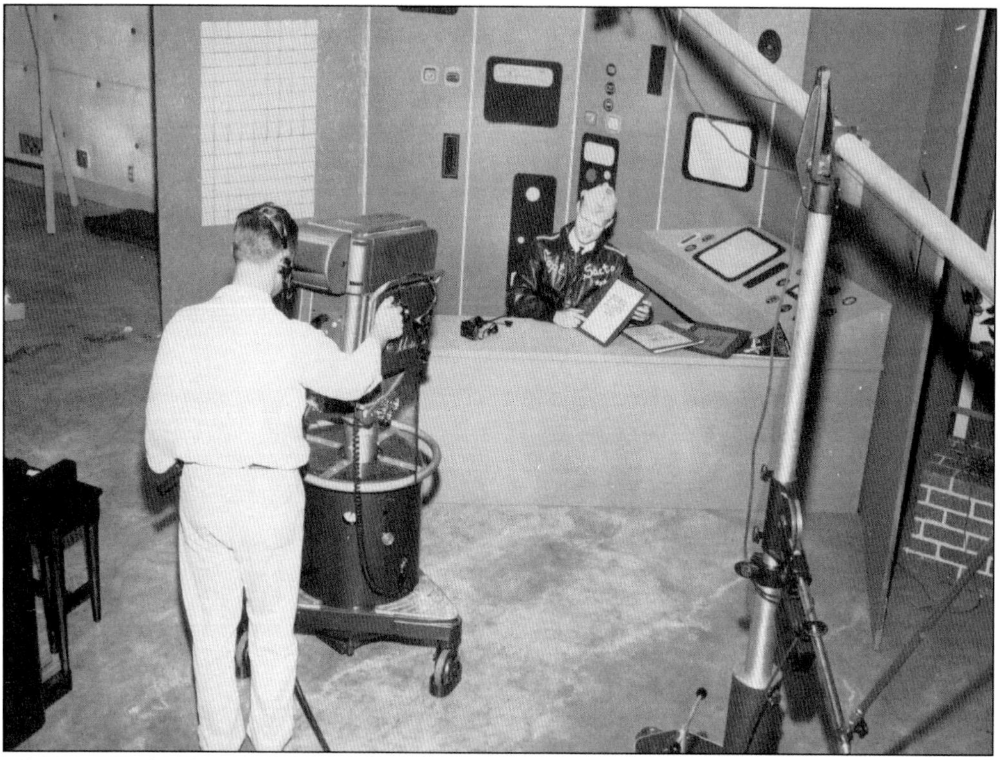

Like many early television employees, Fred G. Wade had to wear many different hats, but before the hats came a pair of boots as the multitasking manager became "Dirty Boots McGee," a pioneering KCRA-TV kid's show that featured a pair of talking boots between cartoons. Wade is best remembered as the station's first Captain Sacto and is shown here on the set designed by longtime employee Bob Miller. Photographer Kenny Blue is behind a new RCA TK-60 in the old Studio A. (KCRA-TV, Sacramento.)

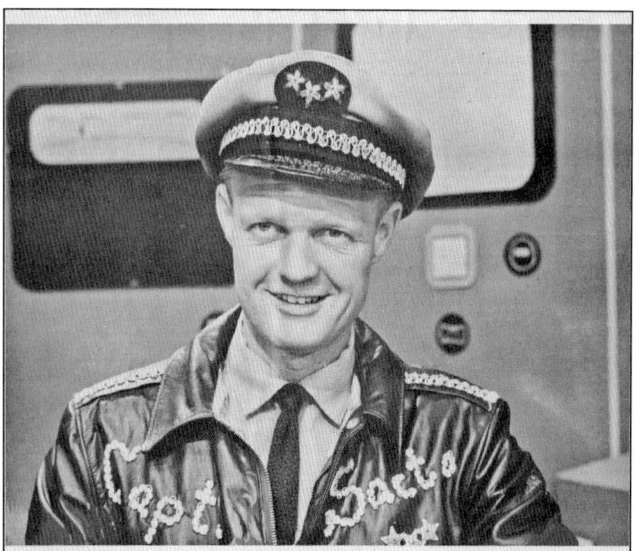

"Captain Sacto" was KCRA-TV's most enduring character, and the first man to don the embroidered jacket and modified cab-driver cap was promotions/production/operations manager Fred Wade, a reluctant hero who was always amazed at being recognized for work done outside of his chosen fields. Among the initial 50 station staffers that opened the enterprise in 1955, Wade was an energetic and innovative force and carried those qualities into his career in advertising, beginning his own award-winning agency in 1962. (KCRA-TV, Sacramento.)

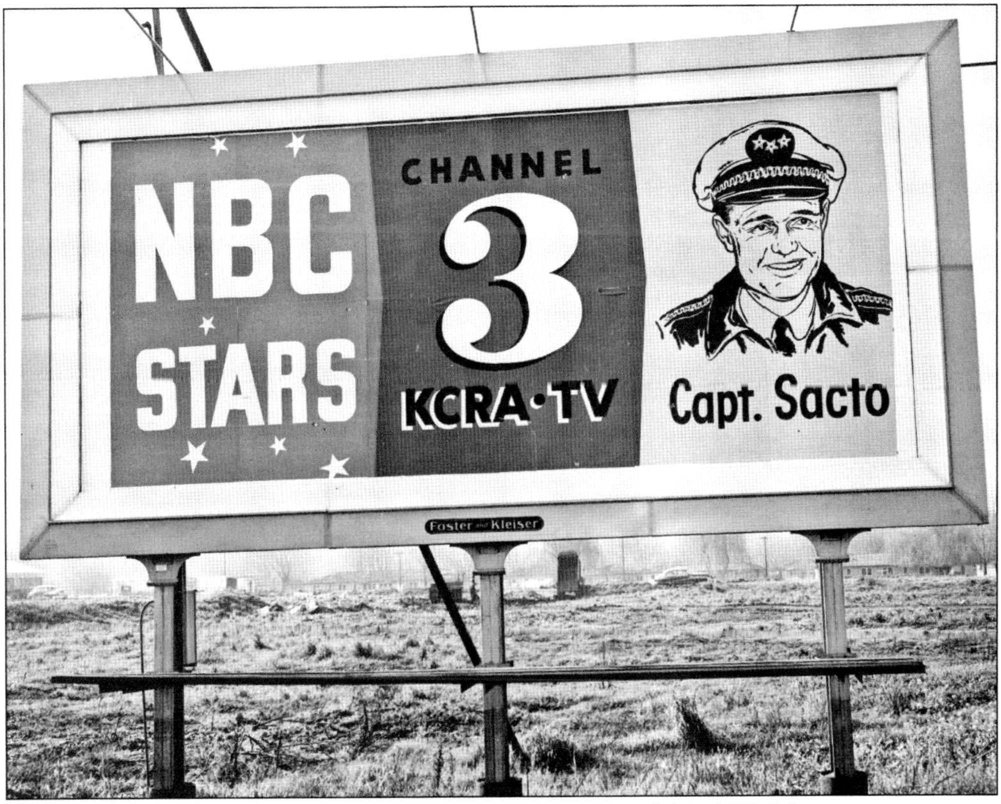

Captain Sacto quickly became KCRA-TV's earliest icon with Fred Wade's image warranting billboard space within a year of his assuming the role. Wade and his character parted ways after a couple of years, but the good captain is still fondly remembered by baby boomers throughout the Sacramento Valley. The Fred G. Wade Scholarship, established in 1982 by the Sacramento Advertising Club, offers funds to college students seeking careers in advertising, communications, or marketing careers. (KCRA-TV, Sacramento.)

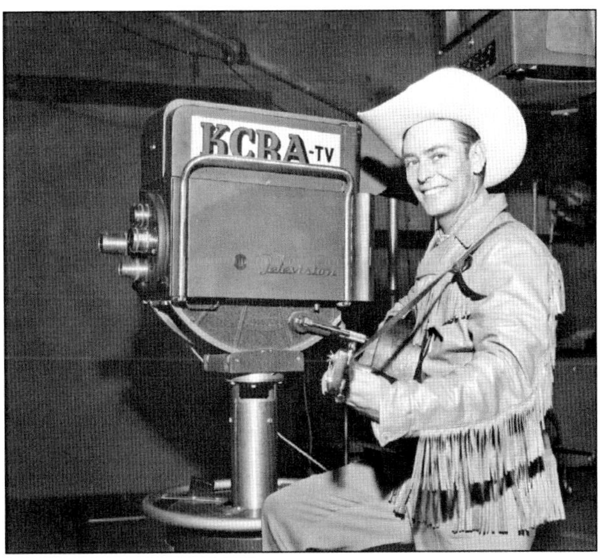

Billy Jack Wills was still in his teens when he started playing in his brother Johnnie Lee Wills's band and later moved to California to join his famous brother Bob as one of his "Texas Playboys," doubling on bass and drums. He led his own band in the 1950s and is among the first country musicians to fuse rhythm and blues, rock 'n' roll, and Western swing. Billy Jack poses here in front of a KCRA-TV camera during one of his many appearances wearing a fringed leather jacket and the crowd-pleasing smile that only faded with his passing in 1991. (KCRA-TV, Sacramento.)

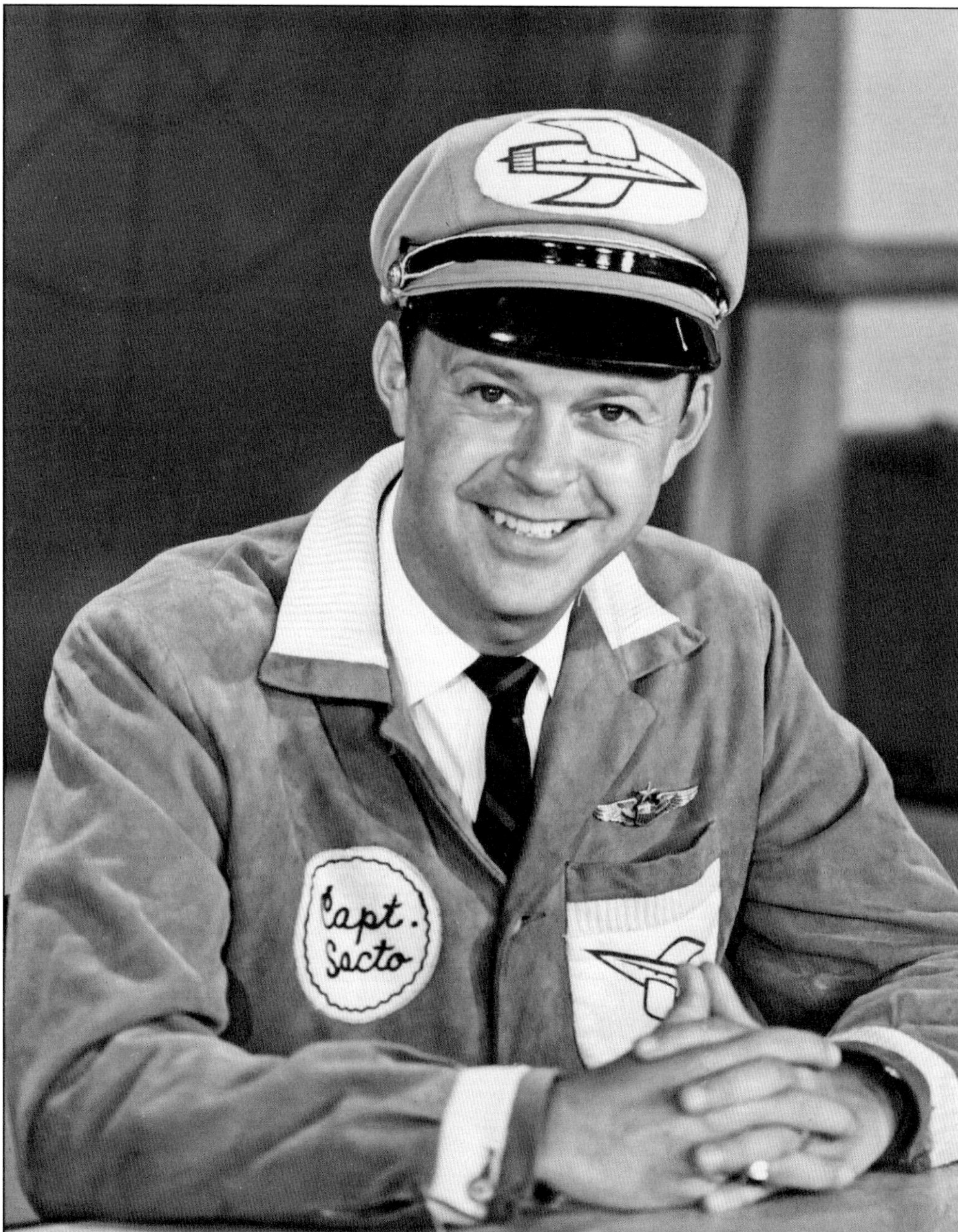

Wearing his movie-star smile, Sacramento's second Captain Sacto, Harry Martin, was *the* television kid's show host for the majority of baby boomers who yearned to soar through the clouds and wear a jacket and cap decorated with rocket ships. Harry Martin became the face of KCRA for more than children's programming and rose from afternoon movie host to conduit to Hollywood. His interviews with the legendary, the famous, and those on the way up in the movie industry put KCRA-TV and Sacramento on the entertainment map and made Martin a celebrity as well. (KCRA-TV, Sacramento.)

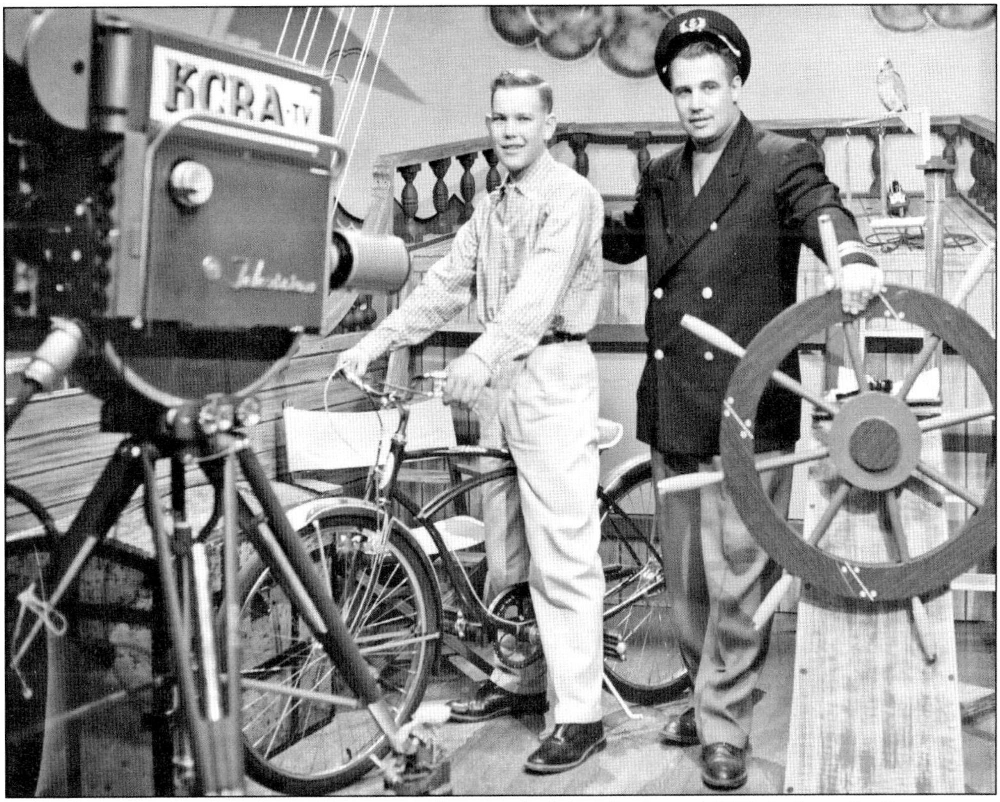

"Skipper Stu" Nahan was one of the nautically named adults who hosted KCRA shows for Sacramento schoolchildren during the 1950s and early 1960s, talking up local kids and offering them prizes and a chance to be seen on television. Nahan was a native Californian who played professional ice hockey in Toronto and Los Angeles before donning the cap and unreeling black-and-white cartoons between reporting sporting events. Shown here on set around 1958, Skipper Stu Nahan sailed on to bigger and better things back East, eventually permanently docking in Southern California where he carved out a career as a broadcaster before passing away late in 2007. Nahan appeared in motion pictures, most notably the popular *Rocky* series, and is the only alumnus of KCRA immortalized by a sidewalk star at 6549 Hollywood Boulevard. (Both KCRA-TV, Sacramento.)

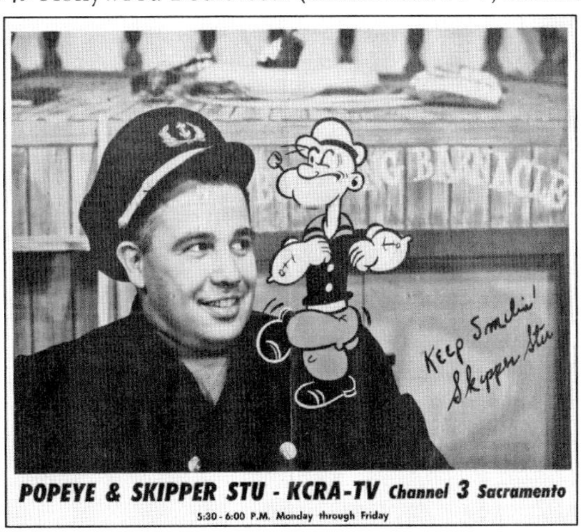

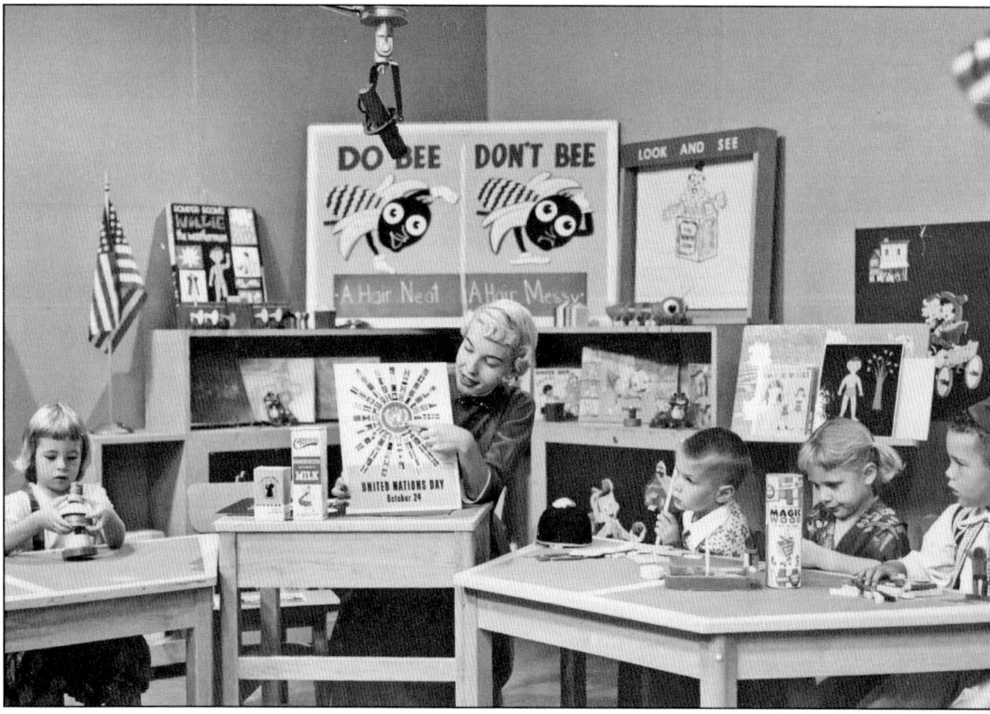

"Miss Nancy" Besst was a veteran of children's television when she arrived in Northern California at the age of 23 to host *Romper Room*, broadcast in the Bay Area and on KCRA-TV Channel 3. "Romper, bomper, stomper, do. Tell me magic mirror who . . . is watching today!" was repeated daily by Miss Nancy Besst, the genial hostess, until she left the playhouse in 1969. In 1997, Besst was honored for years spent gently easing four- to six-year-olds into their place in the classroom. (KCRA-TV, Sacramento.)

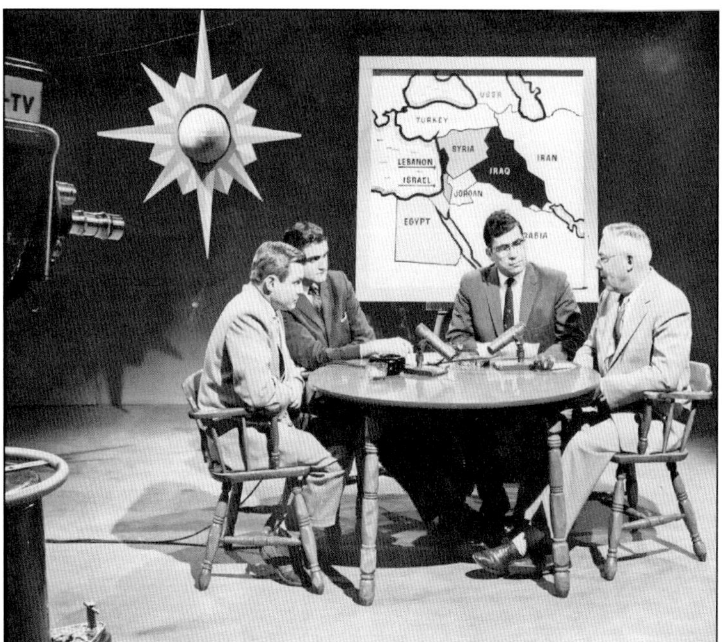

Under the Capitol Dome was an early KCRA-TV program focusing on current events moderated by Jerry Weaver, on the far left, and news anchor Josh Darsa to the right of him. Though the guests joining the reporters around the maple table remain unnamed, the subject of the discussion, the Middle East, remains timely 50 years after this show aired in 1959. (KCRA-TV, Sacramento.)

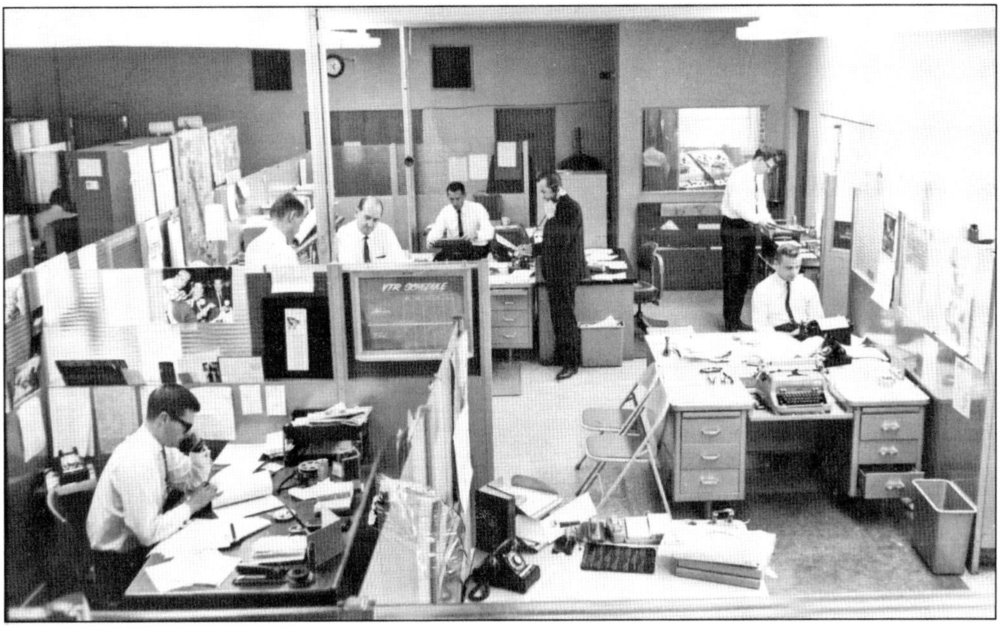

KCRA-TV had been on the air less than 10 years in 1962, but under the guidance of patriarch Ewing Kelly and eventually his sons Jon and Robert, the station prospered. The small newsroom was always busy. Its staff, from left to right, includes Stan Atkinson, Paul Thompson, Tom Breen, Bill Harvey, Don Smith, John Jervis, and Gary Park. Note the reels of film and videotape on Atkinson's desk and the editing room on the far back wall. (KCRA-TV, Sacramento.)

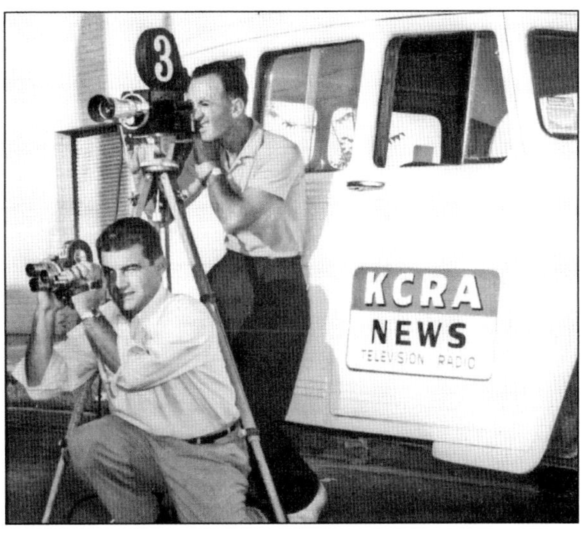

Ace cameraman Harry Sweet poses for a KCRA-TV publicity shot with a Cinephonic 16-millimeter movie camera, while Bob Crete crouches below him with a Bell and Howell handheld camera. Sweet was an aerial photographer at McClellan Air Force Base beginning in 1942 and worked in local television as early as 1953. Crete was a longtime employee and passed away in early 2009, and these two helped set the standard for local news photography. The station maintained Sweet's 1963 Willys Jeep, and he logged seemingly endless miles in it capturing location shots over the years. (KCRA-TV, Sacramento.)

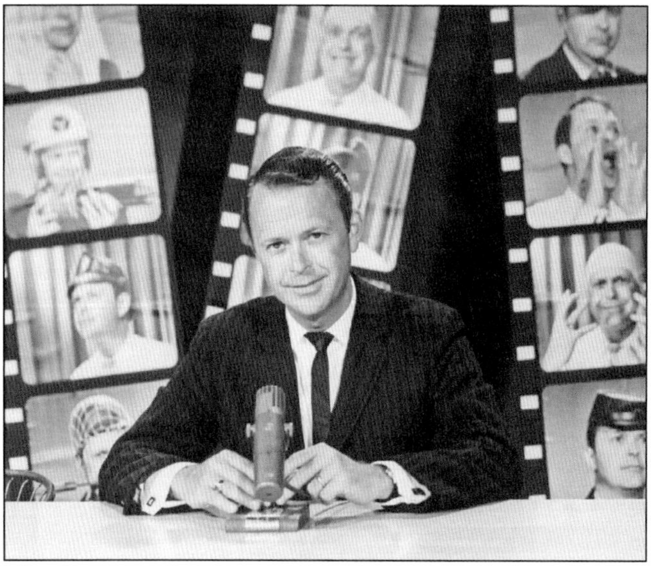

Harry Martin and a microphone went well together, but he and Sacramento were a seamless fit. The urbane-looking gentleman in this photograph was capable of hamming it to the hilt, and all the goofy guys displayed in oversized frames of film in the background are characters he created. Born Harry Martin Uhlenberg in 1927, the World War II and Korean War veteran joined KCRA-TV in 1956 and stayed with the station until retiring in 1989. He passed away in February 2008 at the age of 81. (KCRA-TV, Sacramento.)

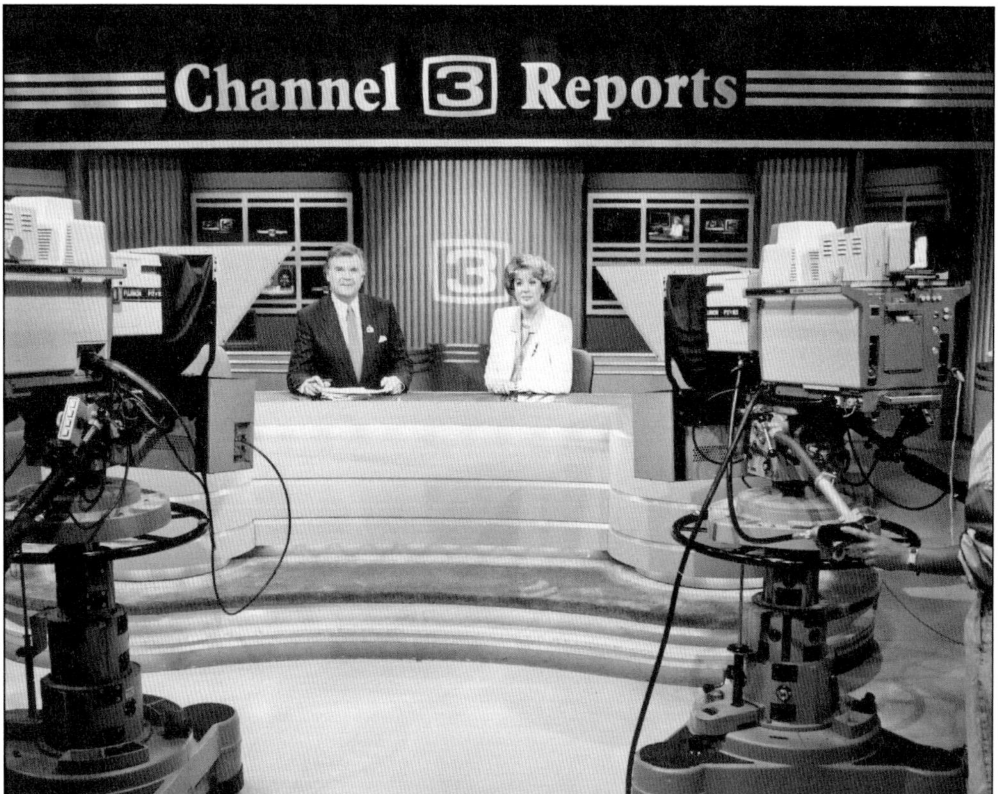

Stan Atkinson and Margaret Pelley, shown here on the set during a 1988 KCRA-TV broadcast, were both popular reporters and news anchors for many years. Atkinson traveled the globe and is well remembered for his war zone reports from Afghanistan to Vietnam and most points between. He retired in 1999 but still maintains a high local profile. (KCRA-TV, Sacramento.)

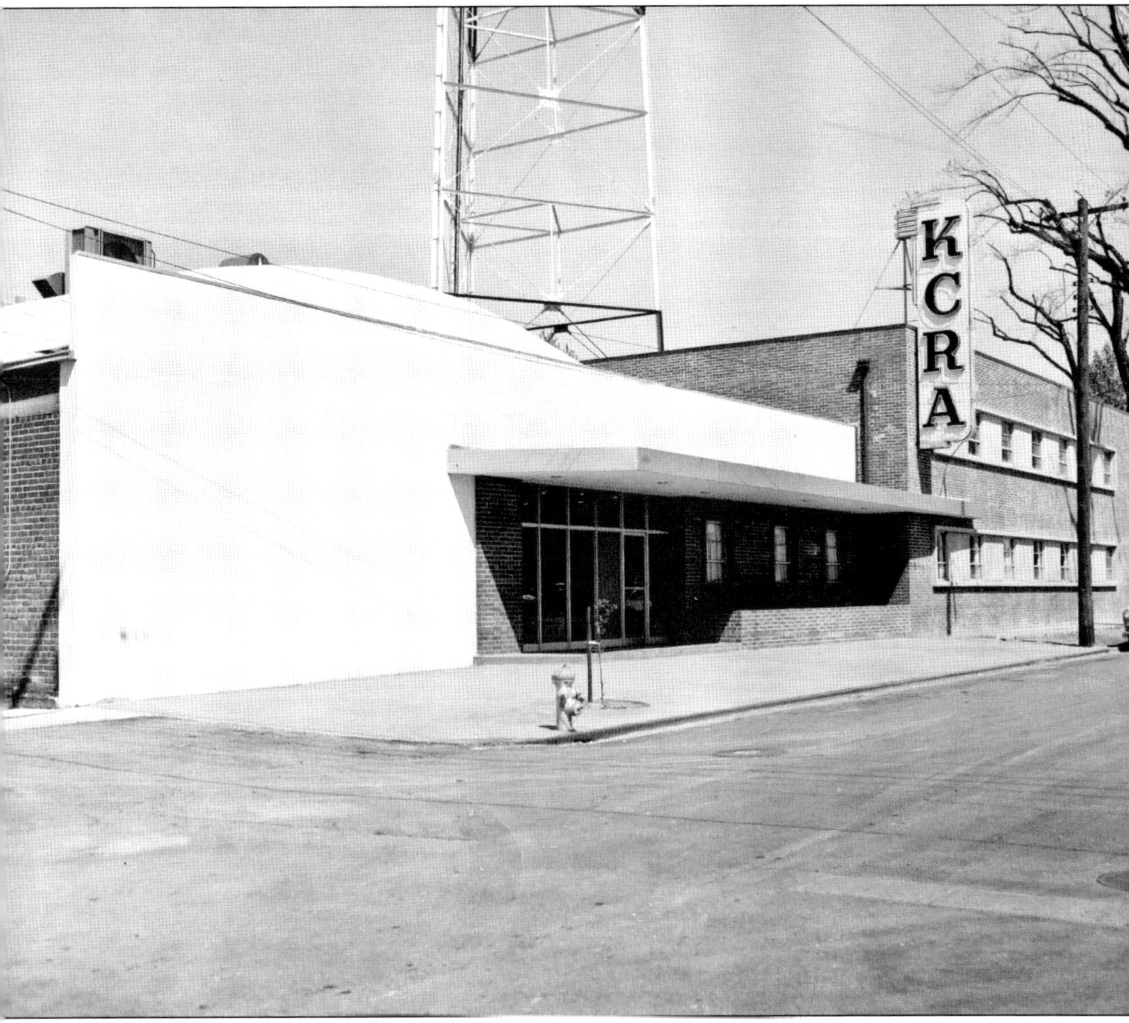

KCRA-TV was owned by the Kelly family, who bought out the original property owners and partners, the family of Crystal Cream and Butter patriarch Carl Hansen, in the early 1960s. In 1999, the Kelly family sold the NBC affiliate to the Hearst Corporation and Hearst-Argyle Television, who have maintained the station's popularity along with their mission and motto, "Where the News Comes First." All but one of the electric letters on the original neon "KCRA" went dark over the years, but the sign refuses to give up and electricians have drawn a blank on what circuit powers the flashing light. (KCRA-TV, Sacramento.)

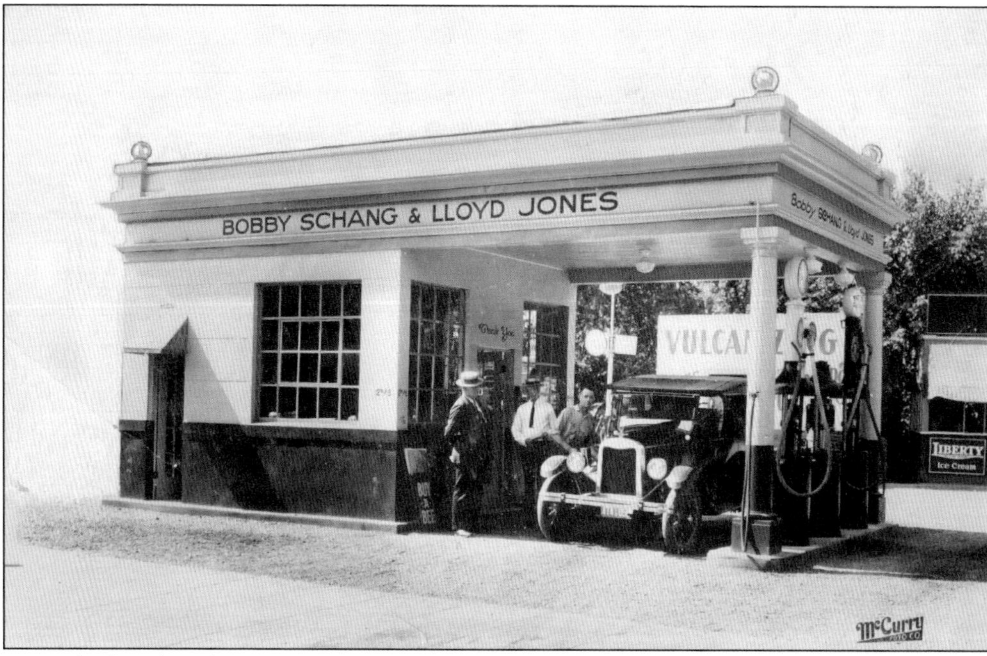

Trying his hand at a burgeoning gas-pumping industry is ex-Sacramento Senator baseballer Bobby Schang. Known as a solid defensive catcher, Schang had his best year with the Senators in 1924, hitting a solid .348 in 115 games. Schang's career highlights included stints with the Pittsburgh Pirates and New York Giants in 1914 and 1915 and a "cup of coffee" with the National League champion St. Louis Cardinals in 1928. (SPL.)

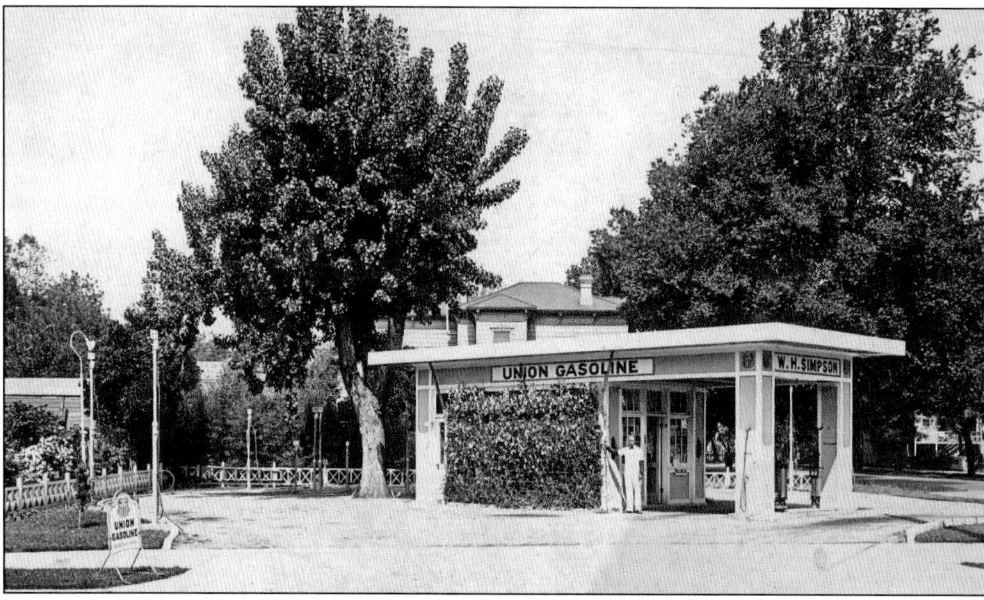

Not long after the christening of the Twelfth Street "subway," William "Bill" Simpson opened his own Union Gasoline service station, pictured here in 1920 at 500 Twelfth Street. It was a savvy move for Simpson, who hoped to capitalize on the growth of the automobile. By the beginning of the World War I, Sacramento led valley and foothill counties in the number of registered vehicles at 6,415. (CSH.)

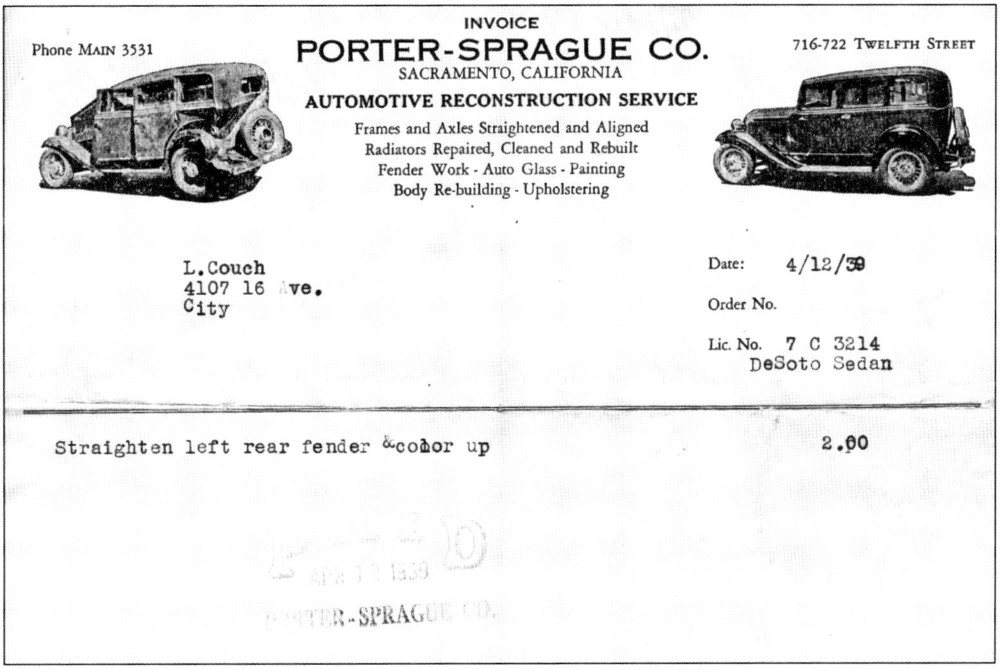

INVOICE

PORTER-SPRAGUE CO.

SACRAMENTO, CALIFORNIA

Phone MAIN 3531

716-722 TWELFTH STREET

AUTOMOTIVE RECONSTRUCTION SERVICE

Frames and Axles Straightened and Aligned
Radiators Repaired, Cleaned and Rebuilt
Fender Work - Auto Glass - Painting
Body Re-building - Upholstering

L. Couch
4107 16 Ave.
City

Date: 4/12/39

Order No.

Lic. No. 7 C 3214
DeSoto Sedan

Straighten left rear fender & color up 2.00

APR 13 1939
PORTER-SPRAGUE CO.

Sacramento saw its first automobile in 1900. If the young city needed time to master the new form of locomotion, auto-body businesses like the Alkali's Porter-Sprague at 722 Twelfth Street would gladly help. The business was founded in 1917 by Wildey Porter and Eddie Sprague. In time, it would become a Sacramento fixture, spanning two centuries and smoothing things over for a capital area clientele that has included mayors, judges, and governors. (Ed Quint.)

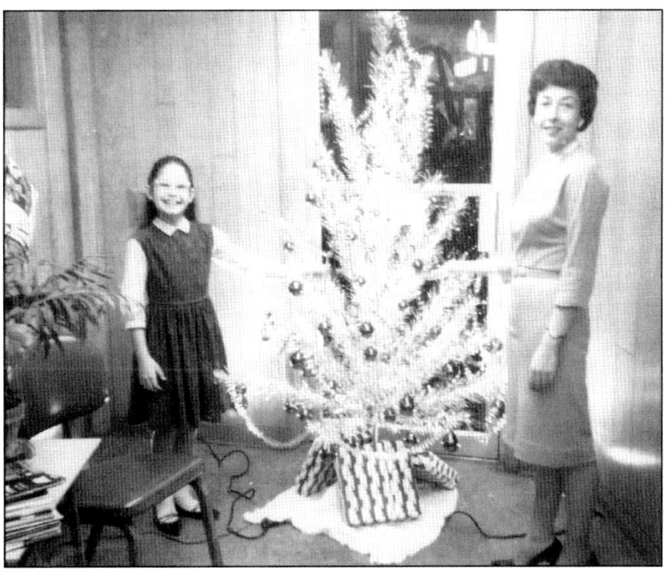

An enchanted Adrienne Oehler and her mother, Carrol "Jean" Quint, illuminate the foyer to Porter-Sprague during the Christmas season of 1964. Oehler, who was nine years old at the time of the photograph, recalls her mother assembling the quintessential 1960s chip-and-dip tray, adorned with pink and purple Christmas ornaments. A company party was held just after this photograph was taken. Oehler still operates as Porter-Sprague's secretary treasurer. (Adrienne Oehler.)

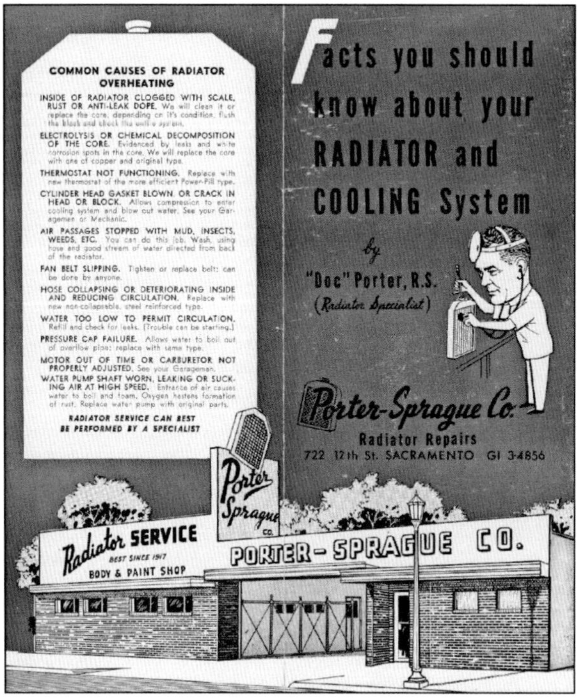

The caricature, so much the marketing rage in post-war America, found its way onto this brochure for one of the first AAA-approved auto-repair shops in Sacramento, the Porter-Sprague Company. The "radiator specialist" is John "Bud" Porter, son of cofounder Wildey Porter. In 1964, Bud sold the business for $5,000 to Harold Hoff and Ed Quint, with the latter still at the helm with business partner and company president Jim Havey, who came on board in 1980. (Ed Quint.)

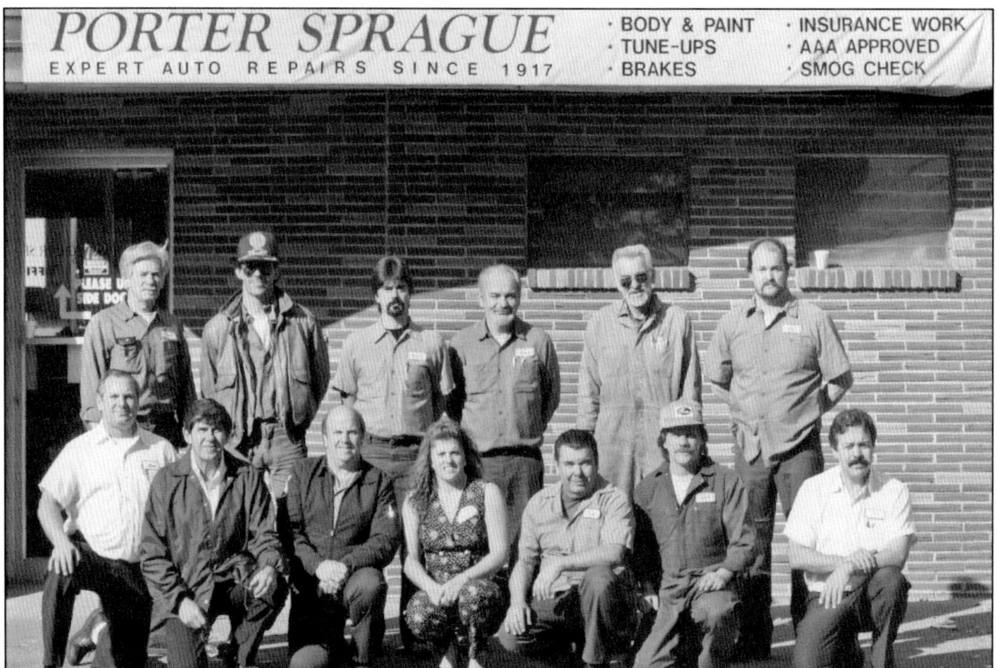

This photograph before the Twelfth Street entrance to Porter-Sprague was taken in November 1992. Co-owners Jim Havey and Ed Quint are pictured in the first row, first and second from the left, respectively. After selling the business in the mid-1990s, Quint reacquired Porter-Sprague in 1998, reopening on February 3 with a sign posted on Twelfth Street that read, "Jim, Ed and the Old Gang are Back." (Ed Quint.)

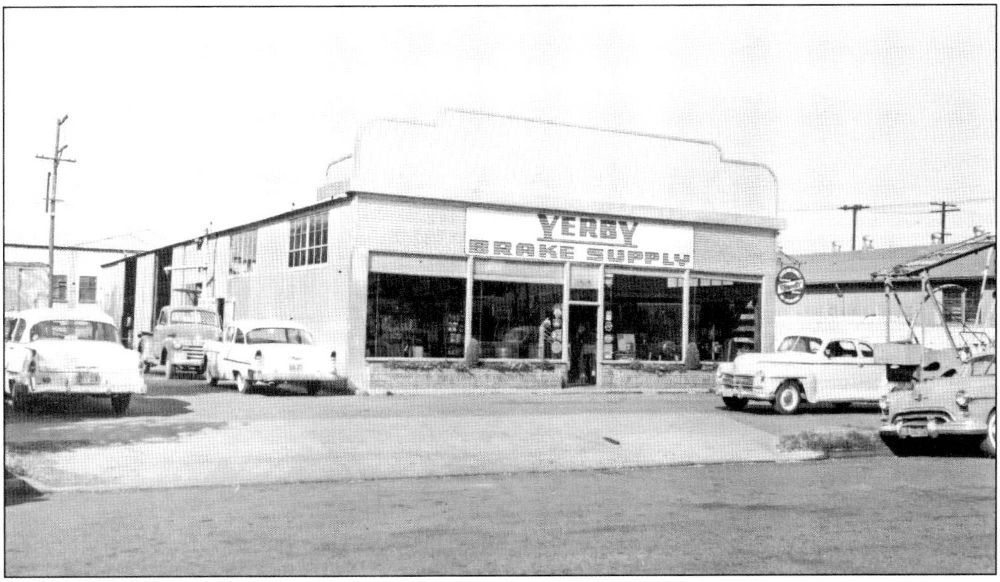

Pictured here in the early-1950s is Yerby Brake Supply at Thirteenth and C Streets, an Alkali business fixture from its opening in 1949 to its recent closure in 2008. Its founder, Thomas G Yerby, was intent on seeing through a "burning desire to get into business"; this pushed him to move from pumping gas and breaking hard candy with his bare hands to settling on a promising career in brake supply and servicing. (Lawry Yerby.)

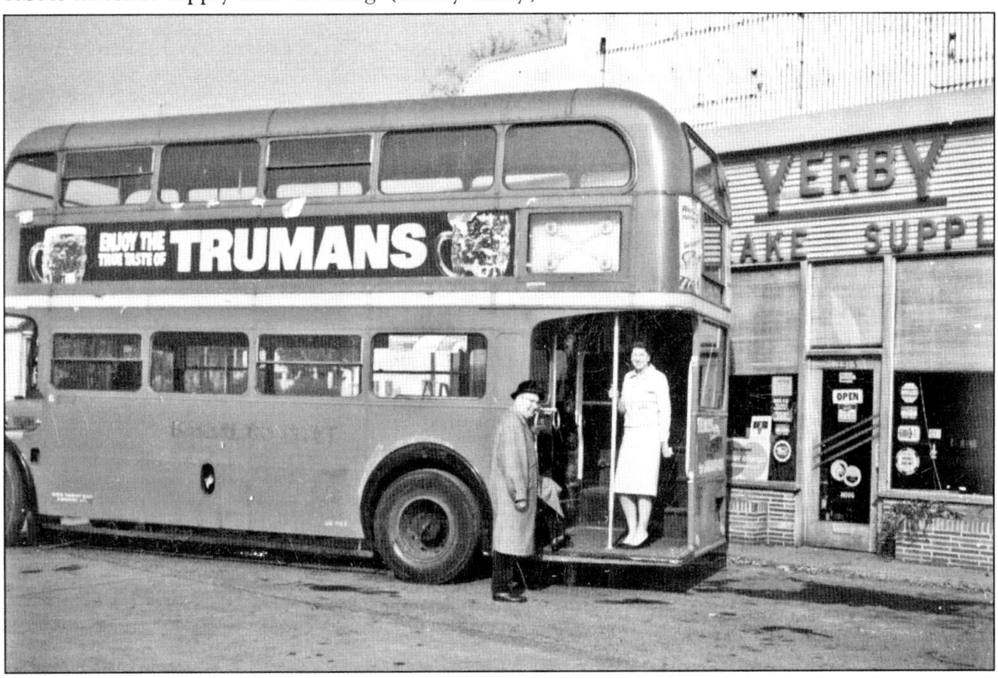

Yerby Brake Supply won the citywide reputation for being able to accommodate the unusual. Perhaps their most exotic job came with London-style double-decker busses, purchased by the students of the University of California at Davis in 1967. Yerby also serviced the trucks of the Sacramento Fire Department and Pacific Gas and Electric. Pictured here are Tom Yerby and his wife, Alleen, posing before a Leyland Motors Titan. (Lawry Yerby.)

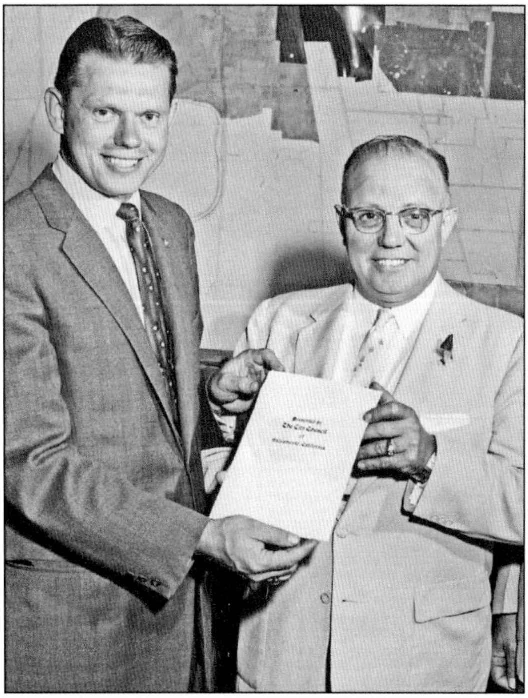

Sales savant Roy Yermol was a driving force behind Yerby's success. The winner of the 1955 National Power Brake Sales Award, Yermol had numerous opportunities to leave the smallish business by accepting offers from such brake giants as Bendix. That said, Yermol was fond of his job and equally loyal to Tom Yerby. Here stands Yermol, pictured to the left of Sacramento mayor Clarence Azevedo, around 1956. (Lawry Yerby.)

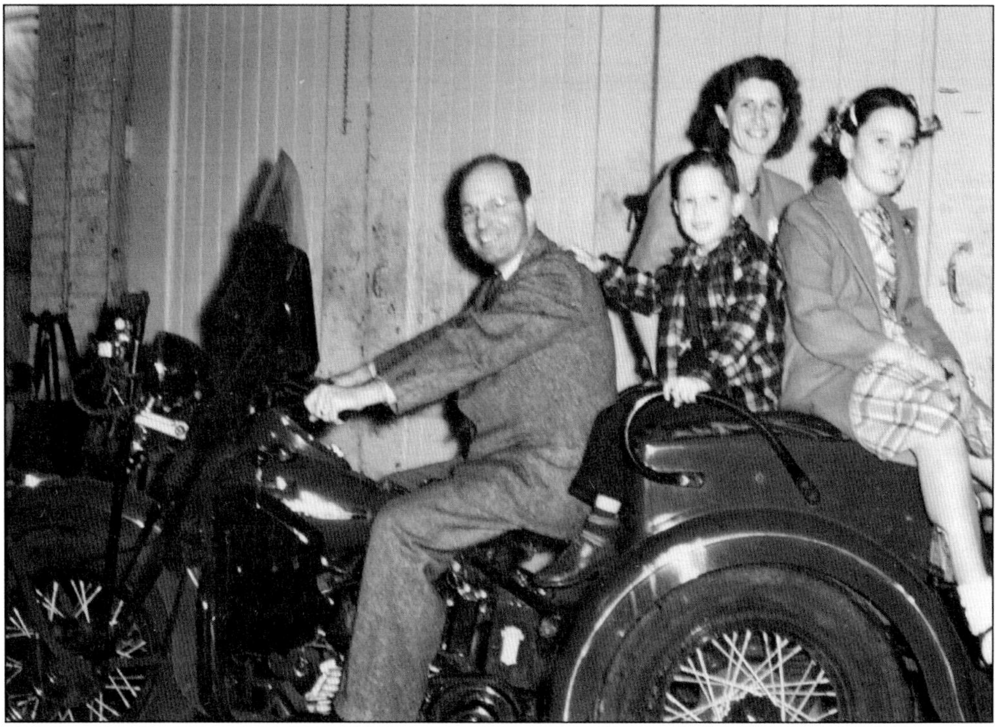

The first family of brake service in Sacramento rests here, around 1950, upon the back of a three-wheeled motorcycle used for towing brakeless cars. From left to right are Tom and his son Lawry, his wife, Alleen, and his daughter Leone. According to Lawry, the bike was one of the many ideas that his father had for improving the business's level of customer service. (Lawry Yerby.)

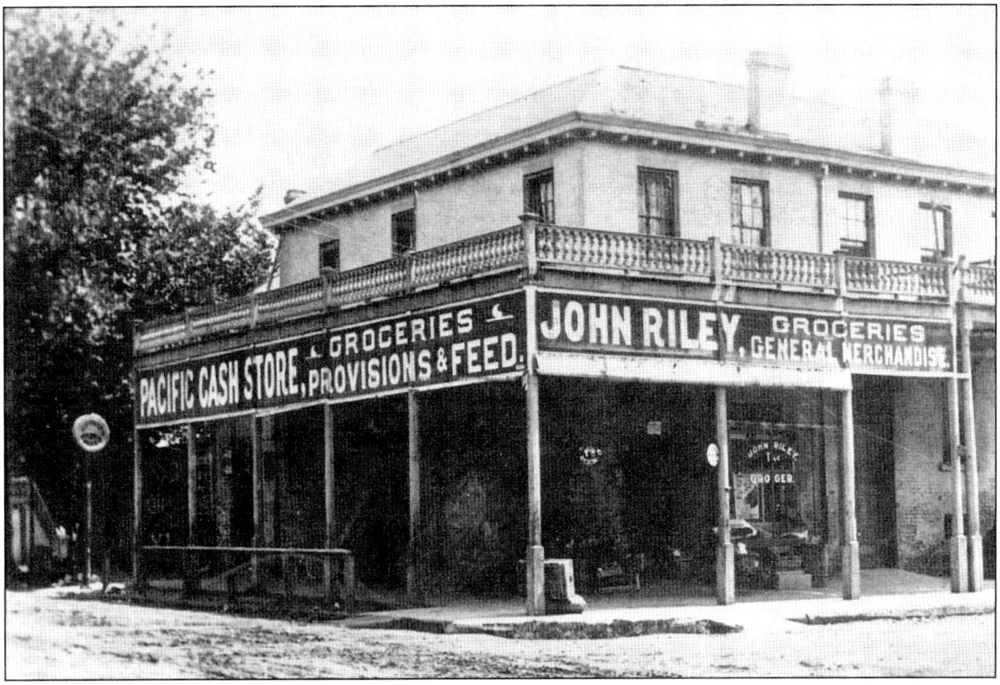

The venerable Tru-Valu Market, on the corner of 10th and E Streets, is Sacramento's oldest grocery store, tracing its origins back to 1868. Through the years it has held the monikers of Wagner's, Riley's, and Dunphy's, all of them witnessing some type of change within the Alkali. When it was Riley's, the store included a stable of at-the-ready delivery horses and a massive canopy and balcony that loomed over patrons as they entered the premises. Just a few decades later, and pictured below in 1929, Dunphy's was experiencing the dryness of the Volstead Act, while also teetering on the edge of the Great Depression. (Above, Saber Shehadeh; below, CSH.)

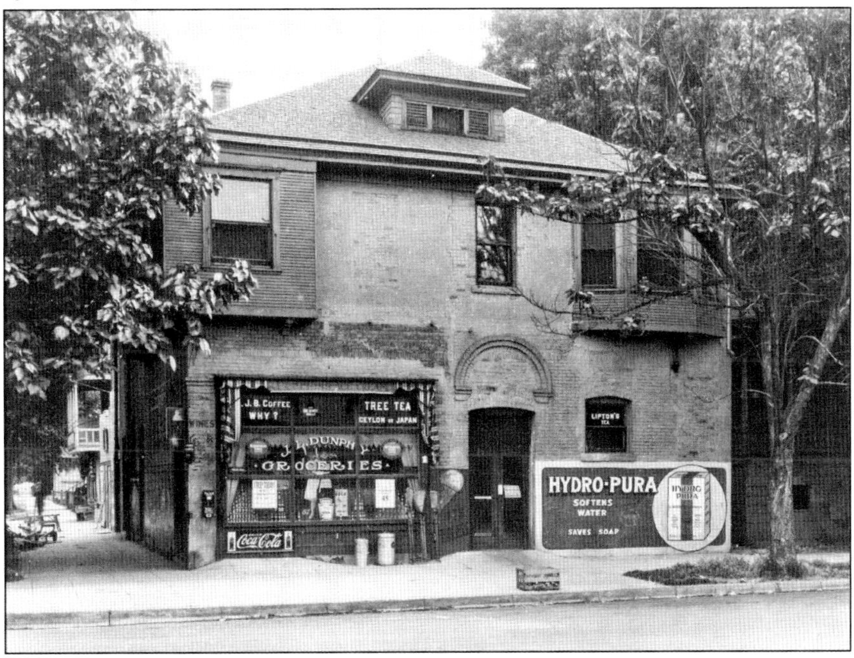

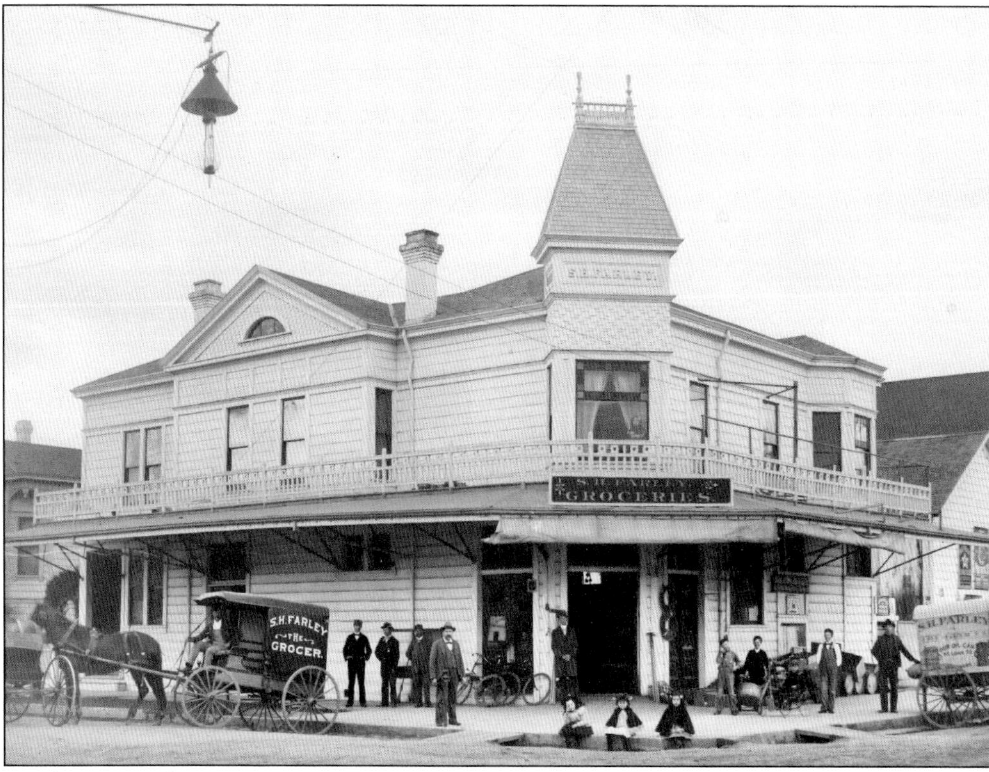

Stephen H. Farley, a Wisconsin native and the son of an Irish immigrant father, opened his general store in 1897 at Twelfth and F Streets, where he dispensed groceries, hay, grain, and feed. His business's distinct corner cupola, inscribed "S.H Farley," exists to this very day. In addition to stocking shelves, Farley found time to serve as city trustee for the city's fifth ward, which covered Alkali Flat. (CSH.)

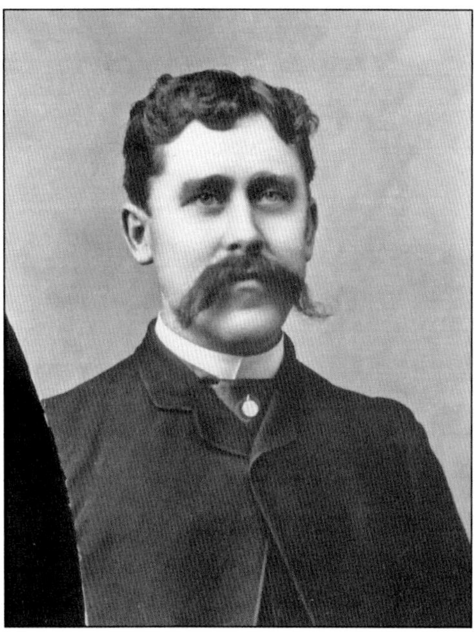

Stephen H. Farley operated his grocery until 1910, when he sold out. After doing so, Farley took up real estate, while also working for the Ruhstallers just down the street at their Twelfth and H Street brewery. It was amidst the hustle, bustle, and heat of the brewery that Farley died of a heart attack in 1912. He was 51 at the time and left behind his wife, Lena, and children Edna, Irma, and Everett. (CSL.)

A New Yorker by birth, William R. Strong came to Sacramento in search of gold. Having found no luck in mining, he became a merchant, only to see three business ventures foiled—two by fire, one by flood. In time, however, he found stability in a produce business that would draw from its own nursery and orchard. He is pictured here in 1880. (CSL.)

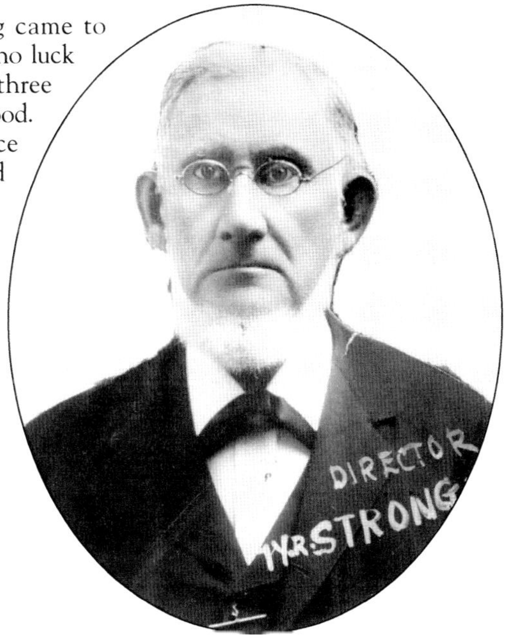

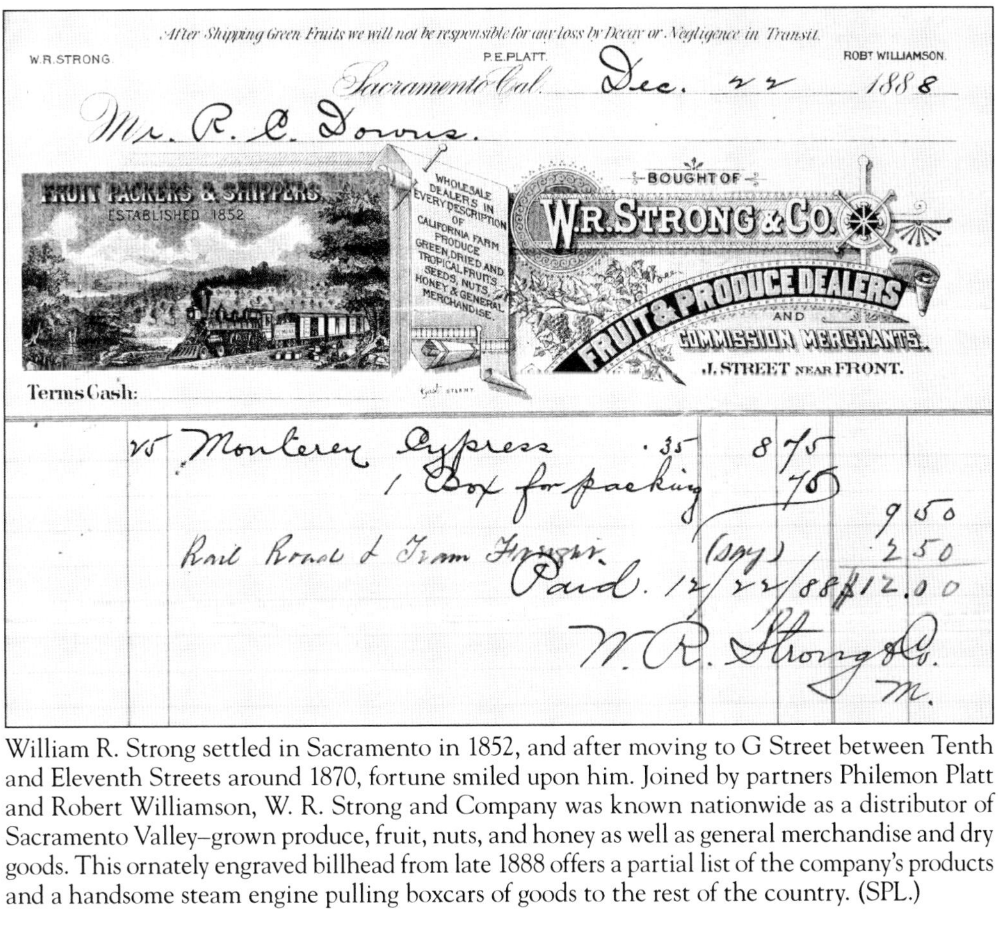

William R. Strong settled in Sacramento in 1852, and after moving to G Street between Tenth and Eleventh Streets around 1870, fortune smiled upon him. Joined by partners Philemon Platt and Robert Williamson, W. R. Strong and Company was known nationwide as a distributor of Sacramento Valley–grown produce, fruit, nuts, and honey as well as general merchandise and dry goods. This ornately engraved billhead from late 1888 offers a partial list of the company's products and a handsome steam engine pulling boxcars of goods to the rest of the country. (SPL.)

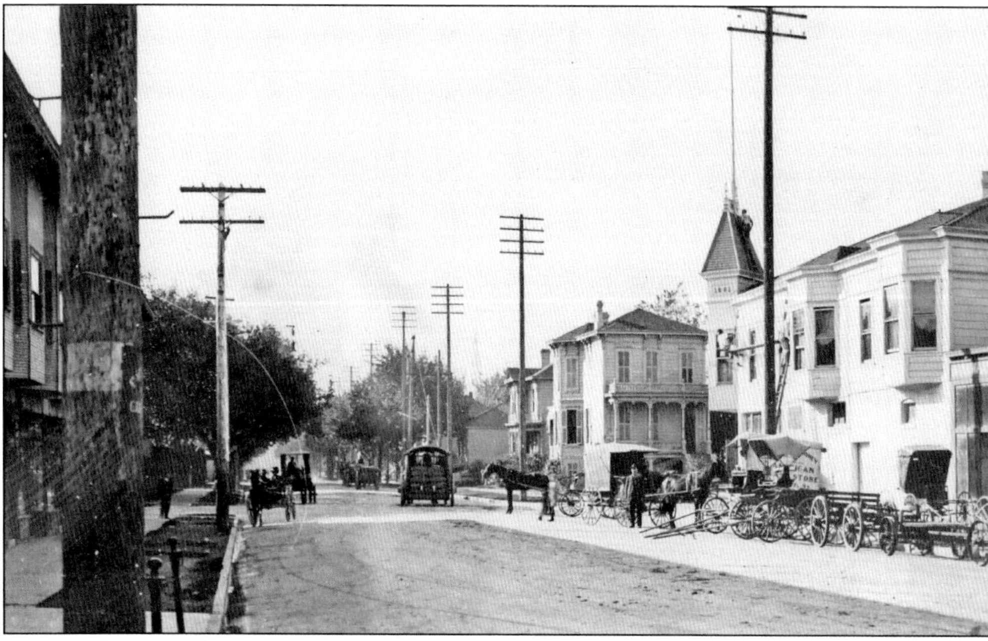

It was in the 1920s that the Twelfth Street Business Men's Association was looking to make Twelfth Street the "Fillmore of Sacramento." San Francisco's Fillmore became a temporary beehive when much of the city's traditional business was pushed there after the 1906 earthquake and subsequent fire. Here is a look down Twelfth Street toward F Street and downtown around 1911. (CSH.)

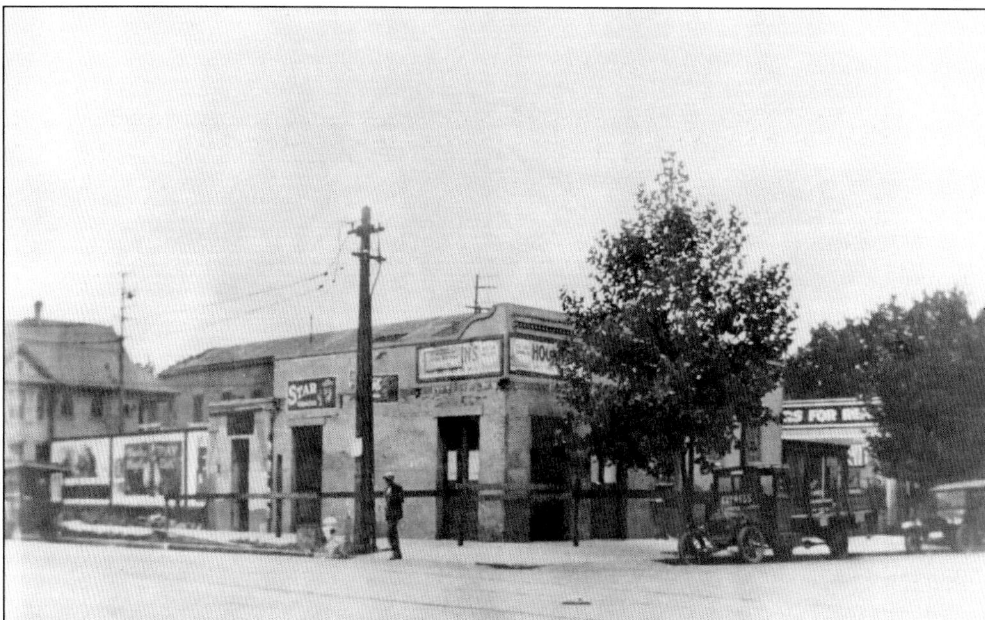

The Volstead Act dried Alkali Flat out in 1920, but haunts like Gus Rudi's, pictured here on southwest corner of Seventh and G, pushed on. Rudi's sat directly between the Southern Pacific shops and hundreds of homes in Alkali Flat. Although reinvented to give the pretense of soda and ice cream shops during Prohibition, many of the city's saloons illicitly sold alcohol under monikers like "speakeasy" or "blind pig." (CSH.)

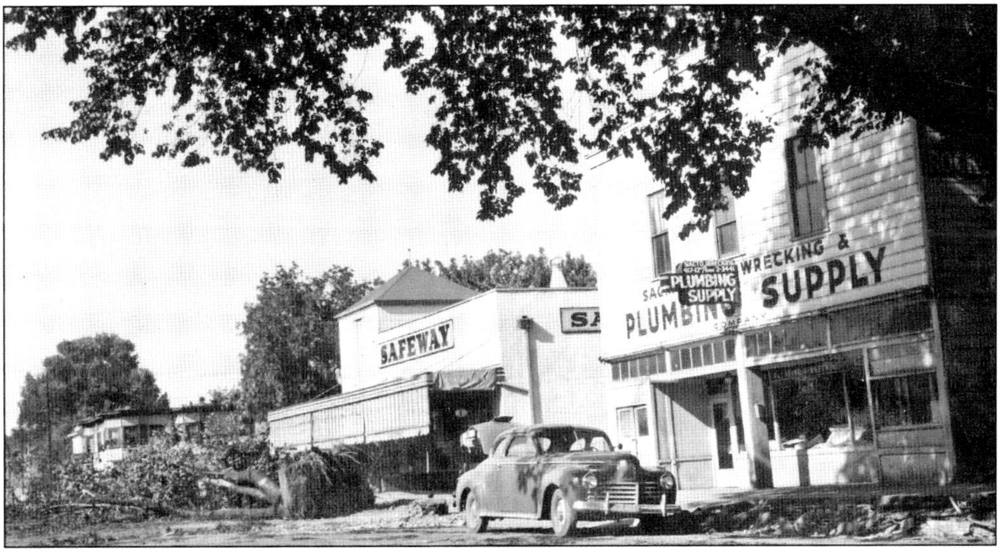

Whispers of post-war change to the Alkali are evident in this 1949 view of expansion on Twelfth Street. The Safeway store to the left was established in 1929, and by the time this photograph was taken, it was 1 of 13 Safeway outlets in the city. By 1952, the market was gone, perhaps falling victim to the construction of stores in burgeoning suburban centers like Carmichael and Citrus Heights. (CSH.)

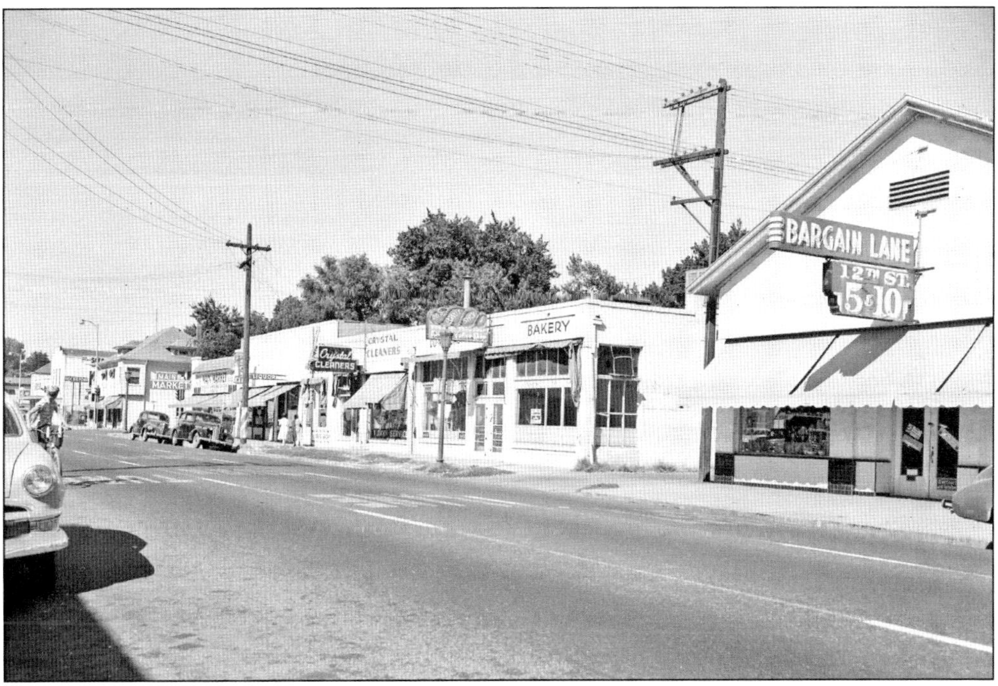

This 1951 view of the east side of Twelfth Street between E and F Streets reveals the indispensables—from groceries to baked goods—of Alkali civilization. Businesses under Chinese, Latino, Italian, and Anglo-American surnames spoke to the growing polyglot face of the neighborhood. The longest lasting of the row was John Riolo's "505 Club," which over time destabilized into a smoky, oftentimes dangerous, haunt until its demise in the late 1980s. (CSH.)

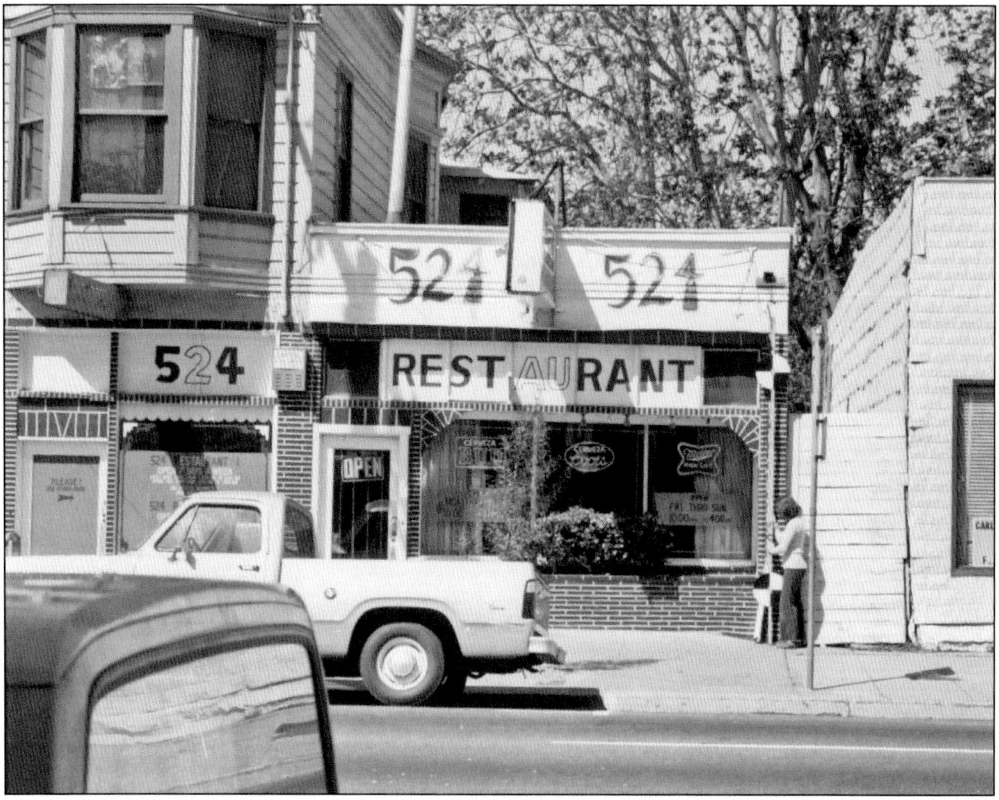

The iconic 524 Restaurant, pictured above in 1984 and ensconced into a building dating back to 1897, was started in 1969 by brothers Miguel and Jose "Pepe" Gomez. Its loyal clientele has included local laborer to state legislator, all of whom could enjoy high-quality food at a reasonable price. The restaurant was gutted by a fire in the summer of 2003, and despite Miguel passing away in 2005, the 524 was resurrected in the fall of 2007 when, after a $1-million renovation, it was rechristened by a party that was attended by Mayor Heather Fargo. Below is a view of the eatery as it appeared, prior to the fire, in 2003. The restaurant continues to serve the city, maintaining several of the founders' original recipes. (Above, Dan Hood; below, Jose Gomez.)

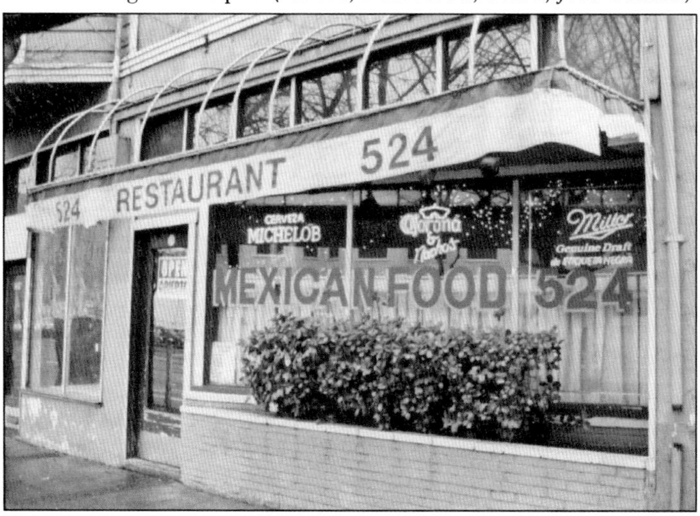

Five

Alkali Lore

by James Scott and Tom Tolley

After fishing, hunting, and gathering their way through an abundance of flora and fauna in the lower Sacramento Valley, the Nisenan would convene and tell stories, weaving a historical tapestry of tales. The presence of no less than four native villages in present-day Sacramento leaves an exciting archaeological legacy amidst the Alkali. One of the earliest Anglo-American accounts of the Alkali was written in 1848 by the founder of the *Placer Times*, as he spoke of a place where ancient oak and sycamore stands surrounded a multitude of ponds and undoubtedly what would become the hapless China Slough. Alkali's rich and famous included none more notorious than California Supreme Court Justice David S. Terry, the "Dueling Judge," or 20th-century mass murderess Dorothea Puente. Young May Woolsey was little known outside of family, classmates, and neighbors, but thanks to a fluke discovery a century after her passing her story is well known today. The Garten Gold Cure Institute was a short-lived but colorful enterprise in the Alkali during the mid-1890s, and near the same time, the transmission of electricity from Folsom to the Sacramento receiving station at Sixth and H Streets was a boon to the city and a huge, but little-remembered feat. One year earlier, hundreds of California National Guardsmen and federal troops camped at Ninth and D Streets to secure the routes of the Southern Pacific Railway and quell an armed strike that threatened to cripple coast-to-coast transportation. An unexploded bomb, the brief passing of a behemoth cannon, and the only recorded death of an Alkali soldier during the World War I are stories grown dim with time, while fads like "Tom Thumb Weddings" are never revived and seem bizarre and possible only during the madcap 1920s. Hard times and Hoovervilles were a way of life in the 1930s and passed into lore, but history has a way of repeating itself and homeless camps bordering the Alkali have been the focus of national attention during the first decade of the 21st century as the neighborhood looks to a new future.

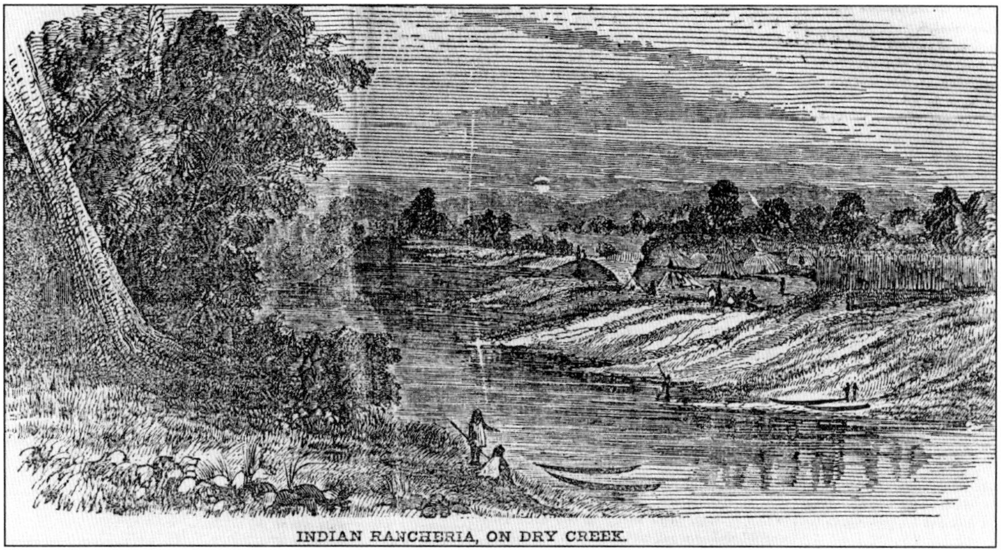

The Nisenan formed the earliest Native American presence in Alkali Flat. Dating as far back as 11,000 BC, this hunting, gathering, and fishing culture occupied the villages of Momol on the northernmost edge of the Alkali and Sa'cum to the neighborhood's southern frontier. A 2003 excavation of the area containing the current city hall, at Tenth and H Streets, yielded enough evidence to suggest that it may have been used as a hunting and fishing camp. (CSH.)

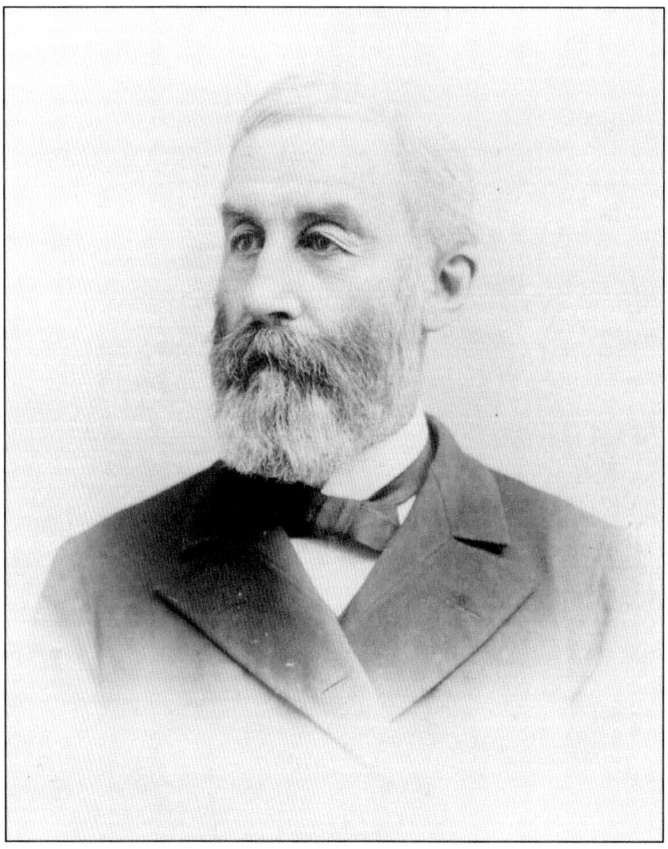

After 20-year-old Edward Kemble visited Sutter's Fort in 1848, he wrote in vivid detail about his journey by "adobe cart" from the Sutter's Embarcadero to the fort, a route that would take him along the southern edge of Alkali Flat, "A forest of Noble sycamores, dense and deep, guarding a mighty solitude like a vast army of giants," he wrote, stood amidst "miniature lakes . . . prophets of the floods that were to drown the fortunes of thousands in subsequent times." Kemble went on to found Sacramento's first newspaper, the *Placer Times*. (CSH.)

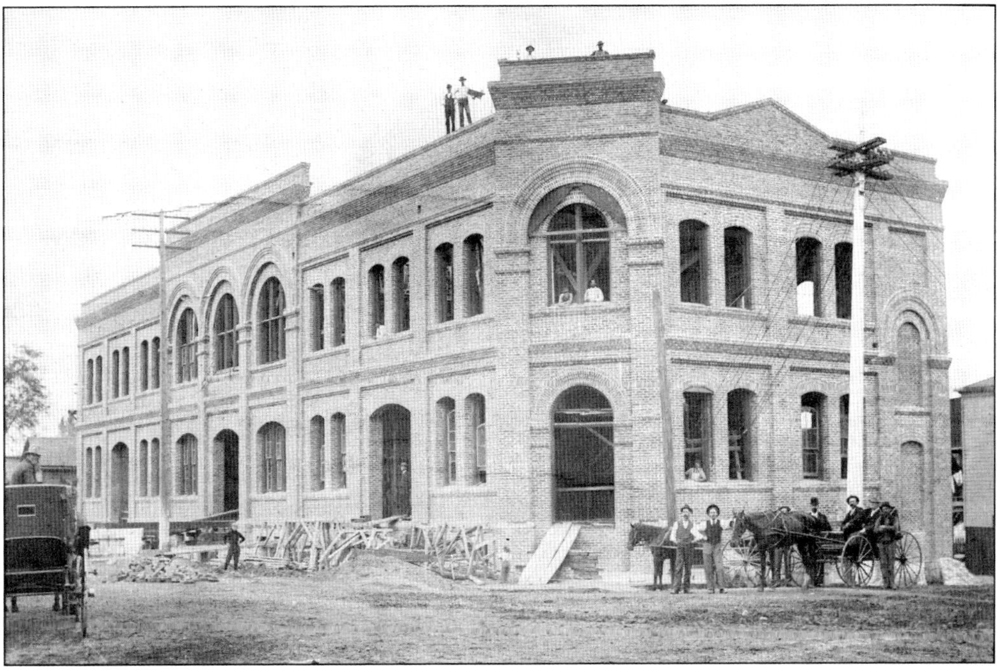

As pristine today as when it first received electricity from the Folsom Powerhouse in July 1895 is Station A on the northeastern corner of Sixth and H Streets. The 22-mile-long transmission was unprecedented and was celebrated by two artillery salvos from Battery B, which had been bivouacked at the temporary "Camp Shock." The station also powered what would be considered, in its time, one of the finest streetcar systems in the country. No one knew at the time that just adjacent to the station was a spot where energy of a spiritual sort had been created anywhere from 500 to 1,000 years earlier. There is indeed evidence that a Nisenan sweat lodge, or *k'umi'mhü'*, and seven Native American burials were located nearby Station A. (Both CSH.)

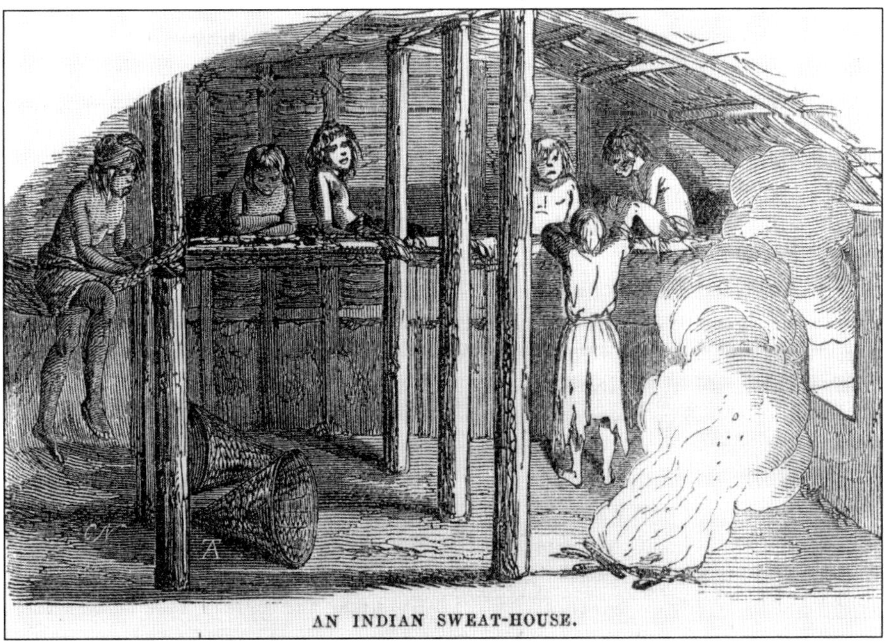

AN INDIAN SWEAT-HOUSE.

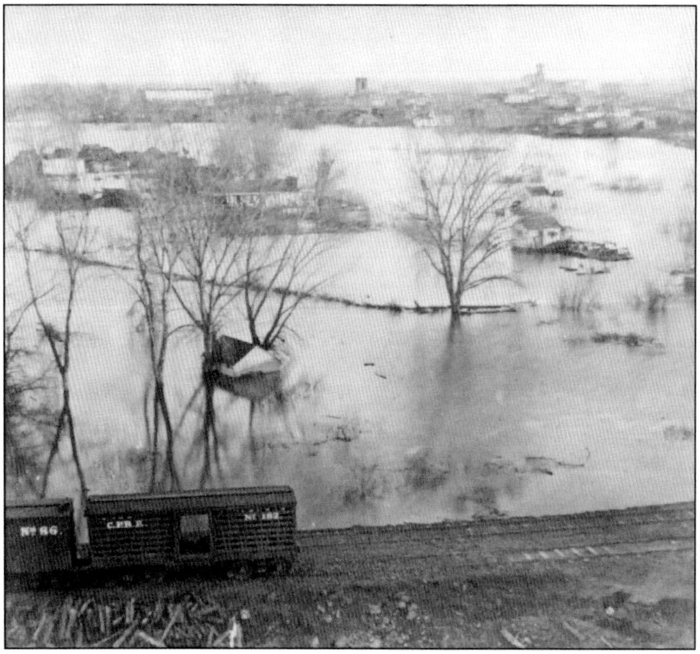

Sacramento's lost lake, China Slough, lapped upon the westernmost boundary of Alkali Flat. The oils and solvents of the railroad shops, plus the sewage and garbage of the residential area along lower I Street, made the slough both unpleasant to look at and notoriously odorous, prompting the city to plant some 3,000 eucalyptus trees along its banks in 1876–1877. Pictured here in 1866 with a view of the Alkali on the far shore, the slough was finally filled in 1910 with Rocklin riprap and river sand and silt. (Library of Congress.)

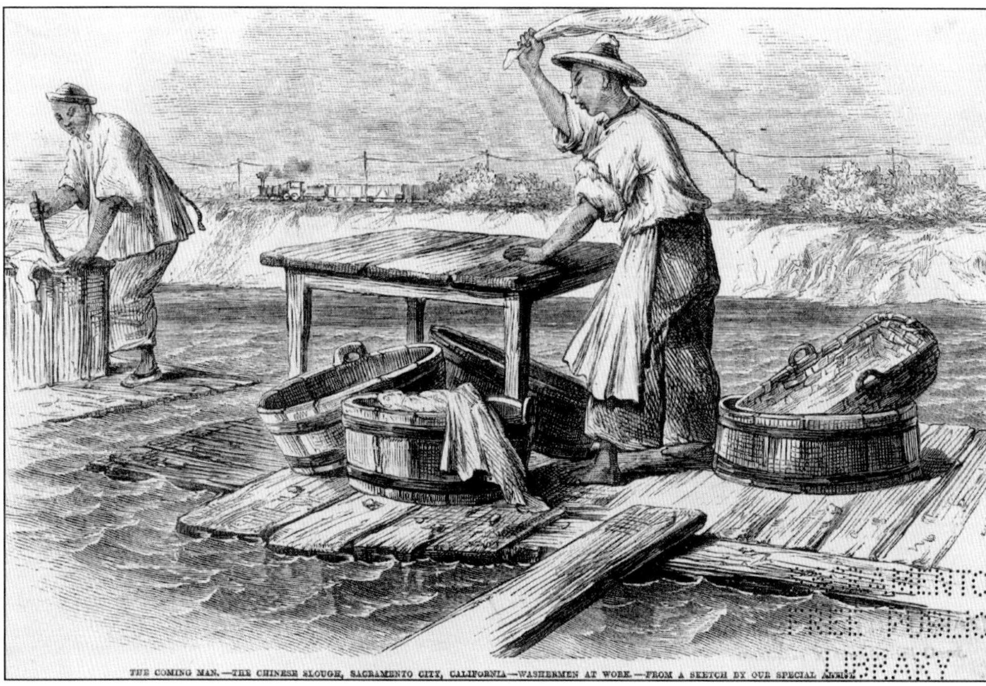

According to an 1852 county census, the city of Sacramento was home to 804 Chinese men and eight women, comprising 12 percent of the city's total population. Around this time, the city's first ethno-racial neighborhood was founded by the Chinese on the banks of China Slough (seen here) and stretching along I Street, between Second and Fifth Streets. As time went on, Chinese Americans settled deeper into the Alkali, both as residents and business owners. (SPL.)

New Englander Albion Sweetser lived at the northeast corner of Tenth and G Streets. Although most of his fortune had been amassed in real estate and insurance, Sweetser spent his early days in Gold Rush Sacramento as an architect. His most notorious creation, in his latter years made from willow poles, canvas, and tarred paper, was the Round Tent saloon, a spot that city historian John Frederick Morse called a place of "naked, unmasked depravity." The irony dwells in Sweetser being an ardent teetotaler. (CSL.)

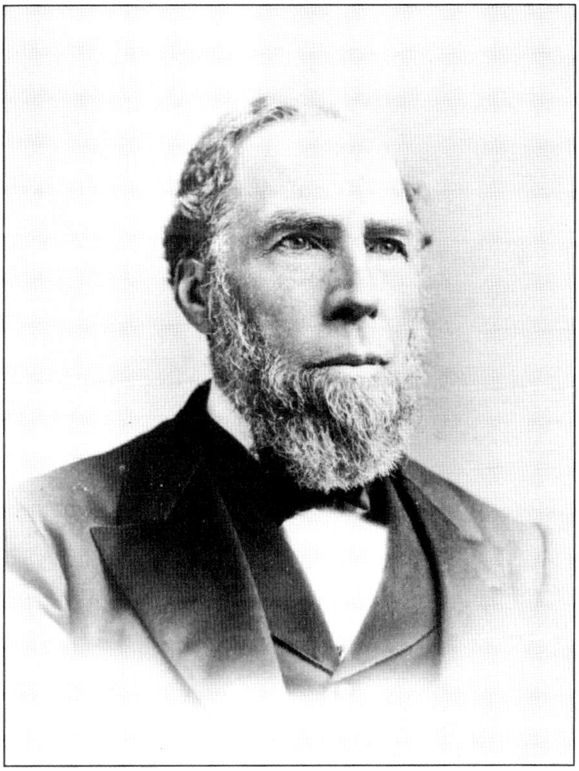

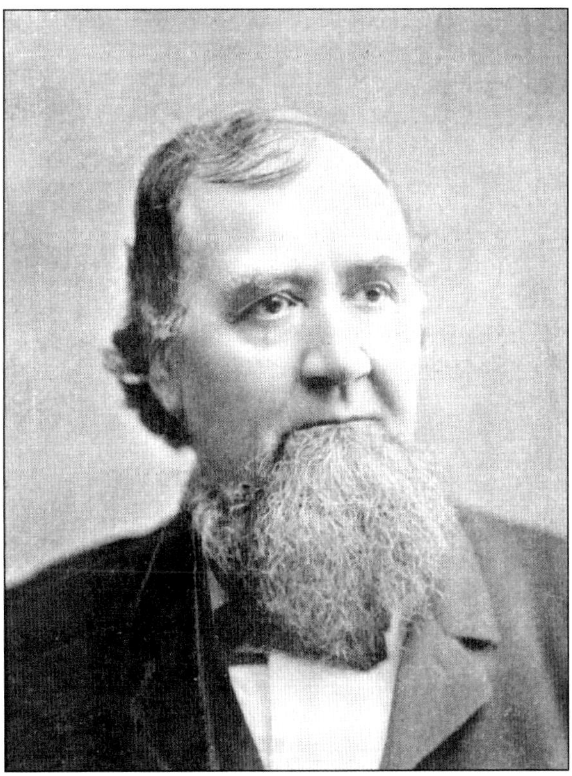

David S. Terry, a native Kentuckian and pro-slavery Democrat, served as a California Supreme Court justice from 1855 to 1859. He resided in what would become the J. Neely Johnson House at Eleventh and F Streets. He will be forever tied to dueling with, and killing, U.S. senator David Broderick in September 1859. The incident was fueled by politics: Terry favored the extension of slavery into California, while the "Free-soiler" Broderick did not. (SPL.)

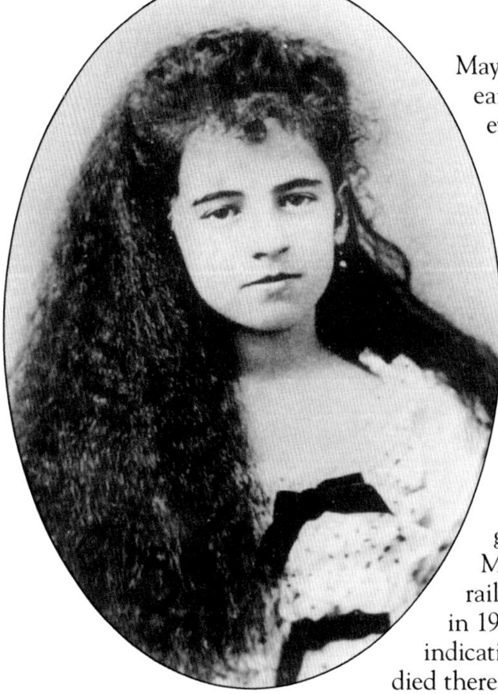

May Woolsey was old enough to dress up and wear earrings for a photograph portrait, but those tired eyes never had the chance to see her own reflection as a grown woman. Taken by encephalitis at the age of 12 in September 1879, May's passing led her grieving parents to pack her favorite clothes, toys, papers, and other possessions into a trunk, which they concealed in a space below a stairwell. In January 1979, the new owner of 916 E Street contacted Sacramento City historian James Henley, and the two of them tore back the fabric of time and viewed little May's treasures almost a century after they were hidden in pain and despair. Among the possessions were her diploma from the Washington School and a diary that revealed a girl who enjoyed friends, school, and social life. May's mother died at home in 1895 and former railroad pattern maker Luther Woolsey did the same in 1914 at the age of 85, neither of them leaving any indication that their beloved daughter had also lived and died there. (Both CSH.)

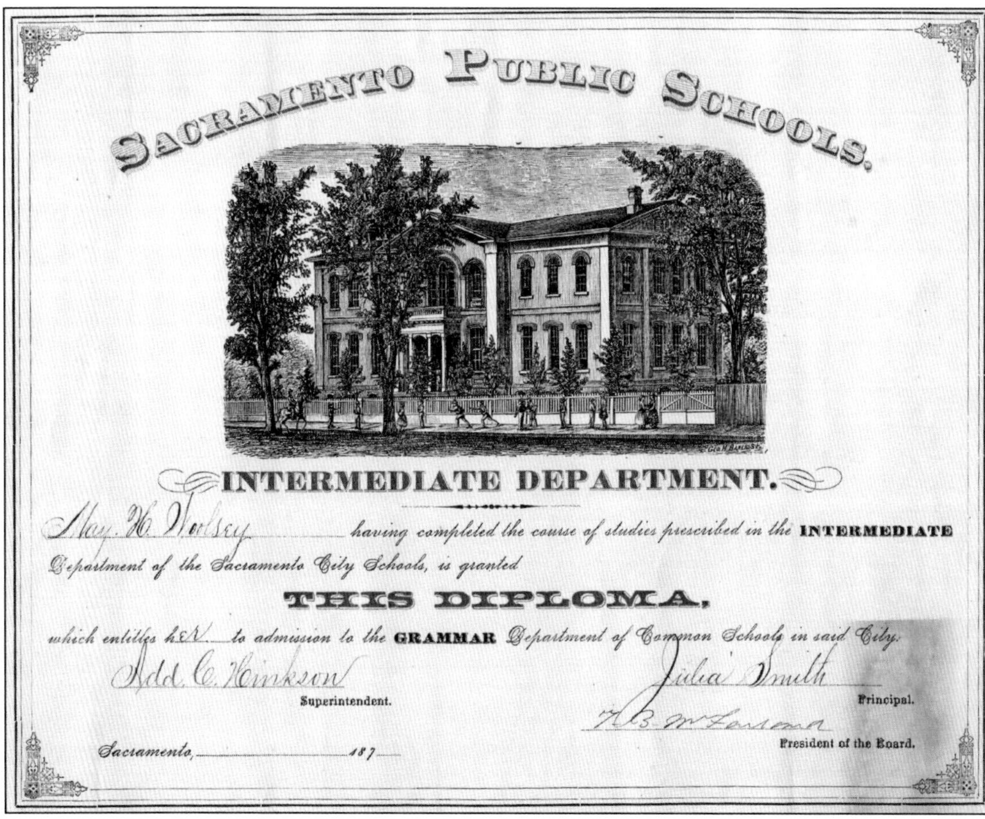

SACRAMENTO PUBLIC SCHOOLS.

INTERMEDIATE DEPARTMENT.

May H. Woolsey having completed the course of studies prescribed in the INTERMEDIATE Department of the Sacramento City Schools, is granted

THIS DIPLOMA,

which entitles her to admission to the GRAMMAR Department of Common Schools in said City.

Add. C. Hinkson Superintendent.

Julia Smith Principal.

President of the Board.

Sacramento, 187

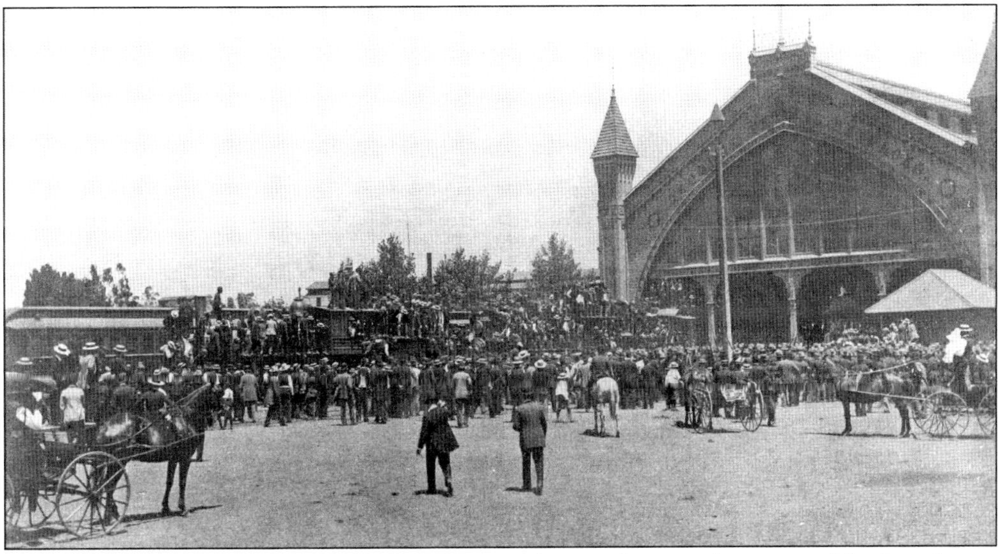

Blocked tracks and fiery oration drew the curious and sympathetic to the center of the disturbance in front of the Sacramento Depot in early July 1894, but it was a serious matter for the giant railroad companies and the businesses and communities dependent on constant carloads of food and goods across the country. Early in the strike, many Californians were sympathetic to the laborers and similar stalemates temporarily halted rail traffic in Oakland and Los Angeles. (CSH.)

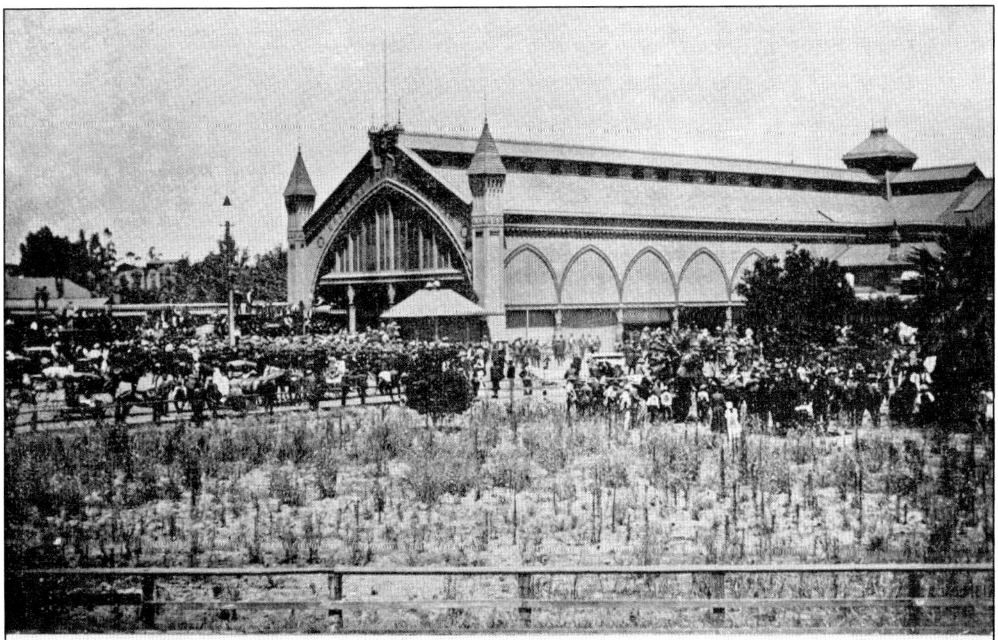

THE DEPOT AT SACRAMENTO, JULY 4TH, 1894.

The California National Guard units from San Francisco steamed into strike-torn Sacramento, disembarked at the station near Twenty-first Street, and marched to the Armory at Sixth and L Streets to join the local units. The Sacramento guards and their Stockton brethren had little stomach for a confrontation with the friends and relatives that swarmed the rail yards on the edge of Alkali Flat, effectively blocking entry to the east, and the tone was tense in those early days of July 1894. (SPL.)

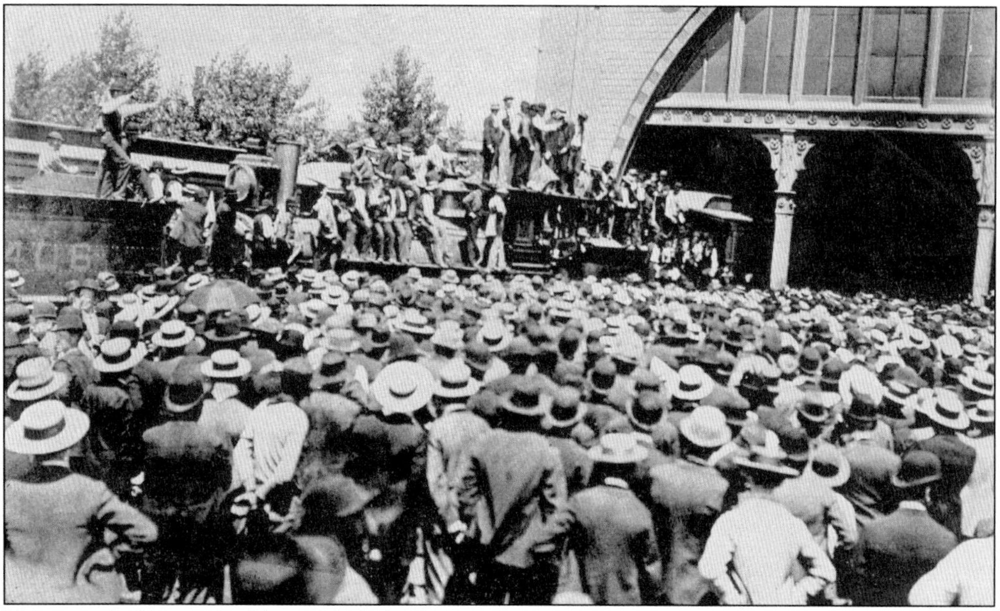

U.S. marshal Barry Baldwin's failed effort to break the human chain that held the nation's railroads frozen in Sacramento led to a state of emergency where hundreds of troops armed with 20 rounds of ammunition each and fixed bayonets formed skirmish lines against strikers and their sympathizers. Knocked to the ground and jeered at as he harangued the crowds, Baldwin missed a union-sanctioned opportunity to send the mail out when he insisted on hooking the hated Pullman cars to the train. (SPL.)

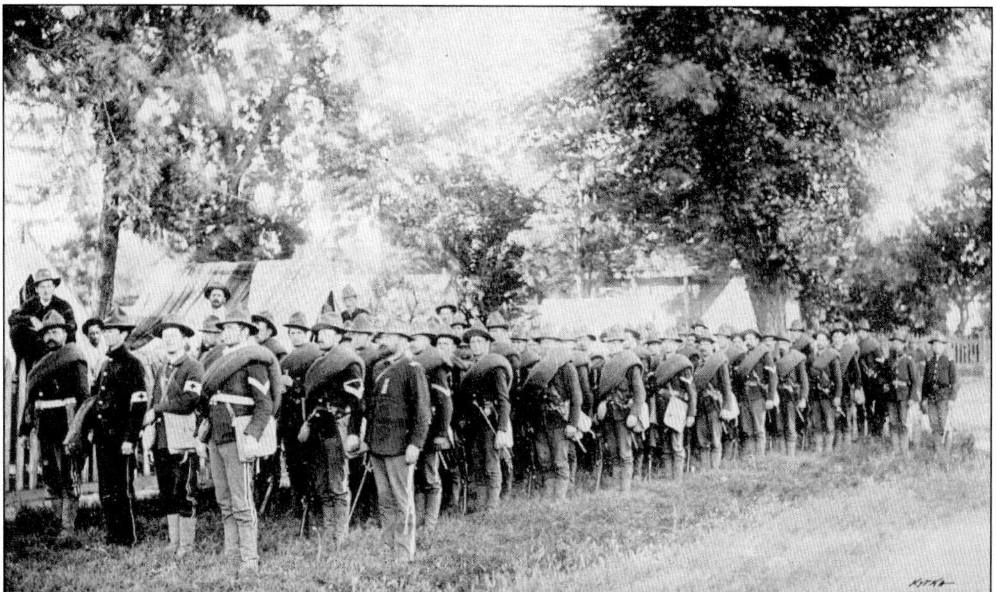

B Company of the National Guard of California stands at the ready in heavy marching order during the sweltering summer of 1894, lined up next to tents positioned along a fence in its neighborhood encampment. The Pullman Strike provided real action, though sometimes in the form of shots fired by skittish sentries that resulted in livestock casualties. On July 18, the troops headed off to guard a bridge on the American River, leaving only litter and a legend. (SPL.)

Factory whistles drew thousands of strikers and supporters to face the National Guard of California during the opening days of what became nationally known as the Pullman Strike, but things were quiet in the rail yards when the first train in over a week left on July 11, 1894, a lone trooper on horseback the only witness to an impending event that would hasten the end of the confrontation. (SPL.)

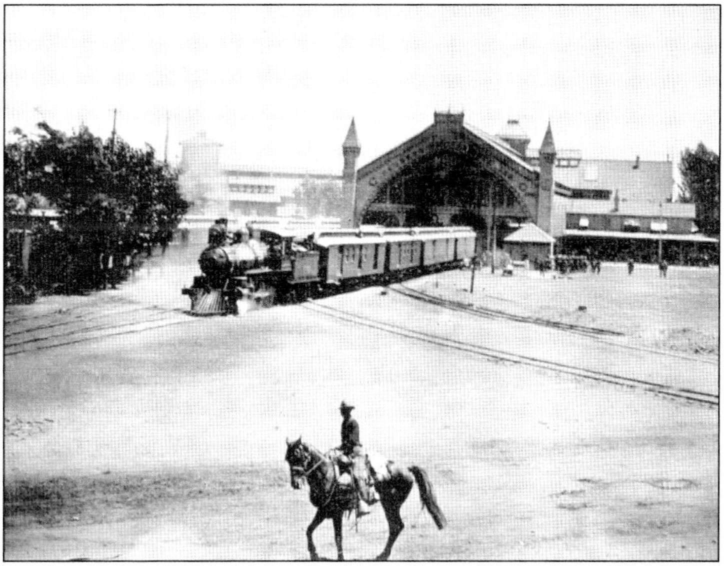

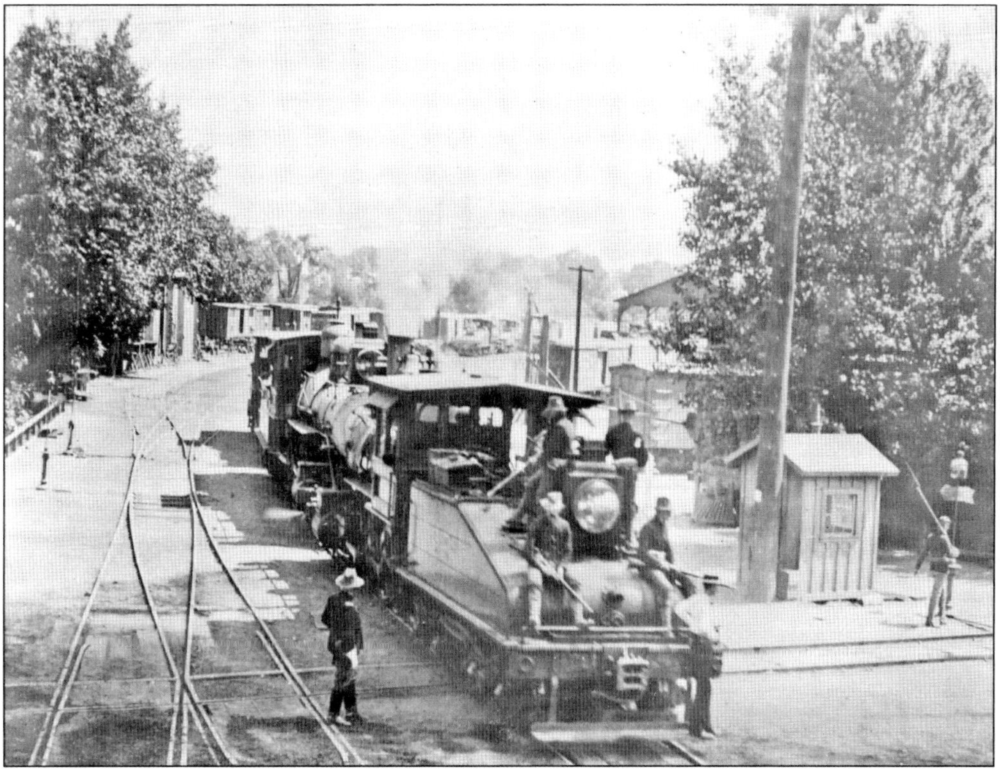

The popularity the strikers enjoyed earlier in the month plummeted with the engine and five cars toppled from a sabotaged trestle bridge 3 miles west of Sacramento on July 11, 1894, that killed railroad engineer Sam Clark and four U.S. soldiers. Taken after the deliberate derailment of the first engine to roll out of the depot in more than a week, this photograph shows a well-guarded train with armed soldiers. Within a week, normal rail traffic was resumed and the troops were sent to deal with strikers further up the line. (CSH.)

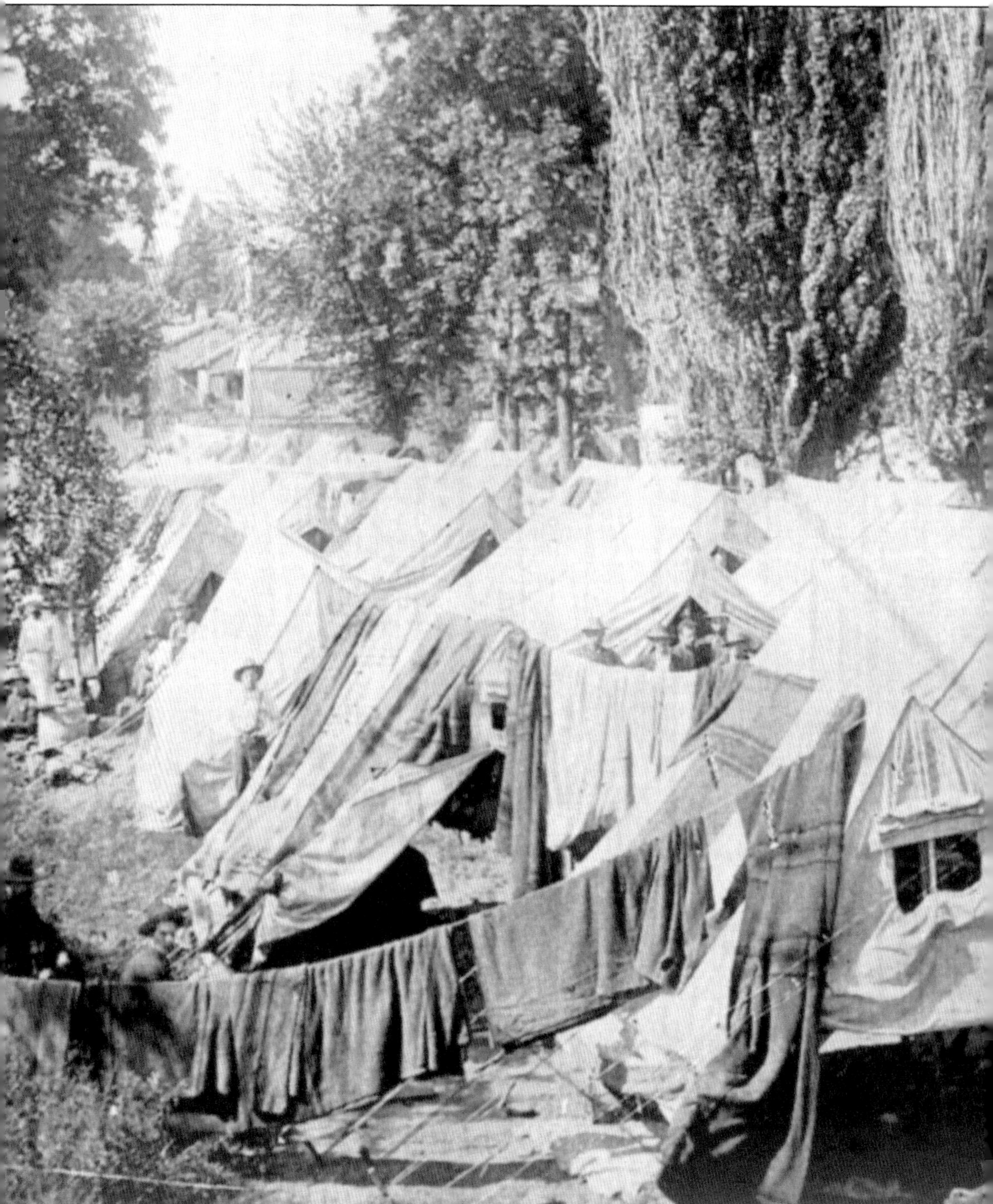

Tents brought by wagon to the camp on the northwestern section of Alkali Flat at Ninth and D Streets stand with open flaps, blankets, and clothing hung on lines to dry in the heat as men mill or go about their business near the empty house used as headquarters by the troops. Friday, July 13, proved a lucky one for the hungry soldiers as the quartermaster and company cook sent foragers a few hundred yards up the tracks to the railroad shops to scavenge materials with which

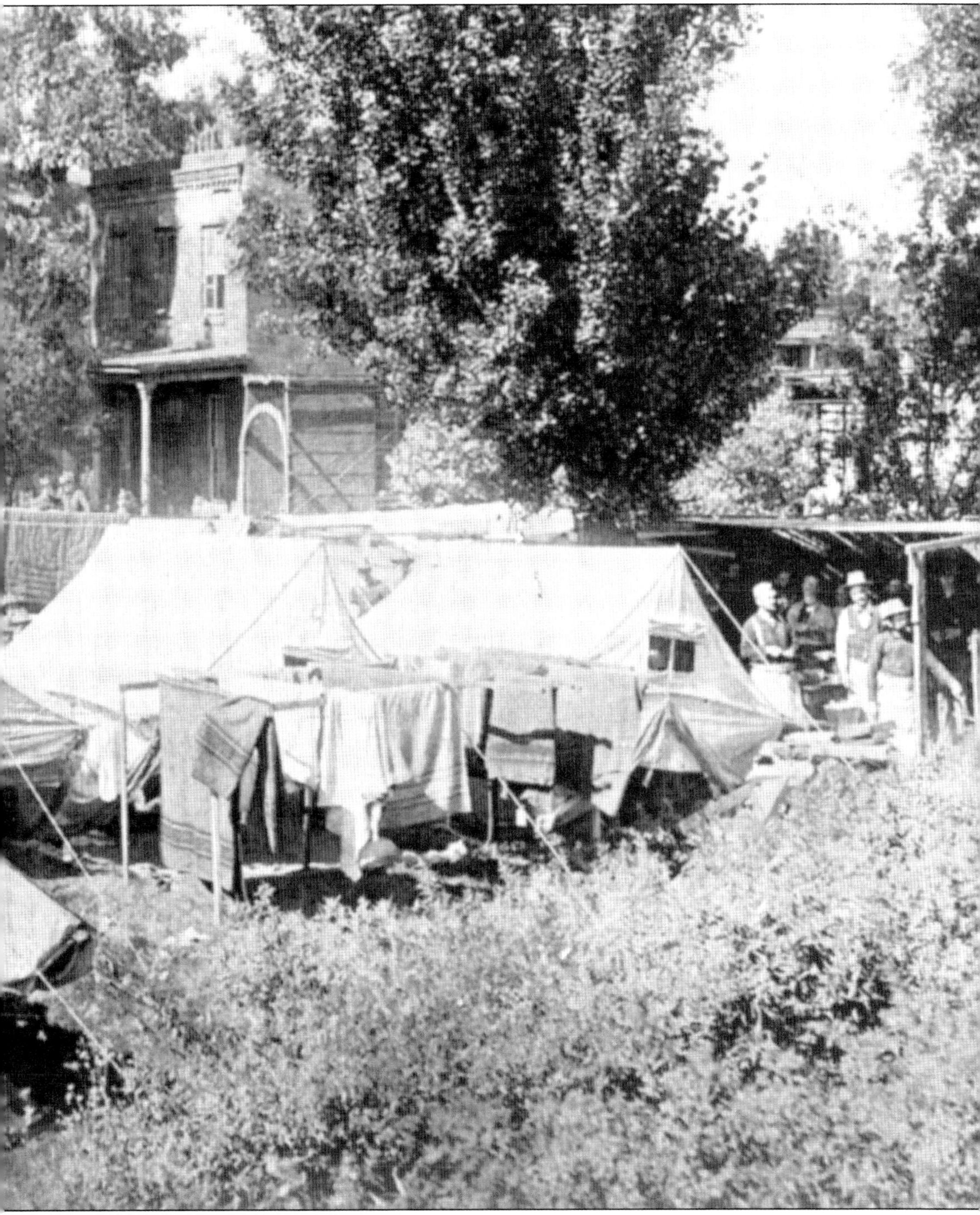

to build a proper company kitchen, including a sheet-iron top and length of iron for a stove top and pipe. KCRA-TV now stands at this corner, where Crystal Cream and Butter originally stood in 1911, and the massive Governor's Village apartment complex covers Ninth Street between D and E Streets. (SPL.)

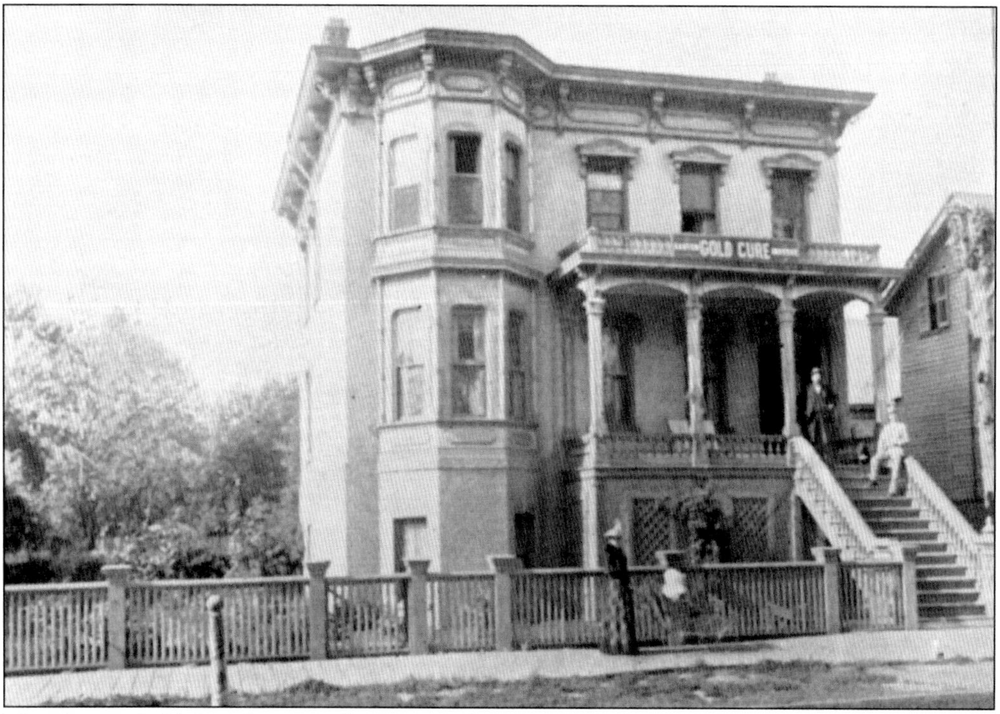

The Garten Gold Cure Institute first appeared in the 1893 telephone directory and was located at the corner of Ninth and F Streets. By the time this photograph was published, it had moved to 808 G Street, across from St. Joseph's Convent. The institute offered "seclusion and retirement" and took the gold from "those addicted to the morphine, cocaine, opium, liquor and tobacco habits." Named for Indiana physician M. H. Garten, the chain failed after a few years, and by 1912 the building had been divided into apartments. By 1944, when this photograph was taken, the former institute had slid into disrepair and was eventually replaced by the new courthouse. (Both CSH.)

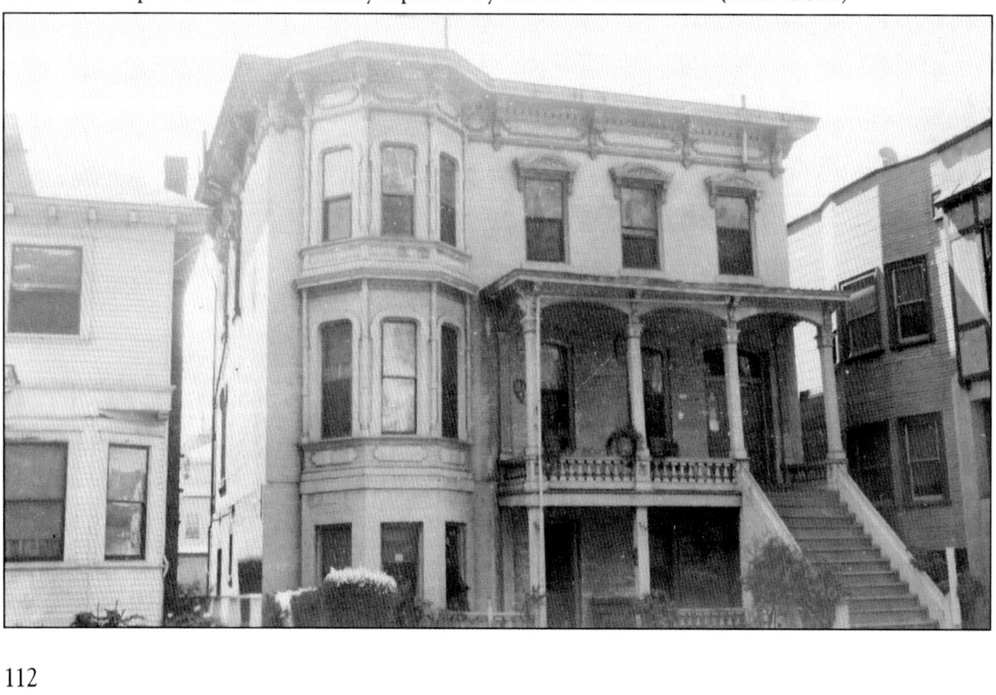

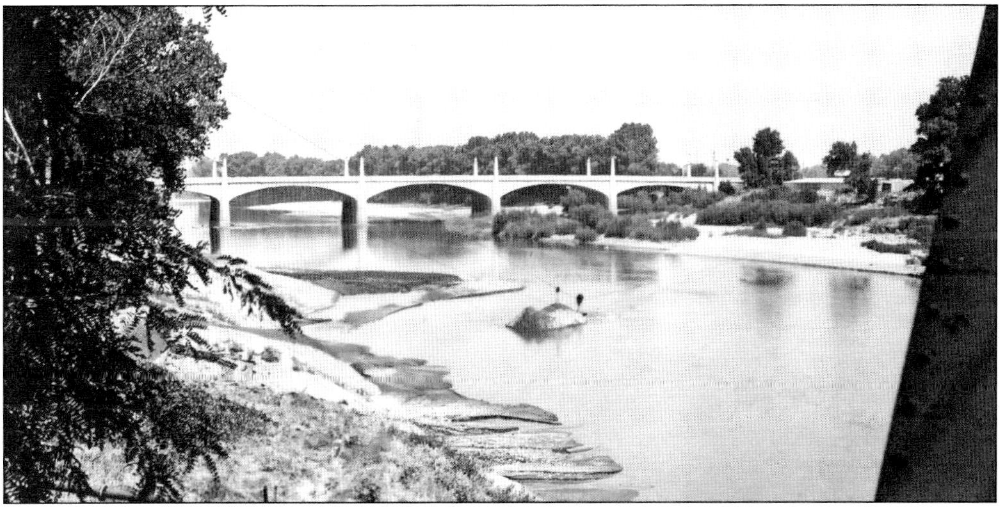

In late August 1917, a man was digging for shelter near the north abutment of the Twelfth Street Bridge when he found a cluster of 45 sticks of high-power dynamite. No fuse or culprit was ever found, but later that year a bomb built of, aptly enough, dynamite, went off at the Governor's Mansion on Sixteenth and H Streets. With World War I raging and the Russian Revolution in full swing, a connection between overseas events and surging agitation by Sacramento Valley devotees to the International Workers of the World, or "Wobblies," is lost to the fog of history. (CSH.)

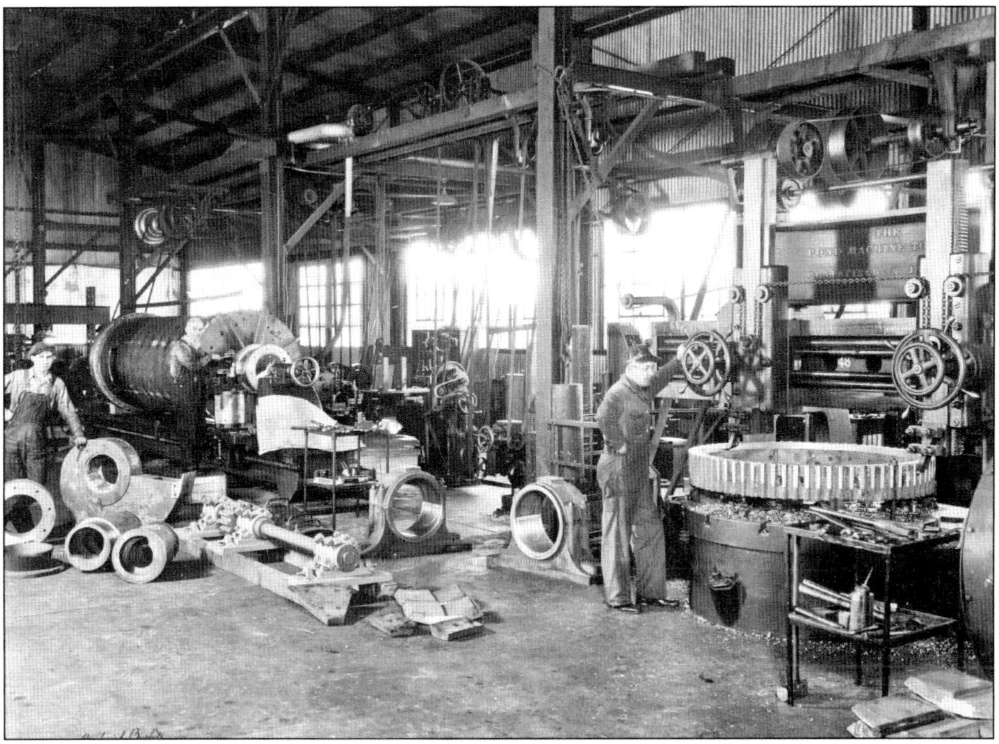

For decades, numerous Southern Pacific shop workers resided within the Alkali Flat neighborhood. The shops, as depicted here in this 1933 image, were fast paced and dangerous. Ill-timed movements of flesh or steel could spell disaster, as in the 1903 case of John West of 515 Tenth Street. West and a coworker were crushed when a boiler slipped from a transfer table while being moved. (SPL.)

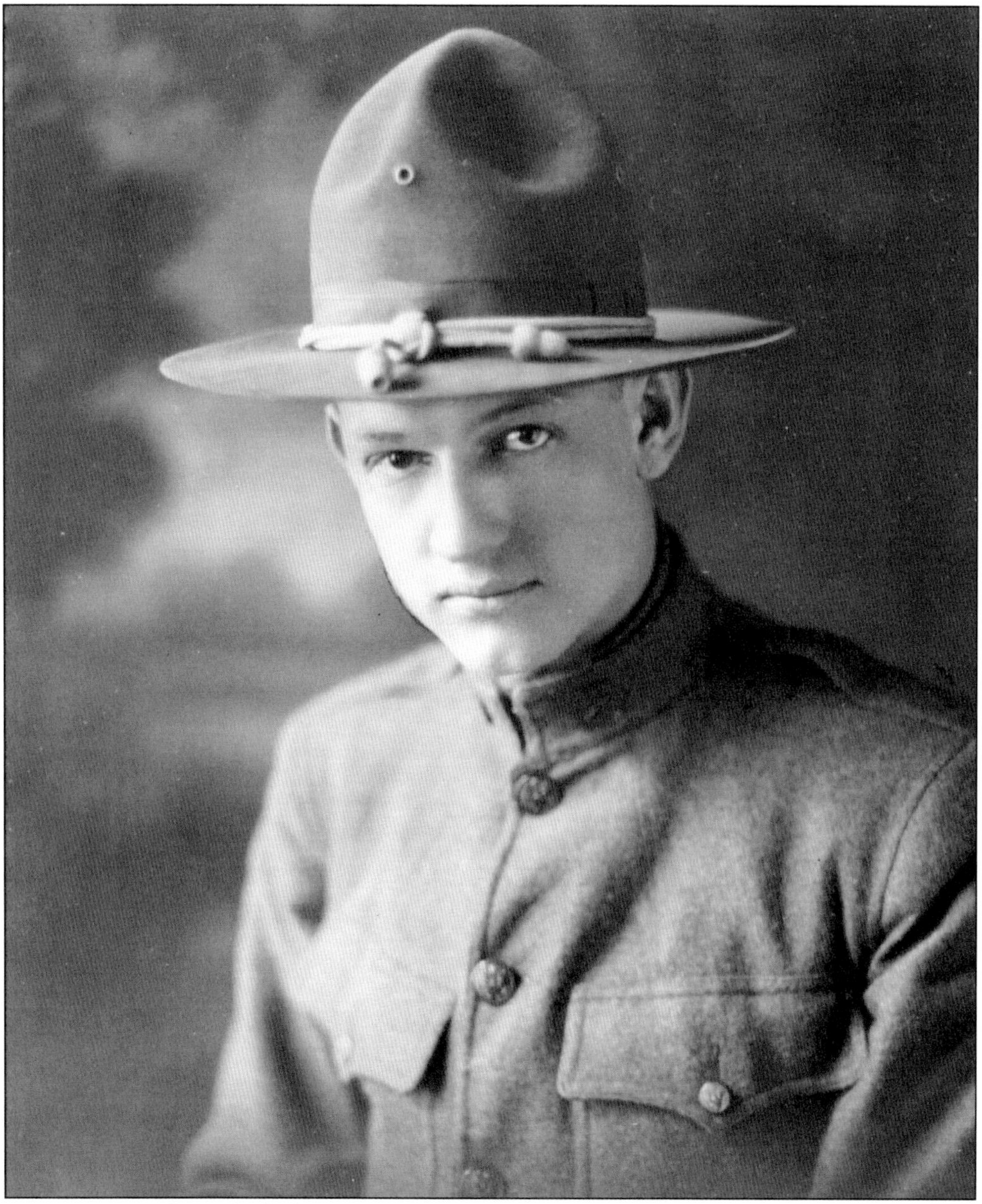

As a young resident of Alkali Flat at 1315 H Street, Hugo Frank Wallner was a 1913 graduate of Sacramento High School and a bank teller at the California National Bank. His German immigrant father, Fred, was brewmaster at Ruhstaller's City Brewery, just a block west from the family's front door. In February 1916, the 25-year-old man won an adding contest at the Travelers Hotel by listing an amazing total of 100 checks in 90 seconds. In the spring of 1918, Wallner was married to Freda Caldarella. Just weeks after marrying, however, he was dispatched to France, serving as a clerk in the 91st Infantry Division. Although holding a task that would seemingly keep him out of harm's way, Wallner was sent into combat in September 1918. According to his lieutenant, he died of wounds suffered during an attack in the Epinonville sector of the Argonne. This made him one of over 100 Sacramentans—and the only Alkali Flat resident—to die in the Great War. His heartbroken Freda never remarried and died in San Francisco in 1983. (CSL.)

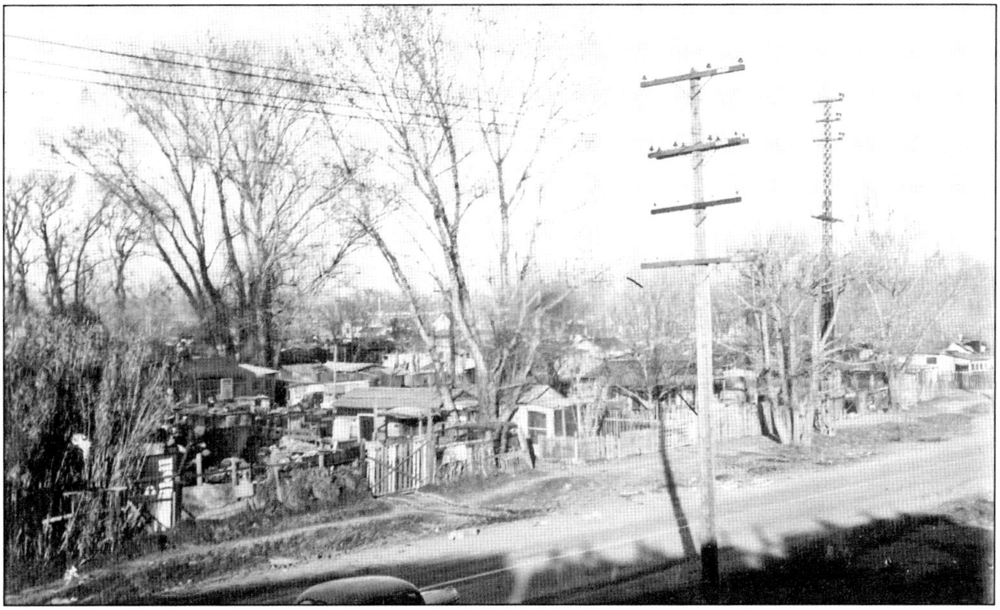

America's economic conflagration of the 1920s and 1930s visited Alkali Flat in earnest in the form of shantytowns, or "Hoovervilles," the latter term a derisive homage to embattled Pres. Herbert Hoover. Amongst the litany of Hooverville's surrounding Sacramento—Skunk Hollow, Rattlesnake, and Rotten Egg—Alkali Flat had its own: Shooksville, named after its eccentric African American leader, Samuel Shooks. Above is an image of the camp from the northern edge of the B Street Levee, while below is the camp as it appears near the city's new water filtration plant. Minority populations were concentrated in Shooksville while its proximity to the city's incinerator and water filtration plant made sanitary conditions nearly unbearable. (Both CSH.)

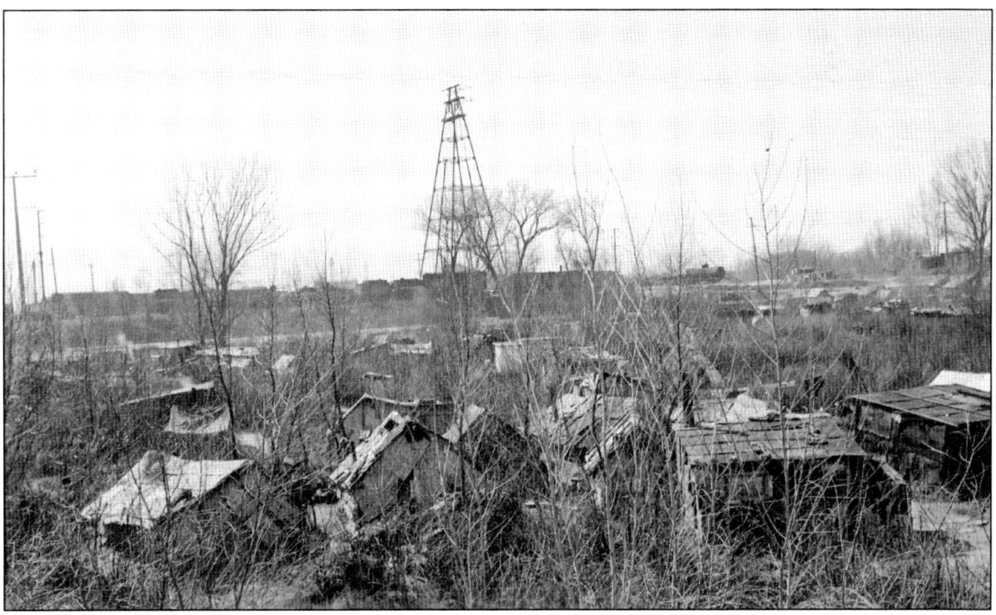

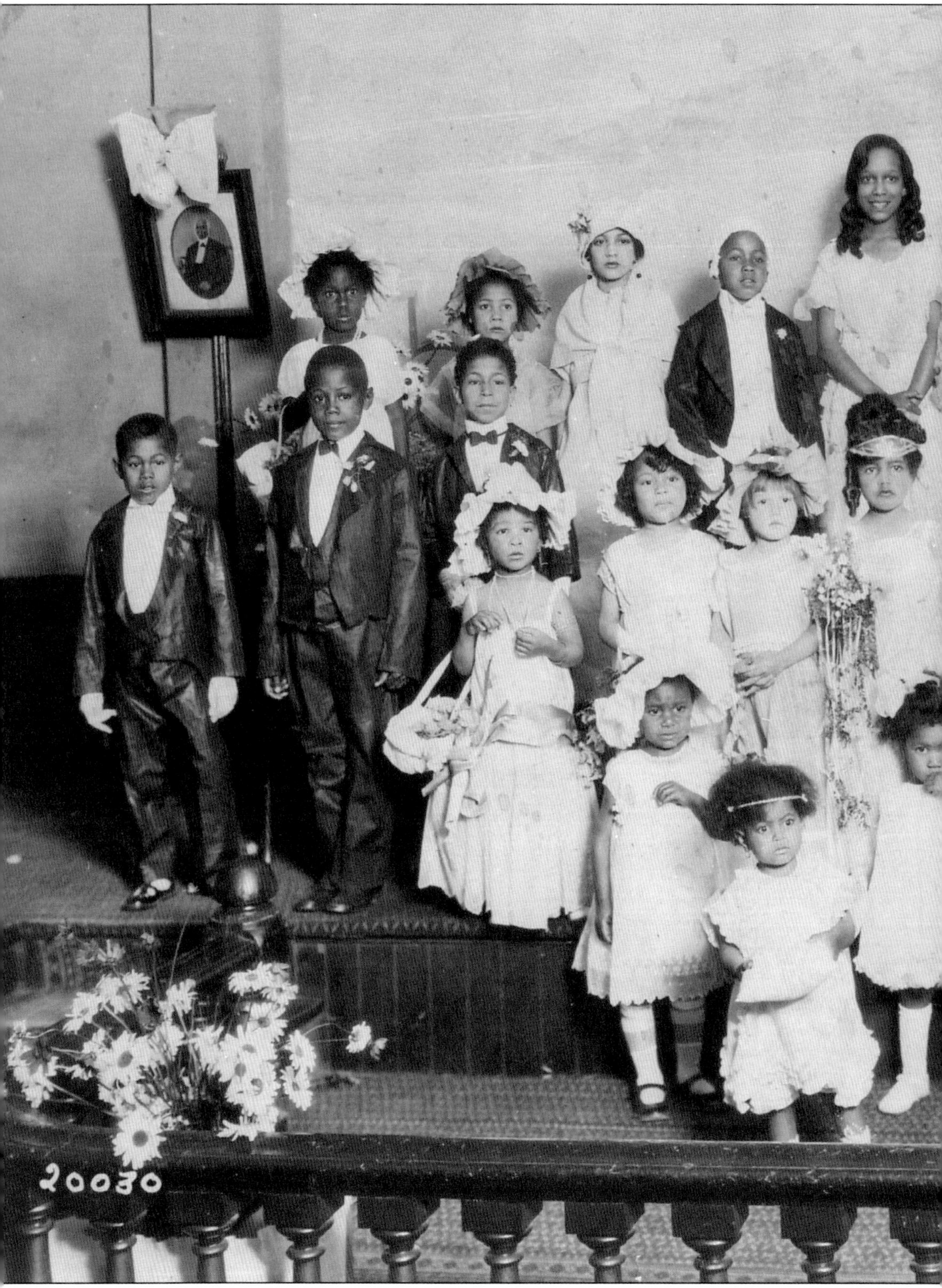
20030

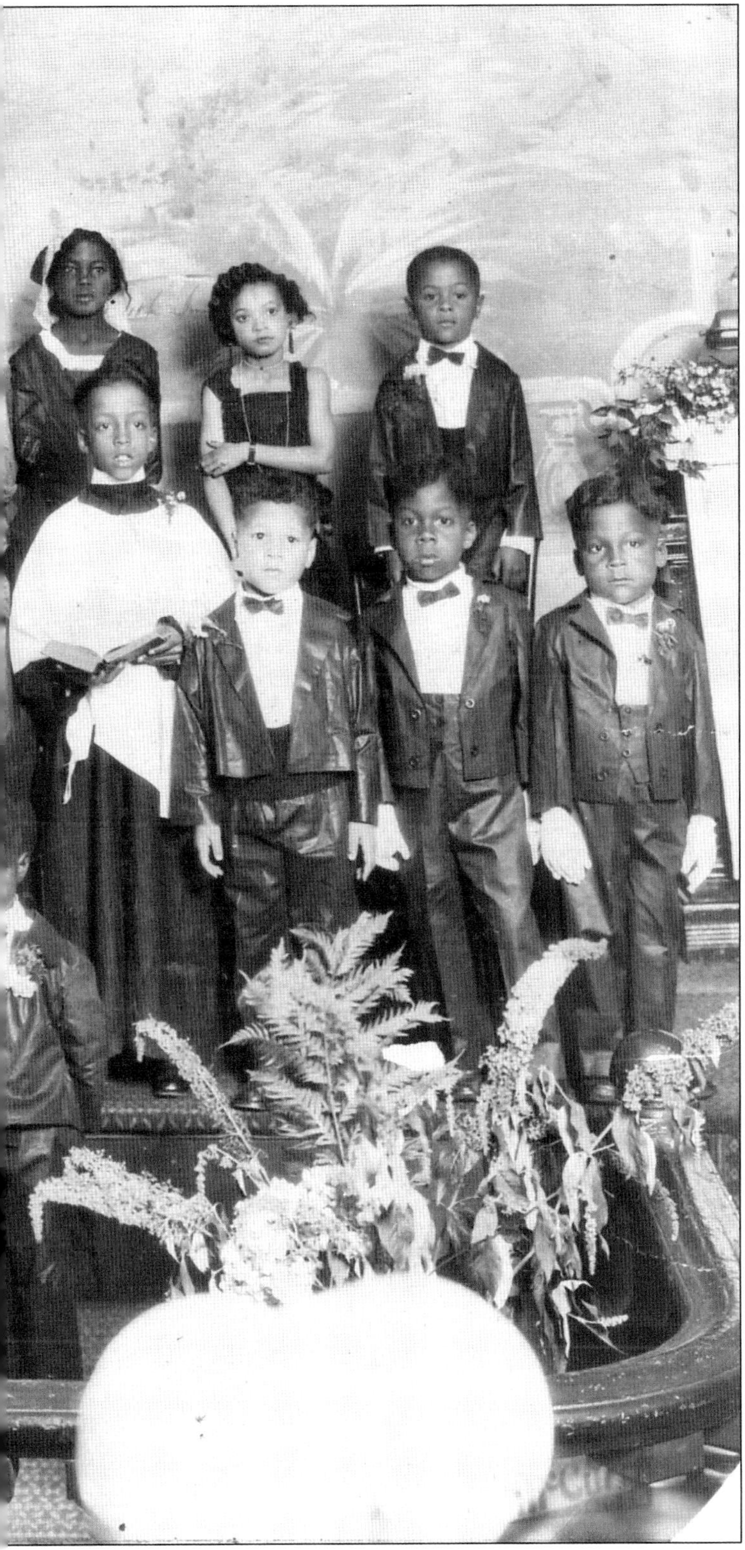

A 1920s fad—the Tom Thumb Wedding—was considered odd even in a decade that spawned goldfish-swallowing and flagpole-sitting acts. This 1926 photograph captures a ceremony at the St. Andrew's AME Church. Four of Bert and Ethel Robinson's children were in the wedding party: Mary (third row, first on the left), Bob (third row, seventh from the left), Bill (last row, first from the right), and Zaretta (last row, fourth from the right). Bert and his family lived at 1223 C when the picture was taken, and he drove for the city garbage department for many years. Ten years after the mock nuptials, Bert and Ethel relocated to 410 Nineteenth Street and Bill, Mary, and Zaretta were still living at home. (CSH.)

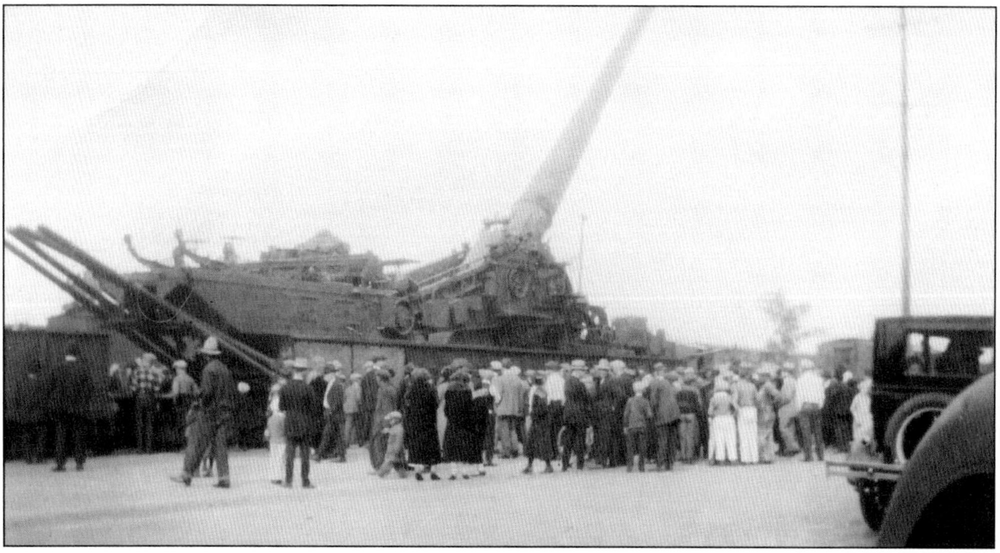

It's a circus-like scene at Seventh and G Streets in the early 1920s as a rail-mounted, 14-inch naval gun, built at the Washington Navy Yard, passes along the Southern Pacific rail yards. While difficult to understand a destination—the Panama Canal Zone or the Harbor Defenses of San Francisco— the weapon nonetheless had astonishing power and range, able to send a 1,400-pound projectile nearly 19 miles. (CSH.)

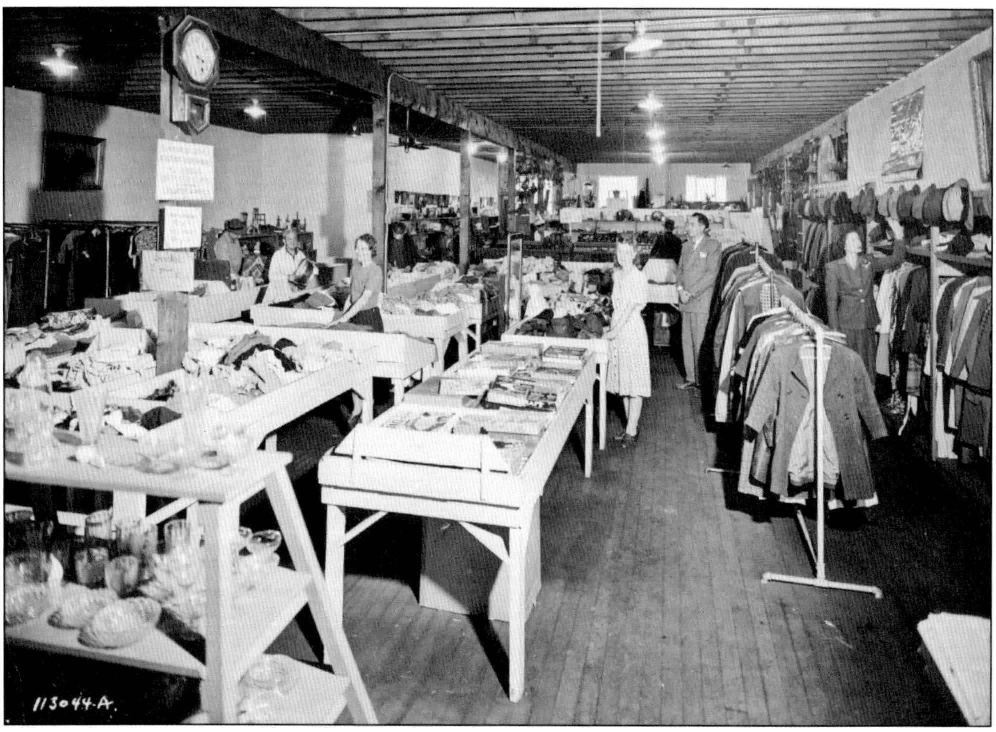

This November 1944 view of the Volunteers of America Thrift Shop at 400 Twelfth Street affords a window into wartime Alkali Flat. Rationing was now part of the national consciousness, and with American GIs and British Tommies making their way closer and closer to the Rhine, the need for America to tighten its proverbial belt grew ever more imperative. (SPL.)

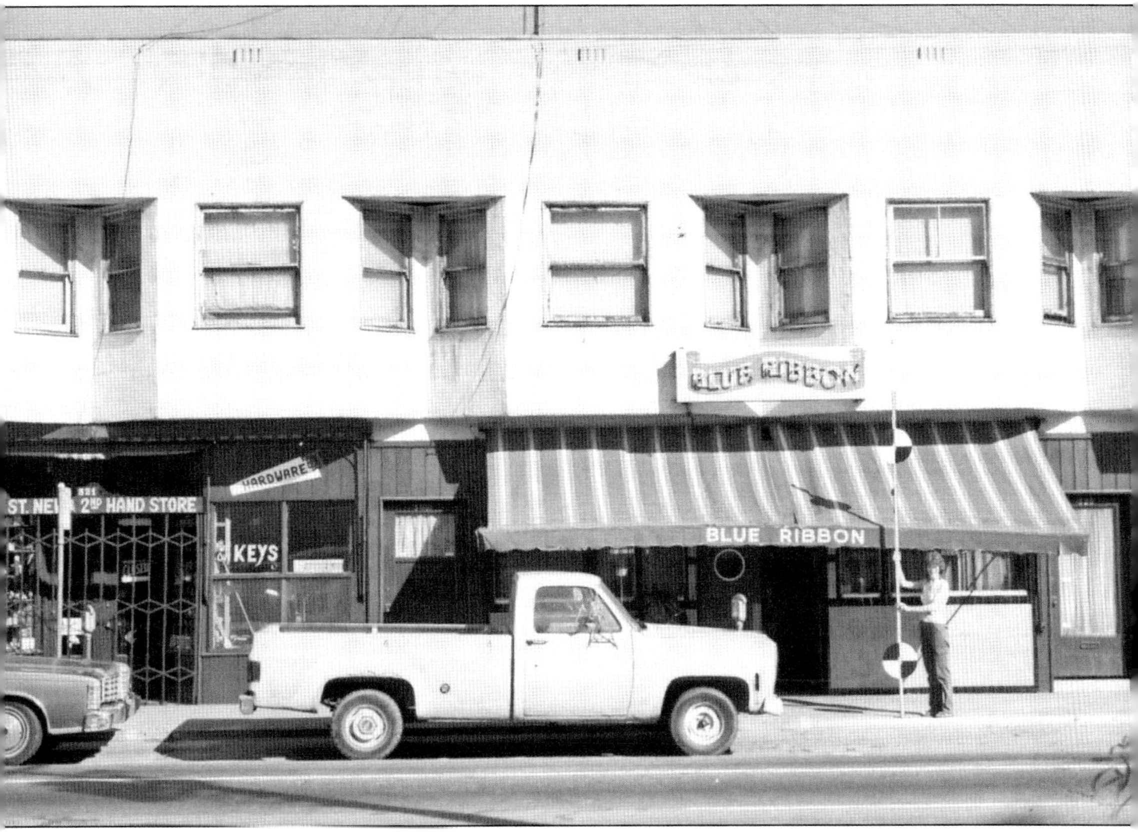

Through the latter half of the 20th century, sooty haunts like the Blue Ribbon and the 505 Club sat along the north side of the Twelfth Street corridor, slaking the thirst of any and all. Pictured here is the Blue Ribbon, whose origins predate World War II. It's gone, but perhaps one of the more stunning crimes in Alkali lore took place there. Just days after the June 1944 Allied invasion of Europe, Frank Heslen visited the Blue Ribbon in a jealous rage. On the evening of the June 15, he blew into the bar searching for his estranged wife, 38-year-old Viola Pearl Knight, whom Heslen suspected of having an affair. After a brief argument, he picked up a paring knife and slashed Viola's throat. Thirty-some onlookers sat in shock as bar owner Jack Fitzgerald bashed Heslen over the head with a beer bottle. Not at all stunned, the killer flew out the door and into the alley between B and C Streets, where he was knocked unconscious by a gallant pursuer. Heslen was sent to the notorious San Quentin for his deed. (Dan Hood.)

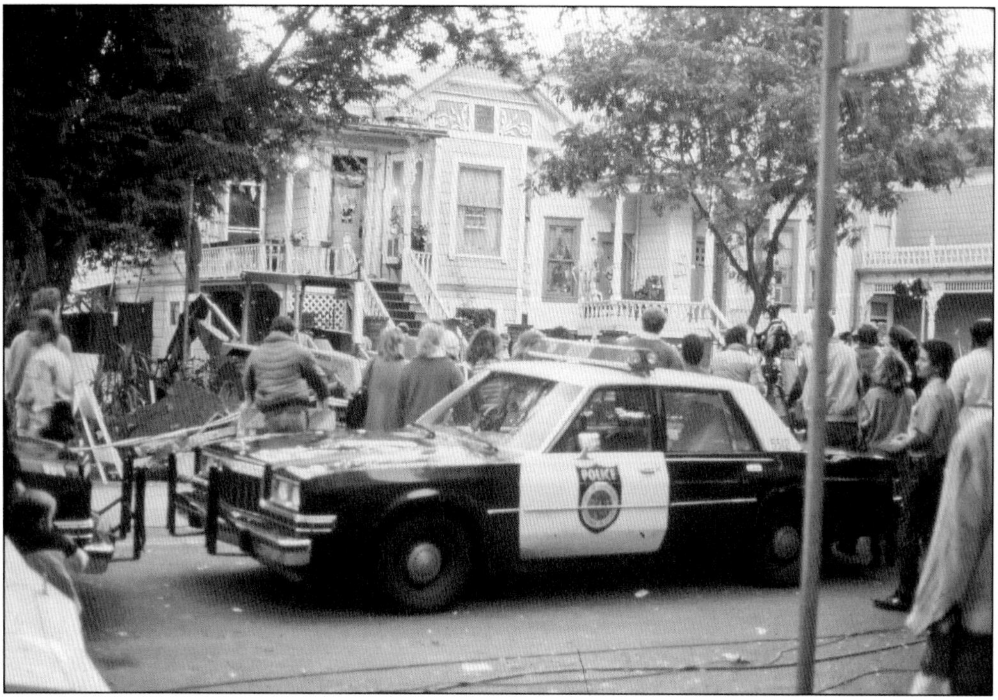

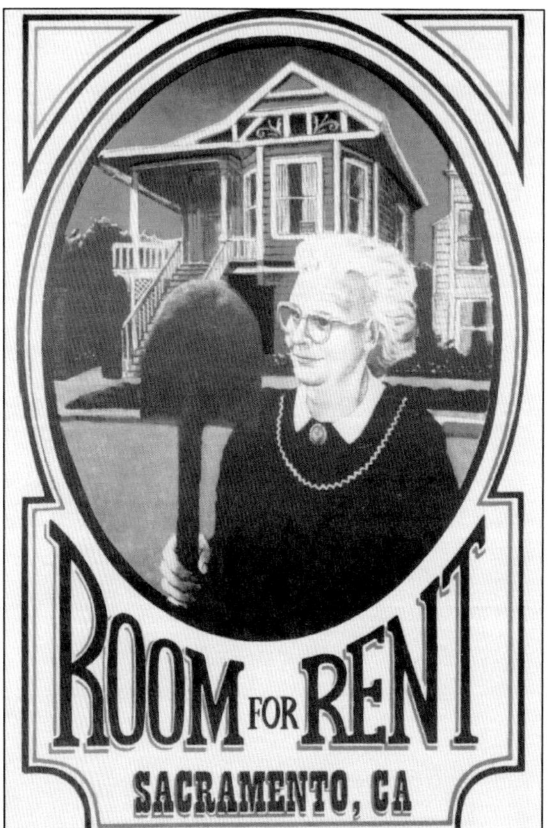

The well-maintained Victorian rooming house at 1426 F Street sits just beyond the accepted boundaries of Alkali Flat, but the horrors unearthed beginning November 11, 1988, went beyond borderlines and shocked the entire nation. Samaritan to many, she-devil to those who crossed her, Dorothea Montalvo Puente led a dual life that ended those of nine men and women, seven of them buried in the ground around the house. Shortly after the above photograph was taken on November 12, the second day of the investigation, the well-dressed Puente was escorted beyond police lines by a detective and quietly disappeared while a second body was unearthed. Caught and brought to trial, the kindly looking old lady was sentenced in December 1993 to terms that placed her behind bars for the rest of her life. (Both Tom Myers.)

Six

Alkali Prospects

by James Scott

In 1990, Alkali Flat resident Roger Lathe referred to his neighborhood as "the cumulative product of many individuals over a long period of time. The result is clearly imperfect, sometimes distressing, frequently frustrating and very pleasant indeed, a living, changing landscape." It's as if Lathe viewed the Alkali as organic—a living, breathing presence that, although "beaten and bruised" (as he would put it), was very much alive, defiant, and ready for future prospects. To walk through the Alkali, a Sacramento neophyte might be shocked to know that the neighborhood was ever in the throes of dilapidation and blight. The Sullivan and Johnson homes are on either side of J. Neely Johnson Park and are grand. A kempt community garden sits on the southern edge of the park and just southeast of that is the Boys and Girls Club, a beehive of busy youth that sits upon what used to be a line of smallish Victorians. The long-coveted rehabilitation and conversion of Globe Mills into loft living sits as a model of adapted use. To contrast this with, for now, the acres of piled cement between the B Street Levee and KCRA, in addition to the crime issues that plague the Alkali's lone light rail station, one can still see a neighborhood assuredly dusting itself off and moving ahead. Some envisage success as the establishment of a static, yet diverse residential population, and one that can stay long enough to develop a sense of community. Others view neighborhood institutions as the key, coming in the form of something as simple as a community garden or as ambitious as a youth center. Whether or not the Alkali can reach its former heights is a matter of community pride—residents are fiercely proud of what they have built and continue to build. Regardless, the neighborhood is moving full-circle; its origins are residential, its in-between years a mix of industrial and itinerant tenancy, and its future arcing toward a place of, yet again, activist and conscientious property owners and tenants who regard the Alkali as home.

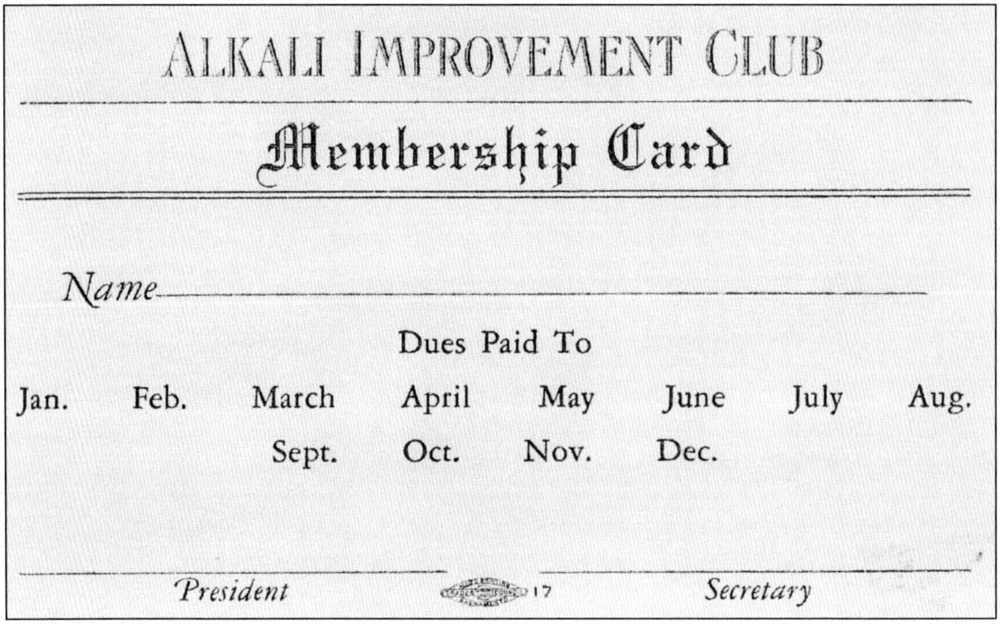

ALKALI IMPROVEMENT CLUB

Membership Card

Name

Dues Paid To

Jan. Feb. March April May June July Aug.
Sept. Oct. Nov. Dec.

President 17 Secretary

Starting with the Alkali Improvement Club, a nongovernmental body born in 1938, systematic ventures to redevelop the area have been common. The city made earnest efforts in December 1948 when, supported by state and federal urban-renewal legislation, a newly formed Sacramento Redevelopment Agency surveyed 220 city blocks west of Twenty-first Street. After the 60-block area, today known as Old Sacramento, the next-highest incidence of blight existed in the Alkali. Efforts were rededicated in the early 1970s with the Alkali Flat Project Area Committee, a group of area residents and business owners who, along with the Sacramento Redevelopment Agency, sought change through "Redevelopment Plan Alkali Flat Project No. 6." Today the Sacramento Housing and Redevelopment Agency and the Alkali Flat Redevelopment Advisory Committee form the aegis under which neighborhood rehabilitation efforts proceed. (Both CSH.)

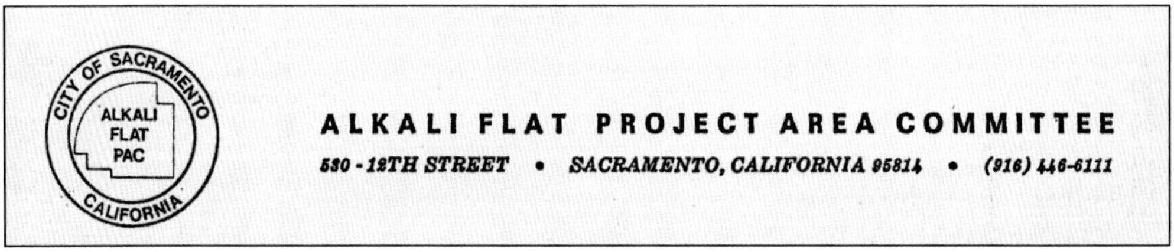

CITY OF SACRAMENTO CALIFORNIA
ALKALI FLAT PAC

ALKALI FLAT PROJECT AREA COMMITTEE

530 - 12TH STREET • SACRAMENTO, CALIFORNIA 95814 • (916) 446-6111

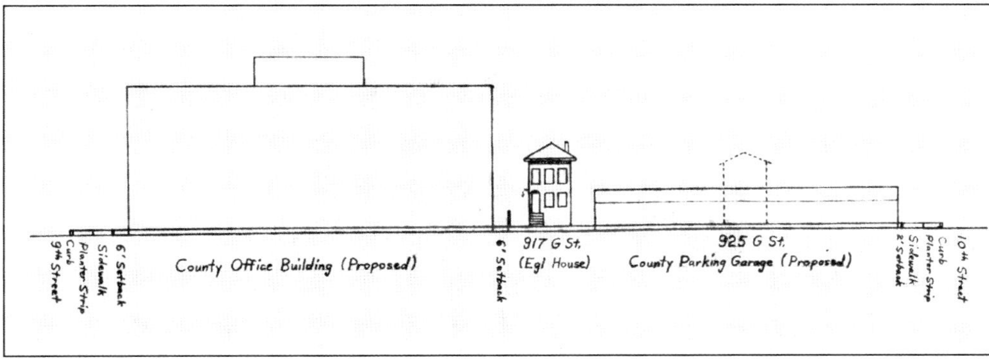

A city planner's sketch of a county project in the early 1970s intimates the Alkali challenge of balancing progress with a passion for architectural history. The John M. Price District Attorney Center was built, but dissension from the preservation community scuttled plans for a garage that would have meant razing the Van Voorhies house on 925 G Street. Had the proposal been carried out, the Egl house at 917 G Street would have, in the words of the attorney representing the owners of the house, been "dwarfed in a cavern of concrete." (CSH.)

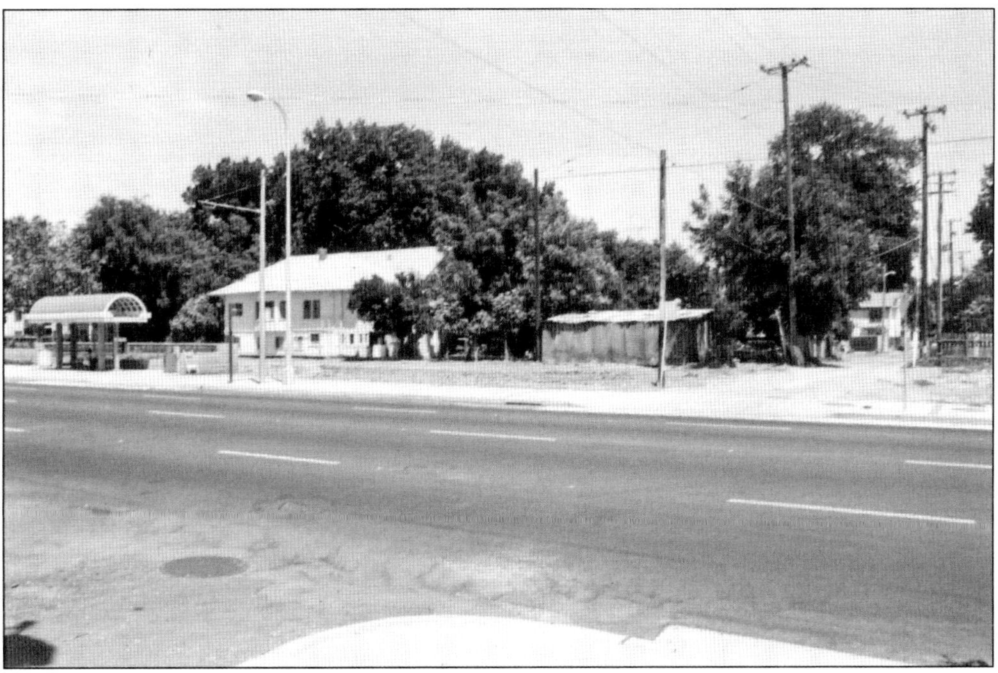

Light-rail service came to the Alkali in 1986 in the form of the LaValentina/Alkali Flat stop at Twelfth and E Streets. Having undergone a face-lift in 1990, the stop is adorned with murals and tile work, symbolic of the neighborhood's dual Victorian/Chicano heritage. Named to honor a heroine of the 1910 Mexican Revolution, Mayor Anne Rudin called it "an everlasting monument" to Sacramento's oldest Hispanic neighborhood. (CSH.)

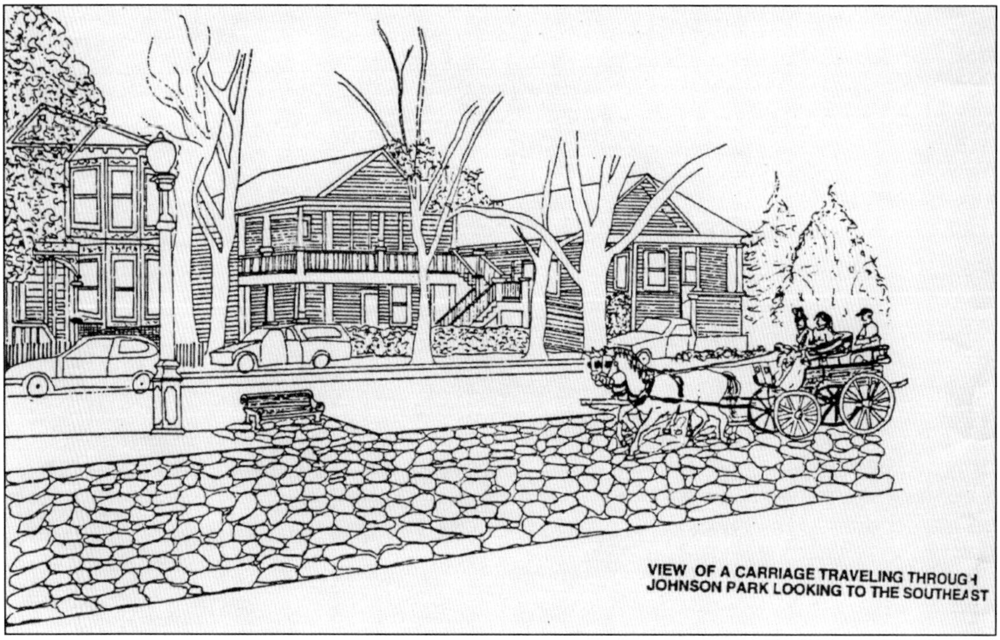

Efforts to revitalize an embattled J. Neely Johnson Park came in the mid-1990s with an eye on resurrecting some of the Alkali's Victorian past. While cobblestone streets, Greco Roman arbors, and gazebos never materialized, substantial change did come on April 1, 2006, in the form of a community garden, courtesy of a Community Development Block Grant and the efforts of a battery of dedicated Alkali residents. The city's landscape and architecture section created a mock-up (below) of the 1.17-acre park and garden in 2004. The garden, which now occupies the spot where a horseshoe pit once was, has stood as a welcoming commons for neighborhood activity, including Halloween and Independence Day parties. (Both Laura Lough and Dan Frankenfield.)

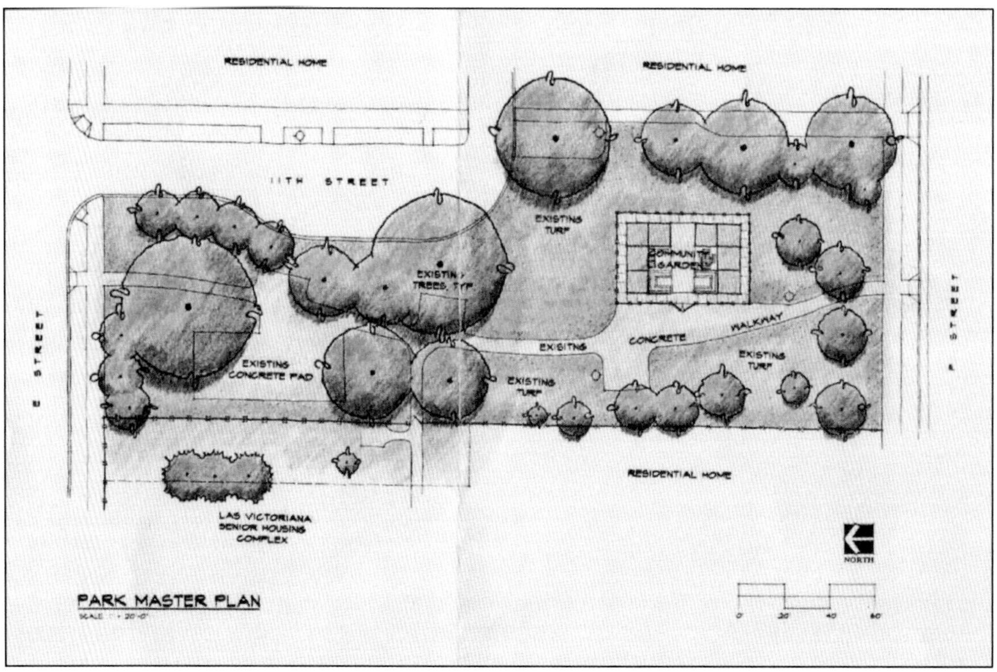

Downtown Sacramento's nearly 4,000 youth received an enormous boost on September 25, 1999, when the 17,800-square-foot Thomas P. Raley Boys and Girls Club—the first ever in Sacramento—opened its doors. Serving between 150 and 200 children a day, the Twelfth and G facility contains game and art rooms, a gymnasium, and a computer lab. The opening-day crowd includes the facility's primary benefactor, Joyce Raley Teel (center). (CSH.)

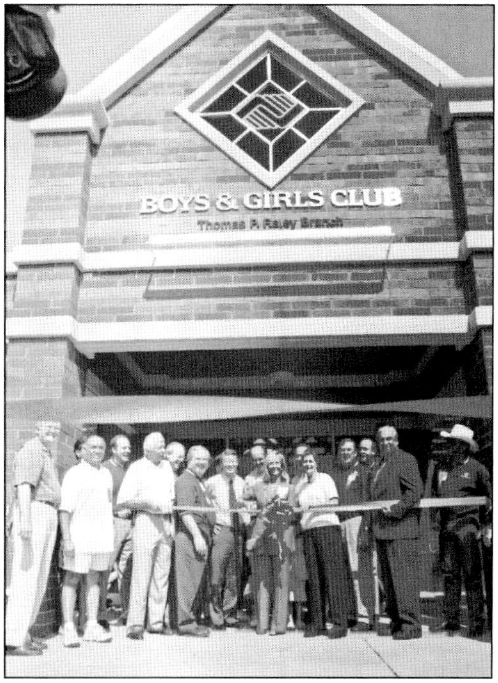

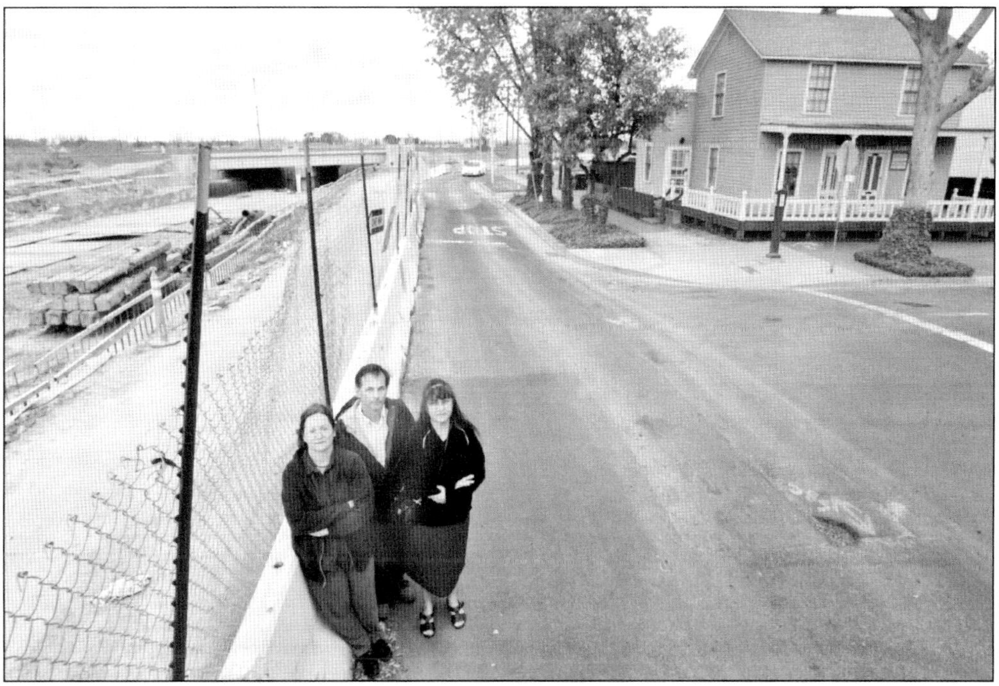

Connecting downtown Sacramento with Richards Boulevard, the Seventh Street Bypass was completed in spring 2004. The project was met with immediate skepticism and fears of increased traffic. After a period of legal haggling and two environmental impact studies, the project was finally completed for $25 million. Pictured here in April 2003 from left to right are community activists Laura Lough, Dan Frankenfield, and Sophia Parra, all of whom opposed the bypass. (*Sacramento Bee*/Jay Mather.)

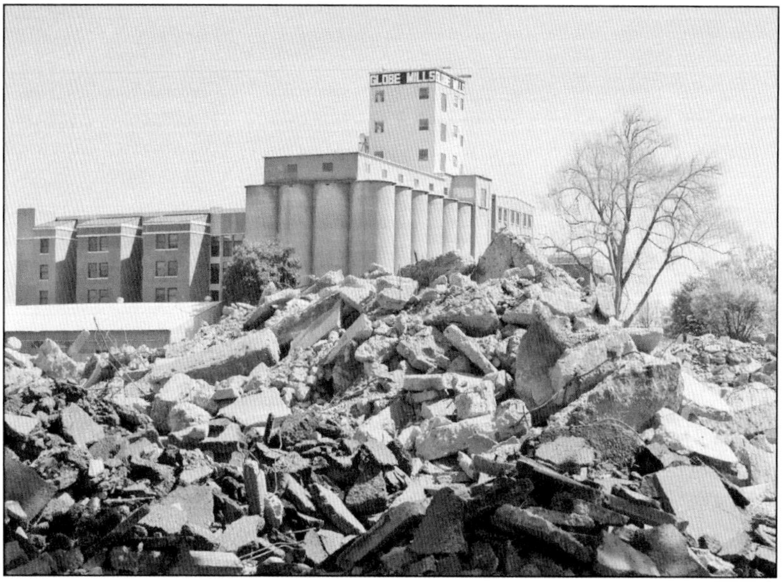

The crumbled remains of the 98-year-old Crystal Dairy are piled below a rehabilitated Globe Mills. The latter is now the home to 146 mixed-income living units, while the Crystal Dairy grounds are slated for development.

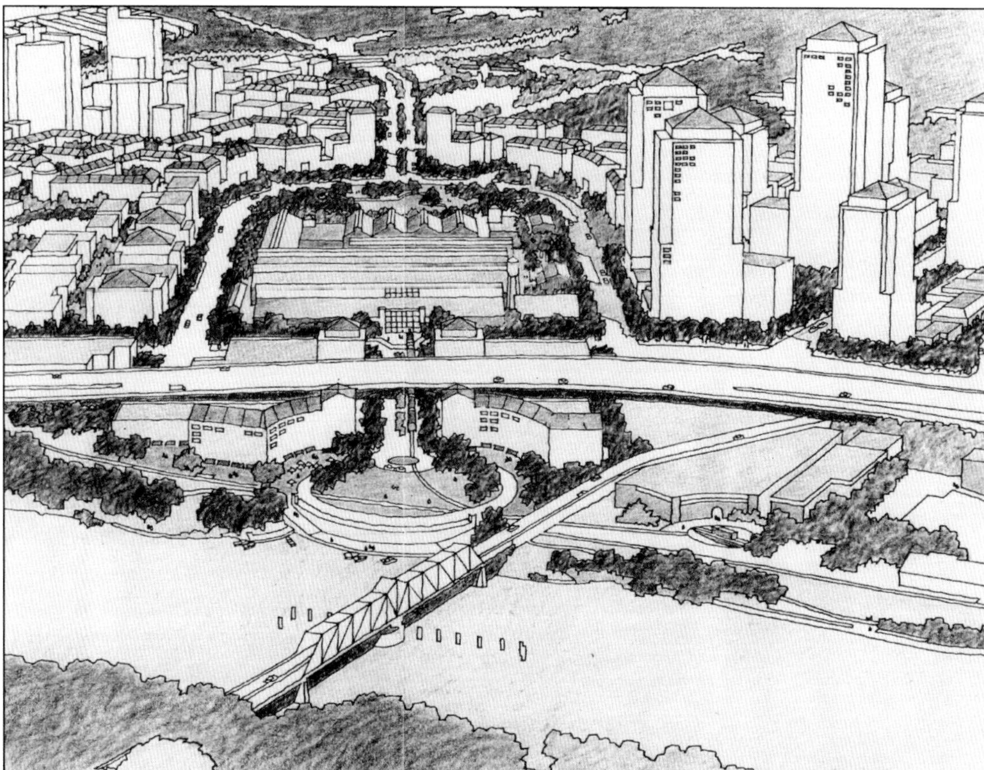

This rendering of an energized Southern Pacific rail yard was put together by the Southern Pacific Rail Yard Development Office. Ground was broken in April 2009 on the 240-acre area, which according to developers stands as the largest urban infill project in the country. Farmers markets, a bullet train depot, and thousands of residential units will highlight the rebirth of an area that, as recently as 2002, was the home to 40,000 cubic yards of asbestos-contaminated soil. (SPL.)

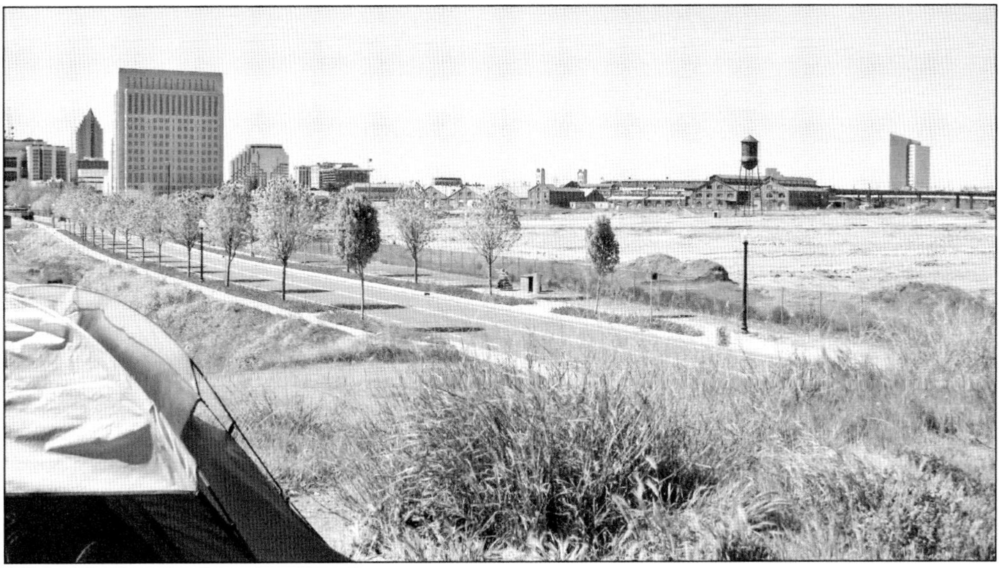

Many of the county's nearly 3,000 homeless seek shelter well in sight of Sacramento's Federal Courthouse, much like the residents of 1930s Shooksville. Like the photograph on page 114, taken some 70 years previous, this 2009 shot was also taken from atop the North B Street Levee, this time looking southwesterly toward the crumbling Southern Pacific foundry and rail shops. (SPL.)

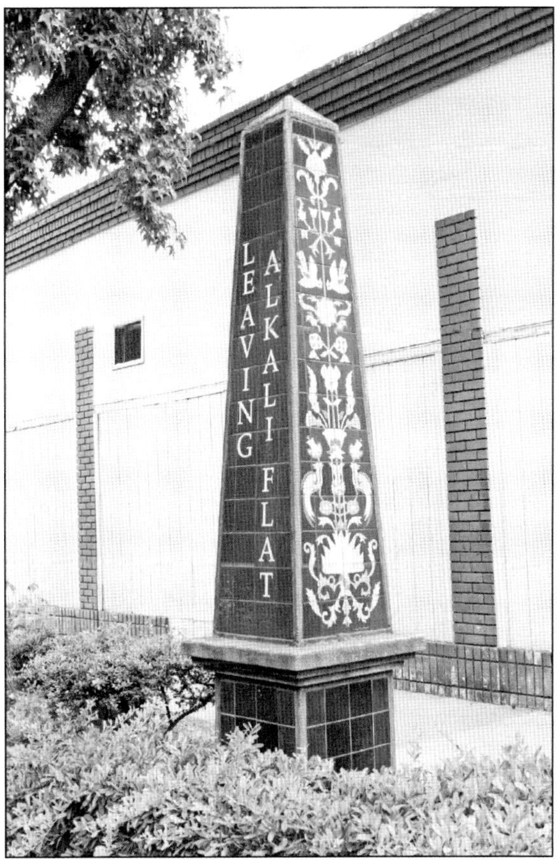

The two mosaic-clad obelisks on Twelfth Street, one upon entering and one when exiting the Alkali, were designed in 1990 by landscape architect John Nicolaus as part of the Twelfth Street beautification plan. Longtime Alkali resident and RCAF member Juanishi Orosco was responsible for the artistic concept on the ornamented tiles. The project was funded by the Sacramento Housing and Redevelopment Agency. (SPL.)

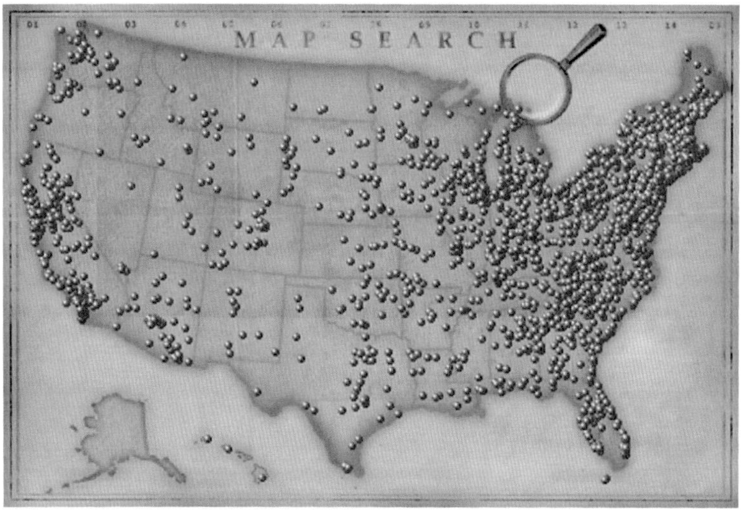
MAP SEARCH